NEW AND OLD

IN GOD'S REVELATION

Studies in Relations Between
Spirit and Tradition in the Bible

Benedict Englezakis

James Clarke & Co
Cambridge

St. Vladimir's Seminary Press
Crestwood, N.Y.

© B. C. Englezakis, 1982

ISBN 0-227-67755-2
USA & Canada 0-913836-89-3

Published by:

**James Clarke & Co
7 All Saints' Passage
Cambridge CB2 3LS
England**

**St. Vladimir's Seminary Press
Crestwood
N.Y. 10707
U.S.A.**

 British Library Cataloguing in Publication Data

Englezakis, Benedict
    New and Old in God's revelation.
    1. Revelation — Biblical teaching
    I. Title
    231.7'4   BS646

    ISBN 0-227-67755-2

Printed in Great Britain by
Redwood Burn Ltd., Trowbridge, Wiltshire and
bound by Pegasus Bookbinding, Melksham, Wiltshire.

PREFACE

I have written the present book in order to tell what I think worth telling about the similarities and, equally important, the dissimilarities between old and new in biblical revelation. I think, indeed, that the book may be described as an essay in the genetics of the Bible. But the biological analogy should not be pressed too far. I have sought the limits between new and old, how the new grows old and the old is renewed, and have tried to find the pattern — if any — underlying this process. I have explored how deeply new revelation is rooted in, and bound by, old revelation, and how far the old determines, or contains, the newness of the new. And I have inquired whether the old might verify or confute the new. These are old and much debated questions, and I regret to say that I too have failed to balance brother Gregor Mendel, of the Abbey of Brunn. I offer this book mainly as an indication of some of the ways along which I believe work might progress in future.

From subject to treatment. In this volume I have been oscillating between two of my quotations: an English one, 'To generalize is to be an Idiot', and a French one, 'L'art d'etre ennuyeux c'est de tout dire'. Depending on the critic's point of view I shall be judged as either 'an idiot' or as 'at least not a bore'. There is little consolation here, and no security. For there is still the more terrible possibility of a kind of hendiadys.

My own opinion is that one can be an idiot by being tiresome. Consequently I have endeavoured to avoid becoming tiresome, without avoiding the particular. For it is the merit of the particular to illuminate, and the danger of too much of it to obscure.

Understanding is never gained without a perspective, and taken in isolation the parts of the displaced reality do not mean anything. Global studies of wholes are, I believe, more necessary than ever in biblical scholarship, and though the specialist will always find points to criticize, the value of the global vision remains unassailable, just because it is a *global* vision. Far from determinists and 'Cliometricians', my concern was, as a recent critic required, 'to manage that delicate and essential enterprise, the striking of a proper balance between generalization and illustration'. Arts that I value much, but which I do not flatter myself that I have attained. Having neither the skills demanded nor the experience of the pitfalls to be avoided, I nevertheless proceeded, believing that there can be no autarchy in the various branches of biblical science. Evidently, no exhaustive examination of all relevant problems can be expected. To avoid generalization as much as possible, I adopted a method of 'exemplary anatomy', *pars pro toto*. Every particular trial-run was

PREFACE

traced and directed with this objective in mind, and in the formulation of conclusions every care was taken to avoid extrapolations.

The present work is based on a doctoral thesis submitted to the
University of Cambridge in 1975. I have made additions and
alterations, but the substance is unchanged. It is well known that a
dissertation does not make an elegant book; I hope, nevertheless,
that the text has been presented in a readable form.

My gratitude goes over and above all to the then Regius Professor
of Divinity at the University of Cambridge, the late Revd G. W. H.
Lampe, who supervised my research and whose help and understanding were inestimable to me. My debt to the Revd C. F. D. Moule,
formerly Lady Margaret's Professor, is hardly less. He helped and
taught me in more than one way.

For valuable assistance of various kinds acknowledgements are
due to Professor S. Agourides, Miss C. Babington Smith, Mrs M.
Bottrall, Dr S. P. Brock, Professor F. F. Bruce, Professor B. Lindars,
and Dr E. Nicholson. I should also like to make here a general
acknowledgement to Professor N. Koulomzine, who many years ago
helped me to a better understanding of the New Testament. I owe
much, even if no definite reference is made, to what I have learnt
from him in the past.

For their competent and generous help in the production of the
book Mr A. Brink and Dr C. Howell of James Clarke & Co. deserve
the profound gratitude of the author and of the reader.

As I look back over and beyond the years of study which this work
represents, I am constantly conscious of one whose love was an
unfailing source of encouragement and support: the late Archbishop
Makarios. I remain more deeply grateful to him than words can
express.

To Archimandrite Sophrony Sakharov should be ascribed in large
part such merits as the book may claim.

B.E.

Nicosia

CONTENTS

ABBREVIATIONS

AB   *Analecta Biblica*
AV   Authorised Version
b   *Babylonian Talmud* (prefixed to the title of a tractate)
BM   *Baba Mezi'a (Middle Gate)*
BO   *Bibbia e Oriente*
BZ   *Biblische Zeitschrift*
CBQ   *Catholic Biblical Quarterly*
F. M. Cross, *Essays*   F. M. Cross, *Canaanite Myth and Hebrew Epic: Essays in the History of the Religion of Israel* (Cambridge, Mass., 1973)
DBS   *Dictionnaire de la Bible, Supplement*
DJD   *Discoveries in the Judaean Desert.* Palestine Archaeological Museum, Ecole Biblique et Archaeologique Francaise (Oxford, 1955ff.)
EHR   *English Historical Review*
ETL   *Ephemerides theologicae lovanienses*
J. A. Fitzmyer, *Essays*   J. A. Fitzmyer, *Essays on the Semitic Background of the New Testament* (London, 1971)
HTR   *Harvard Theological Review*
IEJ   *Israel Exploration Journal*
JBL   *Journal of Biblical Literature*
JJS   *Journal of Jewish Studies*
JSS   *Journal of Semitic Studies*
JTS   *The Journal of Theological Studies*
LXX   Septuagint
M   Masoretic Text
Meg   *Megillah (Scroll of Esther)*
NEB   *New English Bible*
NTS   *New Testament Studies*
A. D. Nock, *Essays*   A. D. Nock, *Essays on Religion and the Ancient World*, 2 vols (Oxford, 1972)
M. Noth, *Essays*   M. Noth, *The Laws in the Pentateuch and Other Studies*, trans D.R. Ap-Thomas (Edinburgh, 1966)
OS   *Oudtestamentische Studien*
G. von Rad, *Essays*   G. von Rad, *The Problem of the Hexateuch and other Essays*, trans E.W. Trueman Dicken (Edinburgh, 1966)
G. von Rad, *Theology*   G. von Rad, *Old Testament Theology*, trans D. M. G. Stalker, 2 vols (Edinburgh, 1962, 1965)
RB   *Revue biblique*
RQ   *Revue de Qumran*
RSPT   *Revue des sciences philosophiques et theologiques*
RSR   *Recherches de science religieuse*
RTP   *Revue de theologie et de philosophie*
Sanh   *Sanhendrin* (Tribunal)
S-B   H. L. Strack & B. Billerbeck, *Kommentar zum Neuen Testament aus Talmud und Midrasch* (Munich 1922-28)
SJT   *Scottish Journal of Theology*
Sot   *Sotah (Unfaithful Woman)*
ST   *Studia theologica*
TB   *Theoligische Blaetter*
TDNT   *Theological Dictionary of the New Testament*
TLZ   *Theologische Literzturzeitung*
TWAT   *Theologisches Worterbuch zum Alten Testament*
TZ   *Theologische Zeitschrift*
VT   *Vetus Testamentum*
VTS   *Supplements to the Vetus Testamentum*
ZAW   *Zeitschrift fur die alttestamentliche Wissenschaft*
ZPE   *Zeitschrift fur Papyrologie und Epigraphik*
ZTK   *Zeitschrift fur Theologie und Kirche*

Note: Dead Sea Scrolls and related literature abbreviations are given according to J. A. Sanders, 'Palestinian Manuscripts 1947-1972', *JJS* xxiv (1973) 74-83 (Reprinted in F. M. Cross & S. Talmon, eds, *Qumran and the History of the Biblical Test* (Cambridge, Mass., 1975, 401-413).

Introduction

VERBUM

To understand how He who is always present comes is a problem inherent in every discussion of the biblical word. For he who comes in the word, carried on the wings of the Spirit, is he not always he who is ever present? Some of the thoughts that brought me to this unimpressive conclusion are offered in the following pages in a number of prefatory remarks. It is well to recollect that, as St Gregory of Nyssa remarked in another place, in these quests, 'It is not one thing to seek and another to find, for the gain from seeking is the seeking itself'.[1]

The beginning of every theology of the word of God is the belief about man as a creation of God. If there exists between God and man a creator/creation relation, a communication is bound to exist between them, at least in the form of a soliloquy between the creator in himself and the creator in his creation.

Man, however, is a creation that can respond to God's addresses with his own word. God aspires to a dialogue with him, and there is in man a congenial opening to the word of God. 'Man shall not live by bread alone, but by every word that proceedeth out of the mouth of God' (Mt iv 4). The word is for man a *desiderium naturae*.

This is the second point for a theology of the word: man is in relation of likeness to God and can be fulfilled only in God. *'Fecisti nos ad te...'*. In the ancient Egyptian and Babylonian texts 'being in the likeness' means being a son similar to his father, participating in his actions and in his powers. Man is a theophanic being, as God is anthropophanic — he can say,'You shall be holy: for I, Yahweh your God, am Holy' (Lev xix 2). Only this 'divinity' of man and 'humanity' of God can make a 'word of God' possible. The moment we reject this relation of likeness between man and God, we have no right to speak any longer of a word, for language is a human phenomenon, *the* human way of communication *par excellence*. If God is absolutely 'un-human', then man cannot communicate with him through language, or in any other way, and so, all having been said, cannot be interested in him as somebody, but only as something. But the other half of the antinomy must equally be preserved intact: God is absolutely Other, and the moment the Word is received only in terms of word, it ceases to be *of God* and, again, we can no longer speak of a 'word of God': God has become a creation of man and in reality we are concerned with a tragic human monologue. Deny the belief in man as God's image and you can no longer speak of a dialogue between God and man, you can no longer speak of any word of God.

What unites the two members of the antinomy of God as being absolutely Other and at the same time communicable is the biblical notion of grace. When, along with modern linguistics, I say 'language means man', I am not saying that God's language is the language of man. I am rather speaking in terms of what certain Latin theologians call the *attemperatio* and the Greek Fathers the *synkatabasis*, condescension of God. The incomprehensible God condescends to man's state and adjusting himself to human strength speaks to man in his own language, the language that he can comprehend. The ultimate divine condescension is the Incarnation of the Word, God the Word emptying himself and becoming man. The Incarnation is the final and most excellent demonstration of man's congeniality with the Word: *'In propria venit'* (Jn i 11). I said the final, because the Old Testament also, 'at sundry times and in divers manners' (Heb i 1), revealed this truth. The Old Testament theophanies, the theology of 'the Face of Yahweh', the glory of Yahweh and the presence of Yahweh should not be easily forgotten. Nor should the mysticism of the *Merkabah* (God's throne) and the *Shekinah* (God's Presence) in Judaism. Isaiah sees Yahweh sitting upon a throne, the hem of his garment filling the Temple (Is vi 1). Ezekiel above the likeness of the throne at the top sees 'a form like that of man' (Ezek i 26). Daniel sees one 'like a son of man' (Dan vii 13). 'Enlightened' men can dismiss all this as sheer anthropomorphism; not the biblical man however: for him, man being in the image of God means the divine Archetype being, *per eminentiam*, in the image of man. This could, incidentally, be one of the primary concerns of the Priestly author in Gen i, anxious to dismiss any theriomorphic or teratomorphic conception or worship of Yahweh.

Some biblical theologians in their great love for the word tend to forget the Old Testament nostalgia for the face, and the New Testament revelation of the Word as Face. Sophistical modern theories about Hebrew knowledge as founded upon the ear and Greek knowledge as founded upon the eye have contributed greatly to the existing partialism and it is time that some almost bureaucratically repeated assertions are dropped once and for all. At best they are inadmissible generalizations; at worst they are Aryan or Semitic arrogances. The simple claim that 'in the Bible God meets man as Word' is half the truth. It would be more right to say that the Bible, or its theology, speaks of God, is a talk about God. But meeting God is a different thing. Both before Christ and especially in Christ God meets man as Word *and* Face. The Bible contains a theology not only of the *Logos* of God, but also of the *Huios* and *Eikon* of God. Every theology of the Revelation must take this into view. Word and theophany go together in the Bible and are intrinsically united in the Incarnation, where the Word becomes man, so that it not only can be heard, but also seen and looked upon, and touched (1 Jn i 1).

The biblical apprehension of man as being in the image of God

begets the 'frightful and fantastic idea' of man's freedom. The
greatness, however, of man's freedom, according to the Bible, lies
not so much in man's freedom *from* God as in man's freedom *for*
God. God liberates man from the rest of creation in order to enter
into an *I and Thou* relationship with him: man is destined for God.
In this lies man's greatness and his tragedy — the tragedy of his
freedom. For man is free to refuse God's call, to refuse an answer,
even to give a negative answer. Nevertheless, what interests us here
is that God can address man as a *Thou*, that man is capable of
entering into an *I and Thou* relationship with God. The word of God
is primordial to man's man-hood: man is man, because he can
receive the word and enter into a relationship with God. Word and
image are closely linked and presuppose each other. The word
establishes the image; but the image is necessary to the reception
and intelligence of the word. 'In the beginning', however, 'was the
Word' (Jn i 1). What makes man is his God-given competence to
receive the word of God and respond with his own free word. This is
what we mean by saying that man is in God's image. If he answers
with an obedient *fiat*, in returning love for love he becomes an
imitator of his God and fulfils himself in his creator. This is what
the Greek patristic exegesis is basically saying in distinguishing
between 'image' and 'likeness' and infuriating Karl Barth. The
moment the exegete looks around him and accepts the idea that even
non-Christians are men (as Barth and his disciples, I trust, do), he
already says that the image is indestructible. The moment I look
into myself, I realize that the image can be dimmed indeed, and
deformed to a degree that makes any claim to likeness insolent. Both
movements are necessary for a right understanding of the nature of
man and the word of God; both conclusions are imposed, the one by
love of the neighbour, the other by self-knowledge. In trying to
describe the 'word of God' or 'image of God', etc., the interpreter
must not look only in the Scriptures; he must first look on the person
of Christ.

The third point, then, to be remembered in every discussion of the
word of God is the fall of man, man's and the creation's fallen state.
This means that God adjusts his word not only according to the
strength of a creature, but to the strength of a fallen creature in a
fallen space, and in a fallen time. The fall in Eden and the sin in
Babel denote a breaking and rending of the unity of man himself
and a division between man and the rest of the Creation,
unwillingly 'subjected to vanity' (Rom viii 20). That vespertine
luciferian attempt of man to acquire knowledge and mastery
without God, outside God and away from God meant the
unavoidable element of objectification in man's perception and
language as we know it (the scandal of the sun being outside us, as
Berdyaev would say), and as God has to accept and use it. It means,
that is to say, that God has to use a fallen language, God's word has
to clothe itself in different human languages, mentalities, and

temporalities.

On the other hand, contemporary linguistic research centred around the names of Ferdinand de Saussure, and, more recently, Roman Jakobson and Noam Chomsky has illustrated that, contrary to the 'Bloomfieldian' claim, we can speak of a human language, and not only of human languages. I believe that Chomsky's argument from the principle of the 'creativity' (open-endedness) of human language is decisive. This should guard us from exaggerating linguistic differences, though, of course, it does not spare us the task of interpretation. Contemporary social anthropology, again, shows us that the arrogant late nineteenth-century myth about the 'pre-logical' mentality of 'primitives' and the 'logical' mentality of Modern Man, has more chance than the primitive thought to be considered a childish superstition. Cultural evolution (after all very short in comparison with biological and inorganic evolution) has not as yet produced a new species of *homo sapiens*. Human nature is essentially one and the same and the hermeneut in his haste to sacrifice to the strange god of 'Modern Man' must not forget this deep truth. On the spatial plane now, modern science helps man to become at last more universal and ecumenical, and I believe that our exegesis of God's word will in the future get rid of its unsound Europocentrism, which asserts that European thought is thought — all other thought is mythology. What a European can accept as true is true — the rest is for the anthropologists. Indeed I am afraid that for all its zeal for history — perhaps because of it — most of our modern exegesis of the word of God will appear to the future ridiculously provincial both in time and in space. In saying this I do not desire in the least to deny history or the fact of man's temporality, and so the need for a *Formgeschichte*: I just want to say that 'man is flesh', but the word of God, despite its human dress, which is a social datum corresponding to a particular experience of life, is eternal and *'stabit in aeternum'* (Is xl 8).

Not least, because the word of God, as I have already hinted, is not just locutive. God's word is not just a message, does not end in the message, but in the reality. God's word is pregnant with the reality, that is why it is theophanic. I mean that the word not only reveals God's designs, but is an 'acting force which begets future events'.[2] We encounter this notion from the very early strands of the Pentateuch and with the Deuteronomist we see it becoming the focal point of a history of Israel. The word must be substantiated and materialized in history; if not itself, then the second word that replaces it. History is for the Bible theophanic, because, unveiled by the word, it proves the word. The word *debarim* itself can mean in the Bible 'history'. 'The *debarim* of Solomon' means his actions, his history. In revelation deed and word are inseparable and, in Augustine's phrase, *'In ipso facto, non solum in dicto mysterium requirere debemus'*. Historically, the biblical dynamistic identification of a word with the thing which it denotes is a common belief in the ancient Near East,[3] and, I believe, in all primitive societies. What is more important for the Bible is that the biblical God reveals himself in history and, especially, that he ultimately enters history personally. I shall come back to this point later.

The theology of the word produced by Barth, Bultmann and their disciples after the first world war debased history, in that it considered history of no great importance. Since then things have changed considerably and a more balanced view has been achieved, though much remains still to be done. Revelation is part of the whole of God's economy and 'history of salvation'. Without history, the word is a chatter of men; without the word, history is a game of gods. Biblical revelation is historical, because happening *in* history and *through* history, it is revelation *as* history — not any history, but God's history, the history of God's encounter with man. Biblical history is a series of encounters between God and man, mainly unsuccessful encounters, which, nevertheless, resulted in God's eschatological encounter with man in his Word made man, Jesus Christ.

In saying that the Bible is the record of those encounters between God and man which prepared, prefigured and brought about their final encounter in Christ, I imply that 'salvation history' must not be viewed in a way excluding universal history, but inclusively, as forming the meaning and the leaven of the universal history. Through the history of Jesus and his ancestors, Israel, God tries to communicate with the whole Adam, all mankind. His word and deeds are meant for all men. Thus, the sacred history cannot be said to be, or be described as, a provincial history, for the Word is 'the light that enlightens every man' (Jn i 9). In this sense, salvation transcends and overflows the narrow horizons of certain *Heilsgeschichte* ideas and must be viewed as the 'secret and marvellous mystery' of the general *recapitulatio in Christo*.

Two historical facts must always be borne in mind in discussing the word of God: a) that the Bible claims to be history; b) that the Bible claims to be more than history. When the reality of the first of these claims is denied, we fall into myth (however modern and sophisticated this myth may be); when the reality of the second claim is denied we fall into pure immanence and secularism, and the word of God becomes a dusty social manifesto. The latter means that the mystery is dissolved into a problem; the former that the problem evaporates into a mystery. Yet neither problem nor mystery can be denied and faith demands them both. 'History', wrote E. Lipinski, 'conditions the rationality of faith and faith deciphers in history the divine *signatum*'.[4]

The problem of the historicity of the believer's history arises immediately. Of course this question cannot be discussed here sufficiently. I shall say that if by history is meant the history written now by historians seated between their radiator and their refrigerator, feet in slippers, then the Bible is not history. The

historians of the Old Testament were very different indeed. They
were impassioned rhapsodists singing the great epic of Yahweh and
his *condottieri*. Sitting barefoot between the Wall and the Temple, or
often between the ruins of the Wall and the Temple, they believed
that certain events in their history happened under God's guidance,
and exalted them as *gesta Dei*. The historian has neither the right
nor the power to contradict this. Miraculous they may be, but it is
precisely as *mirabilia Dei* that they were sung after all. And as the
great Serbian theologian Bishop Nikolai Velimirovich once said, 'A
faith without miracles is no more than a philosophical system; and a
Church without miracles is no more than a welfare organization like
the Red Cross'.[5] This, at least, neither Israel nor the Church ever
claimed to be.

When, following F. M. Cross,[6] I designate the Old Testament
historical narratives as epic, I obviously do not deny the fact of the
myth in the Bible *as a literary genre*. But as a *Recherche du Temps
Perdu* and a global 'resolution' and 'mediation' between life and
death (following Claude Lévi-Strauss' understanding of the term),
myth has no place in the Bible; the Bible does not need it. It is not
through it that it tries to resolve the enigma of human existence and
life (unless God is also to be taken as a myth, which is another
question).[7] Leaving aside cheap vulgarizations, I shall just remark
in relation to Rudolf Bultmann's earnest attempt to demythologize
the Bible that this was a synthetic construct, and a fruit, of long and
complicated German philosophical and historiographical traditions.[8] To quote the eminent Russian Church historian Georges
Florovsky:

> The modern plea is but a new form of that theological liberalism,
> which, at least from the Age of the Enlightenment, persistently
> attempted to disentangle Christianity from its historical context
> and involvement, to detect its perennial 'essence' (*das Wesen des
> Christentums*), and to discard the historical shells. Paradoxically,
> the Rationalists of the Enlightenment and the devout Pietists of
> various descriptions, and also the dreamy mystics, were actually
> working toward the same purpose. The impact of German
> Idealism, in spite of its historical appearance, was ultimately to
> the same effect. The emphasis was shifted from the 'outward'
> facts of history to the 'inward' experience of the believers.
> Christianity, in this interpretation, became a 'religion of ex-
> perience', mystical, ethical, or even intellectual. History was felt to
> be simply irrelevant. The historicity of Christianity was reduced
> to the acknowledgement of a permanent 'historical significance'
> of certain ideas and principles, which originated under particular
> conditions of time and space, but were in no sense intrinsically
> linked with them. The person of Christ Jesus lost its cruciality in
> this interpretation, even if his message has been, to a certain
> extent, kept and maintained. Now, it is obvious that this anti-
> historical attitude was itself but a particular form of an acute

historicism. . . . The study of history was vigorously cultivated by the Liberal school, if only in order to discredit history, as a realm of relativity, or as a story of sin and failure, and, finally, to ban history from the theological field.[9]

The great merit of Bultmann is that he reminded exegetes that biblical exegesis must always be existential, which, however, does not mean that it can only be existentialist, as he thought. For the rest, his work is a tragic series of invariable confusions between myth, imagery, and the supernatural,[10] a confusion of what Henri Corbin has recently distinguished as the imaginary and the imaginal.[11] The biblical interpreter must always remember that much of modern man's inability to accept 'pre-scientific' thought is in fact the inability of the flesh to endure heaven — or hell. It is not so much myth that man cannot bear: in the words of T. S. Eliot, 'human kind cannot bear very much reality'.[12]

History and myth bring us to the problem of time. Once the biblical affirmation is founded on history, the problem of time is bound to arise sooner or later.[13] Much has been said about this question in recent years and a lot of contemporary myths about a 'biblical time' have been dispelled, though their ghosts still haunt our exegesis from time to time. One thing is clear: that there are no such things as a 'Hebrew time' and a 'Greek time', the former linear, the latter cyclical. There are many 'Hebrew times' and there are many 'Greek times'. Greek thought is not uniform, and Hebrew thought is not the continuous monochrome it is sometimes supposed to be. Life is never so simple.

What we can safely say is that the biblical time, as we see it in the light of Jesus, knows a' beginning, a centre, and an end: paradoxically, however, beginning, centre, and end coincide in the person of the Redeemer. Biblical time could (clumsily) be represented as an undulating dotted line, transmuted (I use the word in its biological, but also in its alchemical sense) at the *Cross*-point, — the supreme *mutatio mundi* a line that is neither ascending nor, for that matter, descending. Time can neither bring man to God nor estrange man from God. Time is part of the creation, subjected 'not of its own will' to the fallen state of man (Rom viii 19ff). But though enslaved to the 'bondage of corruption' and in need of redemption and transfiguration, 'in itself' it is 'neutral', and remains good, as the whole of God's creation. That is why I said 'dotted line', because the line by itself can mean nothing and anything; it can lead nowhere. What gives it meaning and direction is the Transcendental continually dotting it from above. Time cannot be redeemed unless crossed from above; it cannot be raised unless it is crucified and buried in the Sepulchre. Only the sign of the cross can mean *plus*.[14]

Biblical time is a time of momentous moments, 'moments in time but not like moments of time', the moments of the 'intersection of the timeless with time', as T. S. Eliot calls them. All revelations, every word and every theophany are such momentous moments and eventful events; the Incarnation being the Intersection of the Timeless in person. The prayer, the sacrament, the annunciation of the word, are they not always the gathering of time past and time future in the *nunc*? Biblical time is a compound of time and eternity (understood as qualitatively, not only quantitatively, different from time), the pattern of the Cross formed of *the moments*, interconnected, similar, contiguous, yet at the same time unique, irreducible and unrepeatable, in a paradoxical union of the *ephapax* with the *eis to dienekes*. In Chalcedonian terms we can say that in the Word time and eternity are united without confusion and without division. Not that the Word is made of time and eternity, but that time and eternity are united in the Word.

The great service of Oscar Cullmann's work on *Christ and Time* is that it illustrated the irreducible and unrelaxed tension between the 'already' and the 'not yet' of the time of the Church and of Christian existence. And that, at a time when history was threatened by historicism, he reminded us that *salvation* is at once accomplished and proffered *in history*. For this he deserves all our gratitude. Mircea Eliade, basing himself to a great degree on Cullmann's work, says:

From the standpoint of the history of religions, Judaeo-Christianity presents us with a supreme hierophany: *the transfiguration of the historical event into hierophany*. This means something more than 'hierophanizing' of Time, for sacred Time is familiar to all religions. But here it is *the historical event* as such which displays the maximum of trans-historicity: God not only intervenes in history, as in the case of Judaism; he is incarnated in an historic being, in order to undergo a historically conditioned temporality.

But as the same historian of religion continues:

And yet it must not be lost sight of, that Christianity entered into History in order to abolish it: the greatest hope of the Christian is the second coming of Christ, which is to put an end to all History.[15]

No theology of the word of God can forget or deny this. Christianity expects a moment when time will cease for ever as we know it and will be once and for all redeemed and raised from the dead. At the same time Christianity believes that this *eschaton*, which is expected in Christ, in Christ is already realized, inaugurated, and anticipated (and when I say 'in Christ', from the purely chronological point of view I mean both before and after the earthly life of Christ, i.e. both in the Old Testament period and in the New Testament). Christianity has not only a past or a present or a future: it is at once past and present, and future in a meta-temporal contemporaneity. The moment the past is suppressed faith, goes. The moment the future is denied, hope expires. The moment the present is absent, there is no meaning, love is dead. The moment of the intersection is the moment of detachment from succession, when past and future are gathered in the present and the word is consummated in the silence. When union transcends communication, words and deeds no longer speak or act; they *are*. Of those moments:

The heart could never speak
But that the Word was spoken.[16]

Revelation *about* God is infinitely poorer than revelation *of* God; knowledge about God incomparable with knowledge of God. For God is greater even than his word.

Between *the moments* the Bible, being a human book as well as a divine, knows all the times of man — and, in this sense, there is no 'biblical time'. The joyful cyclical time of the feast and liturgy; the enigmatic cyclical time of the fruit that falls and the seed that grows; the indifferent cyclical time of the equinox and the solstice; the spiral time of typology; the linear time of the succession of epochal durations, etc. The Bible knows the circle. But it shows that it can be more than depression and anxiety: it can be the time of 'prayer, observance, discipline, thought and action', the fruitful time of the *interpretation*. When man, patient and trustful, 'watches on the tower' (Hab ii 1ff) while:

... the enchainment of past and future
Woven in the weakness of the changing body,
Protects mankind from heaven and damnation
Which flesh cannot endure.[17]

I hope I have at least hinted that there is no physics or philosophy of history or time in the Bible. In affirming that God is the Lord of history and that God has entered history in person, the Bible creates a theology of history, which teaches that history has a *telos*, an end, a goal, a limit, and a fulfilment, and so a meaning. At the same time, the paradoxical affirmation of the almightiness of God *and* the freedom of man excludes any and every idea of a system or an immobile and unchanging structure behind history. The salvation history is seen along with the universal history as a *mystery of salvation and a tragedy of sin*,[18] which cannot yet be said to *be* but to *become*.

Now whoever says word, says language, and whoever says language, says tradition. For the word establishes a tradition in which it speaks. Outside this language the word is incomprehensible; and to try to abstract the language from the word would be absurd. The tradition is the interpretation of the word, in the sense that the word is significant only within the reality of the tradition, i.e. only in relation with the other words. The word is the interpretation of the tradition, in the sense that by its appearance it alters the configuration of the whole and changes the perspective. Obviously, I understand tradition organically, as a whole which cannot be reduced to its elementary parts, the words, for it consists of the words *plus* their relations to each other as created and unveiled by the Spirit.

This means that a single in-coming new word can act on the whole as a trigger, releasing all kinds of reactions, spelling out pre-conceived intentions in the pre-existing words, giving the signal for the reactivation of implicit commands, the revelation of implicit meanings. The whole tradition and each of its components are affected by this trigger and appear in a new light, re-interpreted, re-read, re-set. In the inverse direction, the tradition passes the new word through a series of scanners, filters, and classifiers through which it somehow de-particularises and abstracts it in order to recognize and understand it. For, as Wittgenstein might have said, the word can have a meaning only *im sprachlichen Verkehr* and *im Strome des Lebens,* only in the actual traffic of language and in the stream of life. Thus, the tradition also is creative, though this creativity is a rule-governed one, where the word's creativity is a rule-changing creativity.

All I have said here is implicit in the classical distinction of tradition as both the *traditum* and the *actus tradendi*, the noetic determination of the *traditum* within the people of God. This former is the mystery of the Word, the latter is the mystery of the Spirit of God in the midst of his people. The living and charismatic principle and reality of the tradition belong to the Revelation itself, is itself a divine gift and a divine manifestation, a divine work. In this way the Eastern Church is right to insist always, apropos of the Church tradition, that 'the true and holy Tradition is not reduced only to a verbal and visible transmission of teachings, rites and institutions; but it is at the same time an invisible and actual communication of grace and sanctification'.[19] Of course, this follows also from the very nature of the word of God as an active force and not only an utterance.

Refusal of the tradition is refusal of the word, if not as a sign, as a meaning. For refusal of the tradition is refusal of the communion; refusal to believe in the God who 'quickeneth the dead and calleth those things which be not as though they were' (Rom iv 17); refusal to receive the brother and pronounce the life-giving words of love: '*toi, tu ne mourras pas*'.[20] Tradition is the *communio sanctorum*, as communion both of the *sancta* and the *sancti*, over whom death can have no power. For 'love is strong as death' (Song of Songs viii 6), and 'the souls of the righteous are in the hand of God' (Wis iii 1).

The Bible lives and moves in this communion, its God being 'not God of the dead, but of the living' (Mt xxii 32). In him tradition, far from being a succession of names and words and deeds, appears to the interpreter as a system of significant relations, a language. Jeremiah's prophecy is not something that comes after Isaiah, but is determined by Isaiah and determines Ezekiel in a dynamic relation. In this way for Deutero-Isaiah the 'sources' of Jeremiah are not only Isaiah, but also Ezekiel. For him what is significant is not just the chronological order, but also the relation between and the movement from Isaiah to Jeremiah and to Ezekiel. The same is true of the New Testament interpretations of the relation between Jesus and the Law, or of the Church's understanding of the prophets. The force that continually distends, expands, dilates and stretches the word of God through time is the Spirit, carried by the word in itself. The word is directed by the Spirit horizontally as well as vertically, full of it, God's creative and life-giving power and force, the 'breath of his mouth' (Ps xxxiii 6).

Thus, on the one hand the historical present has behind it historical pasts, and the historical past is a continuity of pasts coming the one out of the other; each one being tradition insofar as it is an actualization of a remote past, and originating tradition insofar as it initiates the subsequent re-presentations. But on the other hand novel revelation in word and deed is added all the time until God's eschatological revelation, when all words are finally re-created and re-presented in the infinitely greater Incarnate Word, Anointed with the Spirit. And these processes must be seen against the more general framework of God's economy in the world. For, as we have seen, God's ultimate desire is not to reveal himself to man for the revelation's sake, but to share with man and to make man 'partaker of his divine nature' (cf. 2 Pet i 4), life, and blessedness. The knowledge of God (da'at 'elohim) to which the word aspires is not an intellectual knowledge of God, but the profound knowledge of the erotic embrace, which transcends knowing and *is*. In this light everything we say about the revelation, the word, the tradition and the Spirit is only an imperfect attempt to describe life, even more, the life of God and man. Every time we forget this and fall to the level of intellectual ideas and definitions, concepts, and notions,

The Word made flesh . . . is made word again ,[21]

and is even reduced to a written text. For we must not forget that in saying word of God, we immediately say Scripture.

Ever since Plato,[22] writing has been considered by the West as an orphan or a bastard, in opposition to speech, legitimate child of the 'father of the logos'. The idea of writing has always (and in all cultures, anthropology claims) entailed an idea of fall and loss of innocence; the primordial innocence of the spoken discourse, where the voice preserves the immediacy of the presence and the meaning. Plato called writing a *pharmakon*, both medicine and poison, and saw the opposition writing/language in the more general opposition of sensible/intelligible, body and soul. At present, however, in certain philosophical quarters thinkers have started questioning the traditional line of phonologism and logocentrism and a philosopher like Jacques Derrida without rejecting the supremacy of speech, calls for a science of writing comparable to that of linguistics; or rather for a science of 'arch-writing' including both language and writing; for ultimately both writing and language are signs pointing back to other elements. These are important evolutions which, it is to be hoped, will in time interest the biblical scholar.

For the Bible, however, the last word is not the writing or the language but the Holy Spirit speaking to the heart. The Scripture in itself, as a book, can be neither a privilege nor a disadvantage. Read by faith it is seen as an excellent act of humility in which the word of God is 'incarnate' in writing, so that man might preserve it exact and unchangeable more easily: He who makes this *in itself* a *for myself* is the Spirit. Without this interior presence of the Holy Spirit the Scripture can never be more than a beautiful corpse — its interpretation an aestheticism of the dead texts. 'It is the Spirit that gives life; the flesh is of no avail' (Jn vi 63). The moment the Spirit overshadows the reader, there is no longer a 'Scripture', he is in the presence of his God and hears Him speaking *to him*. Writing to the Emperor, St Hilary of Poitiers insisted: *'Scriptureae enim non in legendo sunt, sed in intelligendo'*.[23] The Church preaches not a 'Scripture', but 'Christ, the power of God and the wisdom of God'. Beyond any 'debater of this age' (be it Hegel in the nineteenth century or Heidegger in the twentieth), the Word proclaims itself not in speech and words, but 'in demonstration of the Spirit and power' (1 Cor i-ii). For 'as it is said, "every word contests another word", but which is the word that can contest life?'[24]

Chapter 1

AUDI ISRAHEL

In religion the natural inclination of man is to establish for himself gods that he needs and can use, 'the gods whose demands on us are reinforcements of our demands on ourselves and on one another'.[1] In doing so man safeguards centrality for himself: *his* gods are in his image and likeness. Not so in Israel, though. Yahweh creates man in his own image, elects Israel to be his servant, and wants his people to be holy because he is Holy. The God of Israel is beyond any human idea of god, inscrutable, inconceivable. So he is from the first chapter of Genesis until the last Maranatha of the Apocalypse; always 'overthrowing human expectation; by the Cross defeating man's hope; with the resurrection terrifying his despair'.[2] Man does not always know what to do with this Living God, so supremely divine and, at the same time, so disconcertingly human. He just has to go on in obedient following. 'It is Yahweh who goes before you; he will be with you, he will not fail you or forsake you' (Deut xxxi 8).

It is this God's will and word that the prophet as man of God ('is ha-'elohim) announces, and, no wonder, sooner or later he is to be called a 'fool' (mesuga') by people of common sense.[3] His relation to God is dialogical. The word cannot simply pass through the prophet; it is not such a neutral force. 'The prophet', as A. J. Heschel wrote 'is a person, not a microphone'.[4] Being Yahweh's messenger, he is a speaker for Yahweh and a proclaimer, and so necessarily an interpreter, of Yahweh's law; God's overseer and 'vizier'; Israel's sentinel and assayer; her intercessor before God.[5] In the nation's life the prophet is not only the representative of the Mighty One of Jacob, he is a power himself: 'the chariots and the horsemen of Israel' (2 Kings ii 12).[6] A tremendous power, and so a formidable threat not only to Israel's enemies, but to Israel herself: 'See! I am making my words a fire in your mouth .. that it may consume them' (Jer v 14; cf. Hos vi 5). Soul and body, the prophet is the vessel of the word. 'Son of man, let your body eat and fill your stomach with the scroll that I give you' (Ezek iii 1-3; cf. Jer xv 6). The prophet not only hears God, he *eats* the word, and so he exhales the Spirit.

However, the prophets of Israel must not be compared with mystics.[7] In the words of R. C. Zaehner, 'The mystic, simply by being a mystic and therefore incapable of giving expression to his experiences, can have no message from God to man. ... India produces sages, Israel prophets. The message of the first is renunciation of the world in order to partake in an eternal order, the message of the second is the dealings of the Eternal with this world

of space and time. . . . Mystics make no demands; they merely point a
way: prophets make insistent demands, they demand obedience.
They are extremely uncomfortable people'. In another place the
same author pointed to the experience of union with God, so
fundamental in mysticism and so absent from the prophets, and he
emphasised again the exclusiveness and arrogance of the prophets,
this deeply discordant element that 'has scarcely for a moment
ceased to disrupt the concord that more gentle and civilized men
have striven to create and maintain'.[8] The sign of a prophet is the
word, that of a mystic is silence ('non parce que son objet fait defaut
a la parole, mais parce que la parole fait defaut a son objet. . . . Leur
parole est un voyage qu'ils font par charite chez les autres hommes.
Mais le silence est leur patrie').[9]

Called by Yahweh (*nabi'*?), the prophet is appointed (*nae'aeman*, 1
Sam iii 20) and sent (*saluah*, 1 Kings xiv 6) to bring forth Yahweh's
words (Jer i 5), to teach His will and His ways, i.e. *da'at*, the
knowledge of God. The moment of his call and his personal
encounter with God is of the utmost importance, and certainly the
whole of the prophet's message is sealed by this experience. Out of it
spring both his greatness and his misery, his public message and
his personal tragedy. For Yahweh, who has called him, is not a
tractable god that man either needs or can use for the tranquillity of
his conscience, or the welfare of his life. *Jonah* is perhaps the most
instructive story about the prophetic destinies. Jonah was told to
arise and go to Nineveh (East); but he rose and fled to Tarshish
(West). He knew that the outcome of this call would be his cry 'It is
better for me to die than to live' (Jonah iv 28). It was that call to go to
Nineveh and preach repentance which made Jonah a prophet and
which also destroyed his own life. By ending abruptly with a
question by Yahweh and saying nothing about the prophet's
ultimate fate, the story shows to the reader that what is important
for him is *the message* of the prophet, not his life and destiny. This is
the concern of God, not even of the prophet himself — to say nothing
of the reader. It is not the Vomiting of a fish that is important, Leon
Bloy says somewhere, but the message which that Vomiting cried
against the most terrible city of the East, and the repentance with
which it was accepted. (Though no one, of course, would fail to think
that prophets were not made in order to be vomited; or that in Israel
this unhappy servant of God would have been perhaps forced to
beseech his whale to re-swallow him. . . .)

The whole life and existence of the prophet come under the hand
(*yad*) of Yahweh. The very call and first encounter happen under the
pressure of 'the hand'. Yahweh's hand fell upon Ezekiel, was strong,
pressed hard upon him (Ezek i 3; iii 14, 22; viii 1). 'Thus spoke
Yahweh to me when the hand grasped me strongly', says Isaiah (viii
11); and Jeremiah cries that, 'Under the pressure of Thy hand I
have sat alone' (xv 17). It is the experience of being possessed by,
and so possessing, the Spirit of Yahweh. A permanent state and

condition rather than momentary ecstasies — even if this state
starts with an ecstasy and knows its high revelatory moments.[10]
Living in the Spirit of Yahweh, the prophet, as we have seen in the
previous chapter, knows Yahweh's plans, announces His decisions,
and *creates* His word. Thus, he claims, not man's religious life — as
the priest does too often — but man's whole life. Inevitably he
becomes 'a man of quarrels' (Jer xv 10), and his word is a perpetual
source of shame and insults (Jer xx 7ff). He is God's man, and so
contra mundum. Not only a prophet, but a living prophecy himself,
himself both *'ot* and *mopet*, sign and miracle; in his weakness,
ridiculousness and isolation, 'a fortified city, an iron pillar and
bronze walls ... over nations and over kingdoms, to pluck up and to
break down, to destroy and to overthrow, to build and to plant' (Jer i
18, 10) God's city, the Kingdom of God. So, from Samuel's
indignation at the desire of the people to have a king until Ezekiel's
refusal to admit in the city of God David as a *king*: 'and David my
servant shall be their *prince* (*nasi'*) for ever' (Ezek xxxvii 25). For
God is the King.

Prophecy appears in Israel in the period before the united
monarchy, that is at that period of Israel's history which has been
called by G. Ernest Wright 'a period of adaptation'.[11] It is the time
of the guilds of the *bene hannebi'im*. Our subject, however, is the
prophecy of the next period, that of the divided monarchy, the
'period of tradition'. It is the time of the empires of Assyria and
Babylon, when Euphrates, inflated with pride, bursts out to cover
'the waters of Shiloah that flow gently' (Is viii 5ff.). They battled for
nearly three centuries until the people of God refused Shiloah and
melted in fear before the powers of this world. Then the doors of
Jerusalem collapsed, as it had been prophesied: 'If you will not
believe, surely you shall not be established' (Is vii 9). To the prophets
with the powerless miraculous hands nothing of all these
tremendous events was alien. Everything was concurring towards
the writing of a book which was not a kind of *Paralipomena* of God's
acts, but the very mysterious book of his history with his people.

Some (R. Bultmann, for example, in his *Primitive Christianity*)[12]
saw in the prophets one of the causes of Israel's political ruin. Their
utopian requirements, opposing all political and economic progress
as such, undermined the very foundations of the state, drew Israel
out of history, and did not allow her to become realistic. Others
understood the prophetic mission as primarily political and saw in
the prophets great social reformers and political revolutionaries.
Some acknowledge in them 'a keen and unprecedented awareness of
the great historical movements and changes of their own day and
generation', which was not, though, political calculation but
theological conviction (G. von Rad). I have always believed that
Israelite prophecy was a question of revelation more than of
reflection. Religion was for the prophets neither politics, nor
sociology nor intellectual reflection — albeit theological — but life

with God, humble obedience to him in trusting confidence and 'useless service' (cf Lk xvii 10). And this is not unrealistic — not even realistic. ... *'Il y a le reel et il y a l'irreel. Au-dela du reel et au-dela de l'irreel, il y a le profond'*.[13]

We can now proceed to examine some problems of tradition and prophecy in Israel's classical prophets. I shall confine myself mainly, though not exclusively, to pre-exilic and exilic prophecy. Jeremiah will be given special attention because of his extreme importance for our subject. Second Isaiah and Ezekiel will help us to pass over into the next period, which Ernest Wright calls the 'period of reforms', and others the 'period of tradition'!

What is meant by 'tradition' in the period now examined? Very few people will answer today: the Pentateuch or the Law. It would be extremely naive to give such answers so many years after Julius Wellhausen. This is a long story that cannot be related here any better than it has been by W. Zimmerli in his book *The Law and the Prophets*. [14] Suffice it to say that both the Deuteronomic and the Priestly traditions were shaped during this period, and took their final form in the next one. I will just add that I follow neither Wellhausen nor the reaction against him, but the more balanced and cautious thoughts that always prevail after such reactions against overdoses of great intellectual action. The Law is not posterior to the Prophets, nor are the Prophets posterior to the Law; and, though I do not have a Westcott's fondness for such paradoxes, I have to say that the contradiction is very near the truth. In Israel the prophetic movement certainly came after the great works of the Yahwist and Elohist traditions, and of course after the person and the work of Moses himself. This alone would suffice to remind us that a tradition existed before the classical prophets.

First, the tradition of their predecessors, the *bene hannebi'im*. For certainly the great prophets are spiritual sons of those prophetic bands and court prophets of the immediately preceding centuries. It is not for nothing that Elijah became the archetype of prophecy. And Nathan could very well be considered a predecessor of an Isaiah. Samuel I would not hesitate to call 'father of the prophets', by which I do not mean that he himself was just a *nabi*'.[15] Paradoxical though it may appear to some, prophets become themselves tradition, especially the literary prophets, who left their message in written form. Thus we can speak of a prophetic tradition, or an Isaian tradition, or Jeremian traditions.

Secondly, there are the royal traditions in both Israel and Judah, especially in the latter. With David, God's Anointed became an integral part of Yahwism. D. F. McCarthy has shown how the kingship had been integrated into the fundamental relationship between Yahweh and the people, and the relationship reaffirmed, in 1 Samuel viii-xii (a theology that I consider as dating back to the times of the united monarchy and the court prophets of Jerusalem).[16] Classical prophets were among the formative factors of these royal traditions in a degree no smaller than the earlier *nebi'im*. In Judah prophets were trying to direct the royal ideology, in Israel they were its real controllers, the 'Chariotry of Israel and the Horsemen thereof', according to the title of Elijah and Elisha, which has been felicitously compared with the title that Muhammad accorded to his great general Khalid ibn al-Walid, 'The Sword of Allah'.[17] In Israel indeed there was no dynastic royal theology and the prophets, in the name of Yahweh, could appoint and, only too frequently, oust the kings. It must never be forgotten that the prophetic ideal was not in its essence the royal one but the nomadic. In this respect the prophets were not reformers but conservatives. The famous prophecy of Nathan itself (2 Sam vii) is a defence of the traditions of the earlier community. And R. de Vaux was certainly right in saying that, starting from Ahijah, there was a prophetic trend in the North which, while justifying the political independence of the ten northern tribes (i.e. the political schism), condemned, nevertheless, the religious reforms of the northern kings.[18] In Judah the royal theology was linked with the Zion theology, which eventually was destined to survive to this day in the three major monotheistic religions. Here also, as we shall see, the classical prophets both inherited and formed (not only reformed) the tradition.

Yahwism, of which both early prophecy and God's Anointed were parts, is the great religious tradition that stood behind, in front of, above, and below the classical prophets. To say that the prophets inherited this tradition is a mistake, because Yahwism is not only a tradition, not even just a 'religion', but a whole world, within which the prophets were born, to which they belonged. It would be more just to say that the prophets belong to Yahwism than to speak of Yahwism in the hands or in the minds of the prophets. Ernest Wright has rightly indeed called our period 'the period of tradition'. Not only a religious tradition, but also a national and cultural one.

What I mean by national must not, of course, be understood in any modern sense. The consciousness of belonging to twelve different tribes was very strong, the more so as the northern tribes were quite distinct from the southern, and the political schism after Solomon's death froze the situation permanently. Yet an assumed common ancestry and a common religion — blood and election — maintained a national spirit (the people of Yahweh as distinct from the rest of the nations), regardless of the wars between the two rival states. As for the cultural tradition, it must be viewed as a natural reflection of the religion; for, to quote T. S. Eliot, 'in the most primitive societies no clear distinction is visible between religious and non-religious activities; and ... as we proceed to examine the more developed societies, we perceive a greater distinction, and finally contrast and opposition, between these activities. ... A higher religion is one which is much more difficult to believe. ... A higher religion imposes a conflict, a division, torment and struggle within the individual; a conflict sometimes between the laity and the priesthood; a conflict eventually between Church and State'.[19] Even a superficial knowledge of Israel's history would suffice to indicate that by the time of the classical prophets Yahwism was already a 'high religion', with all that this means. The literary products of the period would alone be enough to show what a degree of culture Israel achieved at this time, and the material remains offer a similar testimony. The 'ivory house' of Ahab (1 Kings xxii 39) can be reconstructed by the imagination if one stands before the Samaritan ivories of the British Museum (ninth to eighth century). Had Collingwood known well the 'Succession Document', he would have hesitated to assert that, as compared with Near Eastern and Hebrew theocratic history and myth, Herodotus is the first proper historian in the world.[20] This Document can surpass in many ways both the scientific zeal, the historical research, and the humanism of Herodotus. Classical prophets found a high religion and made it higher. If dress and food are signs of refined culture, the descriptions of the ladies of Jerusalem by Isaiah show the degree of refinement, not to say decadence, that Judah attained by the eighth century among its high and civilized classes ('the dwellers in cities'). The conflict had started, and by the time of Jeremiah it was already a struggle within the individual. Prophetic conflict between prophets, prophets versus priests, prophets versus State, prophets versus their own selves. Religion was no longer a problem of *adhesion* (as in Canaan and the ancient world generally) but a problem of *conversion*. We shall come back to this later.

Prophets never have a private language. 'Even the most personal and transcendent mystical experiences', writes Mircea Eliade, 'are affected by the age in which they occur. The Jewish prophets owed a debt to the events of history, which justified them and confirmed their message; and also to the religious history of Israel, which made it possible for them to explain what they experienced'.[21] The Exodus, the Covenant of Sinai, the Mosaic institution with its law and priesthood, the Judges and their 'justice', the early prophets, Israel's Anointed, and before all these, the Patriarchs and their history and traditions back to the Creation 'when God began creating the Universe'; all this history and religion, is the world that I call Tradition. And the relation of Prophecy to this world is what I will try to examine in what follows.

If Tradition is everything that passed, or was believed to have passed, before the time of the Prophets between their God and his people, then Tradition is not a fetter that binds, but life and grace affectionately preserved and appropriated. It has nothing to do with endless laws, meaningless rituals in incomprehensible languages, squeamish priests, etc. Tradition is a dynamic principle of life, always young and always in need of rejuvenation, continuation, and progress. This is of the essence of the Old Testament's historicism, of its meaning and sense as signification and direction.

In case I did not make myself clear in the first chapter, I shall not
hesitate here to restate that for me everything is not always history
and only history. The Tradition about which I speak is not just
history. It is revelation too, and not just revelation through history,
but through history and word and theophany. (Scriptures indeed are
not Scriptures because they relate the history of salvation, but,
primarily, because they are written under the inspiration of God.)
History is a very ambiguous thing to be so ultimately trusted; its
interpretation very human to be believed, mortal, and so incapable
of an everlasting youth and appeal. And I am not speaking either of
myths or of symbols or reflections, beautiful as they may be and
even able 'to make dreams truths; and fables histories'. I am
speaking of true things and prime historical facts that for centuries
have been so believed by some men — eighth century B.C. Hebrews
or twentieth century A.D. Greeks — who put their trust not in
history but in God: a God who, though revealing himself through
history, is above and beyond it. The Hebrew man never forgot this.
His God was the *Deus absconditus* of the Scriptures *'qui posuit
tenebras latibulum suum'* (Ps xviii 11).

How far is prophecy rooted in the tradition, and to what extent
does it surpass it, bringing in a new element? New not in the sense of
form but of content; for we are not concerned with literary analysis,
source criticism, or history of forms, but with the history of
revelation. Fortunately, the problem was posed very early, and
different solutions have been proposed ever since. This is indeed one
of the most discussed problems in contemporary research on
prophecy — the relation between prophecy and tradition. The story
has been told many times. Debate started with Wellhausen, reached
a climax with O. Procksch, and in recent years goes on under the
rival flags of G. von Rad and G. Fohrer; though one is inclined to
think that neither von Rad nor Fohrer would recognize themselves
in much that is attributed to them by both friend and foe.[22]

I shall pass immediately into what I have called 'exemplary
anatomy' and I will comment on von Rad and Fohrer after these
tests. Three different subjects will be taken as samples: the cult, the
traditions of Zion and David, and the covenant.

The Cult and the Prophets
The exaggerations concerning the prophetic attitude to the cult are
well known. After the liberals had imagined the prophets as their
own predecessors in rejecting cult, and everything like it, for the
sake of *'das Wesen'*, the age of 'pan-liturgism' came, when prophets
were viewed as little more than sanctuary servants. Liberals were
unable to distinguish between prophecy and morality, and the
propounders of the 'cult prophecy' theories unable to distinguish
between prophecy and divination. Some scholars went so far as to
seek in the prophet's association, or lack of association, with the cult
the criterion of his truth or falsehood.[23]

In matters of *essence*, there can be only one twofold 'essence' in
ancient religions, 'the rite, which was thought of as a process for
securing and maintaining correct relations with the world of
uncharted forces around man, and the myth, which gave the
traditional reason for the rite and the traditional (but changing)
view of those forces'.[24] Ancient civilisations agree in their cultic
approach to time. In the hierophanic duration of ritual, mythical
time is restored. Now this mythical, cyclic vision is not 'theocratic'
thinking, as some appear to imagine; on the contrary, it is a
biological conception of time. And here again the uniqueness of
ancient Israel stands out: hers is an historical time. There was a
beginning (be it the covenant or the creation).

Moses necessarily emerges. Was he the ghost that received life
from his grave, as M. Noth wants us to believe?[25] Or was he rather
'the certainly monotheistic founder of Yahwism' of W. F.
Albright?[26] I should say that he is the mediator of the Sinai
covenant and the charismatic leader of Yahweh's people. In relation
to Yahweh and Israel, Moses is 'the friend of the Bridegroom'. No
more, and certainly no less.[27] After him Israel shall have no other
God but Yahweh: 'I am the Existent' (Ex iii 14) — mystery of the
Transcendent existing for a people.[28] The monolatry of the nomad
divinity of the Patriarchs ('the God of the father' [my/your/his])
becomes an injunction towards a practical monotheism. (The first
commandment presupposes the existence of other gods.) There is no
need, I hope, to expand on the enormous consequences of this for the
cult. Israel's worship is to be the worship that Yahweh expects from
His people. With the entry of the people into Canaan problems
appeared that were never to vanish as long as Israel existed. In spite
of political developments and cultural interplays, Israel would be
hindered from following the common 'path of the nations' —
accepting new worships not as substitutes but as useful supplements, which do not involve taking a new way of life in the place of
the old. This is *adhesion*, a way forever blocked to Israel by Moses.
For Yahweh desired the *conversion* of His people, 'a turning which
implies a consciousness that a great change is involved, that the old
was wrong and the new is right'.[29]

'In the great individual prophet', says G. Fohrer himself, 'the
religious impulses of the Mosaic period came to life once more — if
not in identical shape, then in purified and expanded form. They re-
experienced Yahweh's miraculous activity and his inflexible will,
requiring a decision'.[30]

The cult could not, naturally, stay outside their horizon. Some of
them were priests (Ezekiel), or of priestly origin (Jeremiah), others
were cultic prophets perhaps (Nahum?), and still others had nothing
to do with cult and belonged to the court rather than to the
sanctuary (Isaiah); some used liturgical language, others not; some
preached in the official royal sanctuaries, others not. There were
many classes of prophet. What is important is that they all were

'men of God'. Prophets when they opposed the cult, opposed it not
because Yahweh did not need external piety and cult, but precisely
because it was not the cult that Yahweh instituted and wanted, it
was not *His* cult.

Let us take one of the most notorious clashes between prophet and
priest: Amos versus Amaziah. Not the prophet versus the priest, but
God's man against a priest who serves the king rather than God; a
priest for whom Beth El, 'the House of God', is 'the king's
sanctuary, a house of the kingdom' (Amos vii 13). The prophet
attacks the priest not because he is a priest, but because instead of
being Yahweh's priest he has become the Crown's servant. For this
reason 'the high places of Isaac shall be desolate, and the
sanctuaries of Israel shall be destroyed, and I will rise with the
sword against the house of Jeroboam' (Amos vii 9). It is not the King
and his priest who will drive God and His prophet out of His house,
it is God who will ruin the king's house, his sanctuaries, and his
priest (Amos vii 16). Neither throne nor altar can usurp God's
sovereignty.

Israel's right condition in the Covenant is to depend entirely on
the gifts of Yahweh, as at the time of her desert life, when she had
nothing yet to offer Him. This is the meaning of Amos v 25, a
rhetorical question which does not need to be taken literally.
Sacrifices were common to all the Near Eastern countries and there
was nothing specifically Yahwistic about them (cf. Jer vii 22). On
this principle, sumptuous cult and human embellishments of the
ritual are to be condemned too. In the desert 'Did you carry the tent
of your King and the footboard of your God that you made for
yourselves, House of Israel?' (Amos v 26).[31] Baldachins and
footboards (symbols of the royal throne of Yahweh) are human
inventions which have nothing to do with the foundations of the
covenant history.[32]

After the exile the prophets become the champions of the
restoration of the Temple and of the cult, though their criticism is in
no way silenced. Malachi, the last prophet of the canon, will criticize
fiercely the cult of his day and its servants, proclaiming at the same
time that 'from farthest east to farthest west my name is great
among the nations, and in every place a sacrifice of incense is
offered to my name, and a pure offering ... says Yahweh Sabaoth'
(Mal i 11).

It can be concluded that the classical prophets, whose works have
been preserved for us in the canon, stood not against the cultic
tradition of Israel, but against proud human interpretations and
embellishments of the tradition. In so doing they were neither
independent of the tradition nor interpreters of it. After all we must
in no way overstress the continuity of Israel's cultic tradition. Cultic
reforms were all too frequent in the period of the monarchies.
Prophetic tradition played no less great a role in preserving Israel's
memory of the past than the cultic tradition. A static image of the

cult as an unbroken continuity of tradition cannot be vindicated historically. For the prophets the cult ought to be the liturgical expression of that unique covenantal relation between Israel and Yahweh her God. This flows out of their message naturally, it was neither their own reflection nor an interpretation of previous tradition, nor a refusal of the efficacy of God's past actions or institutions. Through his prophets Yahweh refused to all intents and purposes to become a nature god, one of those gods that natural man 'needs and can use'. This was the first front of the prophetic criticism: the 'popular' Canaanizing interpretation of worship. The second front was the 'official' interpretation: Yahweh absolutely refused to become a Canaanite state deity, the god that the king 'needs and can use'. It was not he who was to be the vassal of the king, it was the king who was Yahweh's vassal. Classical prophecy and royal cult clashed on this point until the royal cult collapsed in the catastrophic events of the end of the seventh and the beginning of the sixth century.

This final crisis (with all the doubts that it aroused concerning the efficacy of Yahweh to save his people) and the hard circumstances of the post-exilic period were asking for a new message. Disappointment was leading to indifference or neglect of the cult. Reforms like that of Josiah proved to be insufficient. History was proved untrustworthy. The prophets of the exilic and post-exilic periods discovered the cosmic dimensions of Yahweh's power and saving activity and preached the absolution and the inward renewal of the nation before the coming of the time of salvation. The Temple had to be built (how modest indeed) before the coming of Ezekiel's eschatological Temple; cult had to be a true cult; priests had to be dedicated priests. It fell to a prophet to give perhaps the profoundest description of both the greatness and the predicament of the priest: 'The lips of the priest should guard knowledge, and his mouth is where instruction *(torah)* should be sought, for he is the messenger of Yahweh Sabaoth. But you, you strayed from the way; you have caused many to stumble by your instruction; you have corrupted the covenant of Levi, says Yahweh Sabaoth. And so I in my turn have made you despised and abased before all the people, inasmuch as you have not kept my paths but have shown partiality in your instruction' (Mal ii 7-9). Exilic and post-exilic prophecy reformulated Yahwism in the face of the new historical events and, at the same time, bore witness to greater things. Does not the expiatory sacrificial death of the Servant implicitly involve not only the radical desacralization of sacrifice, but, also, the abolition of the expiatory sacrifice?

Zion and David
Jerusalem was brought into relation with Israel quite late, but after the days of David and Solomon it acquired a significance which went beyond Judah. This importance of the city of the sanctuary

was never to decline, even unto this day. The literature on the traditions of the election of Jerusalem is enormous and I have already mentioned earlier in this chapter two very fine essays by R. de Vaux and M. Noth. Certain works of G. von Rad, Th. Vriezen and O. Eissfeldt — to mention some of the most eminent names only — are of no less importance.

Jerusalem was the city of David, but, primarily the city of Yahweh. Along with Judah it formed the realm of the Davidic rulers. (Not Judah and its capital Jerusalem, but Judah *and* Jerusalem, cf. Is i 1 etc.) In the period of the monarchy it appears as the historical Jerusalem; eventually as the mythological Zion of the origins and of the future, the new Jerusalem of Qumran, the heavenly Jerusalem of the Seer of Patmos.[33] Deuteronomy spoke of the 'election' of the (one) place of the cult. When this place was identified, by Josiah, with Jerusalem, new glory was added to the city of the Ark and of the Anointed. It is possible that David chose Jerusalem just from cold political reasoning — a non Israelite, neutral city liable to be accepted by all the tribes as the king's capital. By transferring to it the Ark, he made it also the central shrine of the realm and a place of pilgrimage. The city paid him well: to him and to his descendants the Canaanite city offered, if not actual patterns of divine kingship, at least hints and suspicions of a divine-king ideology.[34]

We have seen that Ahijah, the prophet of Shiloh, was already the first to distinguish between the fate of the dynasty of David and that of Jerusalem, the city of Yahweh. Much as the accounts of 1 Kings betray the hand of the Deuteronomistic[35] editorship(s), critics like M. Noth and R. de Vaux can still discern the truth. One is indeed astonished to discover that Ahijah's line remained that of all the prophets until the very end, and even beyond the end: the Davidids and Jerusalem are to be distinguished.

God's promises to David through His prophet Nathan remained inviolable for all His prophets. It could not be otherwise, since the same God who had sent Nathan was sending them also. Despite everything, for Amos, Isaiah, Micah, Jeremiah or Ezekiel, a Davidic Anointed is for ever assured of the diadem, the testimony *('edut)*, and his coronation name, a son unto God. To quote only a famous oracle of Yahweh in Isaiah:

Truly to Us a child is born,
to Us a son is given,
and dominion is laid on his shoulder,
and his name will be called:
'Wonder-Counsellor, Mighty-God,
Eternal-Father, Prince-of-Peace'.
(Is ix 6-7)[36]

Even in the dark days of Zedekiah, Jeremiah will not hesitate to utter a promise of a true David, who will come after this puppet so called *Sidkiyahu* (Zedekiah: the throne name that Josiah's son

Mattaniah took on his accession, meaning 'Yahweh is my vindication'):

Behold, days are coming — Yahweh's word —
When I will raise a true 'Shoot' to David;
As true King he shall reign — and wisely,
And do justice and right in the land.
In his days shall Judah be saved,
And Israel shall dwell in safety.
And this is the name by which he will be called:
'Yahweh-*sidkenu*'.
(Jer xxiii 5-6; cf. xxxiii 14-16)

He-who-brings-to-pass-our vindication' will be the future ideal (Messianic) king of David's line.[37]

As for Jerusalem, for the prophets it was the City of Yahweh. The Deuteronomic doctrine of the election of Jerusalem appears only in Zechariah (iii 2). For the prophets Yahweh *founded* Jerusalem; it is His creation (Is xiv 32). He lives there (Is viii 18), and from there His voice is heard (Amos i 2). Zion is 'the mountain of the house of Yahweh' (Mic iv 1-2). If the promised David will be *'Immanu-'el*, God-is-with-us (Is vii), the city's name will be *Yahweh-sammah*, Yahweh-is-there (Ezek xlviii 35); for in that day not the Ark, but the whole of Jerusalem shall be called 'Yahweh's throne' (Jer iii 17).

A very good test case for us is the tradition of Zion's inviolability and the attitude of the prophets to it. Not a general complex of traditions, as in the case of the cult, but an individual tradition, part of the broader complex of the Zion traditions.

T. W. Overholt tried to expand the view that the falsehood of the pseudo-prophets rests in their faithfulness to the past, i.e. in applying God's old message to new situations; in being (as we would say) 'traditionalists'.[38] I will not linger over Overholt's excessive claim that the whole of Jeremiah can be explained by the notion of falsehood, nor on the problem of the prophetic conflict (on which we have now the works of Quell, Osswald, Crenshaw, Hossfel and Meyer showing, among other things, that the opposition of prophets to prophets holds a very much smaller place in the Old Testament than their opposition to kings and politicians).[39] What interests us here is that in describing Jeremiah's opponents Overholt, following Quell, H.J. Kraus,[40] and some other scholars, claims that 'Hananiah in fact stands firmly within the tradition of the prophet Isaiah, who was convinced that Zion would never fall'.[41] Can we really speak of Isaiah's theology as of a salvation theology founded in election and covenant? Did Isaiah really ever hold Hananiah's belief in the inviolability of Zion?

There is no doubt that in pre-exilic times a tradition existed that Jerusalem was inviolable and unshakable for ever. When this tradition appeared for the first time we are unable to say. J. Bright would see it as springing from the miraculous deliverance of the city from Sennacherib in 701 B. C. J. H. Hayes considers it as a pre-

Israelite belief attached to the temple of 'El 'Elyon in the Canaanite Jerusalem.[42] R. de Vaux, in his above-mentioned lecture, found the truth between these two extreme solutions: the tradition was a very ancient Canaanite theme incorporated in the belief of Jerusalem's election by Yahweh and established by the dramatic events of 701 B.C. That certain court circles were very much attached to the tradition, every good historian can detect (cf. certain royal Psalms). That certain of Isaiah's disciples embraced it, we can understand (cf. Is xxxvii 34b-35, which, following Th. C. Vriezen and R. de Vaux, I am inclined to ascribe, along with other material in chapters xxxvi-xxxvii, to some disciples of the prophet), but certainly not Isaiah himself. Such a belief would go against all his message and everything that we know and understand about him. Amidst the conglomeration of traditions in the narratives of 2 Kings and in his book itself, Isaiah, in his undoubtedly authentic prophecies, emerges as the man of faith: and a preacher of faith can give no guarantees of whatsoever kind. I do believe that the *hope* that Zion would remain unshaken was never abandoned by Isaiah; but this was a *hope*, not a *belief* — much more, not a national dogma. For as Hayes has shown, and de Vaux confirmed, Isaiah modified radically the old tradition in two fundamental respects. First, he placed a condition of salvation and protection: faith in Yahweh — 'If you do not believe, you shall not endure' (Is vii 9b). Second, he placed the enemy's activity within the field of the action of God. We can see this in many places and preeminently in the Oracle on Ariel. 'You will be an Ariel for me, like David I will encamp against you, I will blockade you with palisades and raise siege-works against you. . . .' (Is xxxix 1-10). Isaiah seems never to have preached the annihilation of the chosen city of Yahweh, upon which his whole work centres. Not because he believed in its miraculous inviolability but because he never failed to hope in the miracle of faith. This is, after all, why he is the great Isaiah, who can at the same time sing the City on the Hill (Is ii 2-4),[43] and — a fact that very few want to notice — call this very city Sodom, and its people the people of Gomorrah (Is i 10). For Yahweh 'lays in Zion a stone of witness, a precious cornerstone, a foundation stone' (Is xxviii 16), the starting point of the congregation of the future, the holy remnant (Is i 9; xiv 32; xxx 17). As for the destiny of the present city, the depth of her humiliation will be utter: she will become like a ghost whose thin voice is to sound from low in the dust (Is xxix 4). The great Jerusalemite cannot help his despair — 'Turn your eyes away from me; let me weep bitter tears; do not try to comfort me over the destruction of the daughter of my people' (Is xxii 4). In truth, there is nothing of a Hananiah here. The real successor of Isaiah is Jeremiah. One has but to open one's eyes in order to see.

Micah, a younger contemporary of Isaiah, brought the same message from his Lord and, against those criminals who were still saying 'Is not Yahweh in our midst? No evil is going to overtake us',

He prophesied the ruin of Zion (Is iii 9-12).[44] At the accession of
Jehoiakim (609-8 B.C.) Jeremiah reminded those who trusted in
Jerusalem and in the Temple of the fate of Shiloh, where Yahweh
'made His name to dwell at the first': 'I will make this house like
Shiloh' (Jer vii 13-15; xxvi 4-6). Hananiah? One of those eyes that
Yahweh closed, and one of those heads that He veiled (Is xxix 10).
Ezekiel threatened not only the city itself but even those left behind
in the city: they were not the remnant of 'Israel', and the land would
not be their possession. For all these prophets there was no security
in either city or Temple. The catastrophe would be complete and the
end final.

But as always '. . . the end precedes the beginning, and the end and
the beginning were always there, before the beginning and after the
end'.[45] God's 'mighty act', beyond man's power to accomplish, shall
again appear, something as stupendous as the original act of
creation. This need of salvation, is it not always the corollary of the
sense of sin? How many pages of scholarly distinctions and
criticism about *Heilspropheten* and *Unheilspropheten* are indeed
before God 'like chaff which the wind drives away'. The texts resist
every attempt to come back to the errors of Duhm and Marti, and
nothing can be gained by insisting on presenting pre-exilic prophets
solely as prophets of disaster.

The prophets saw that national triumphs — whether of Israel or
her enemies — in the realm of temporal affairs are no proof of the
divine favour, as is falsely supposed in dreams of political
messianism. God uses his nation and the other nations — his
vassals — as instruments; and the instrument is always expendable. Pre-exilic prophets reminded Israel of this, mainly in
regard to her own position: she was but an instrument in God's
hands and she would soon realize that instruments are expendable,
if they are of no use. Second Isaiah and post-exilic prophets
reminded Israel of this in regard to the nations: they are also but
instruments in God's hand; expendable as well. A new creation and
a new Exodus and a new Conquest (as a pilgrimage to Zion this
time!) are about to take place. Jerusalem will be 'radiant', and the
city of Isaiah (Is ii 2-4) joins the marvel of Trito-Isaiah's lx 1-22 and
Haggai's ii 6-9, where the entire cosmic order is overturned and the
primeval peace (plentitude, totality, integrity) which was shattered
by the irruption of violence (*hamas*, cf. Is lx 18 and Gen vi 11,13) is
again given by Yahweh. 'For this is like the days of Noah to me: as I
swore that the waters of Noah should no more go over the earth, so I
swear to be no more angry with you, no more to rebuke you. For even
although mountains depart and hills remove, my grace shall not
depart from you, and my covenant of peace (*berit salom*) does not
remove, declares Yahweh, who has compassion on you' (Is xliv 9-
10).

The promises of Second Isaiah were never fulfilled in the post-
exilic period; we have to admit that. It belonged to Trito-Isaiah, in

his re-publication of Second Isaiah's message, to dissociate Yahweh's advent and the era of salvation it inaugurates from any concrete historical event, from history itself. Not the return of the exiles, but the pilgrimage of all the nations to Zion will ensue on God's coming salvation (cf. Is lx 1-22, xl 9ff). The covenant with David was also reinterpreted. As the last Davidids waned, it might have appeared broken in the eyes of many. Second Isaiah, a true prophet, had no dreams to preach. In one of his greatest proclamations, lv 1-5, not only does he take Nathan's promise to David out of the political and royal sphere, and transfer it to the whole nation (Volz, von Rad, Westermann), but, as O. Eissfeldt showed, he actually places it 'before the fate of Israel and its royal house and declares its eternal validity. In so doing, he relates the promise to the mission of Israel in the world, a mission which is Israel's destiny and which will bring her honor and recognition'. If Ps lxxxix displays a static, rigid conception of the promise of Yahweh, and Haggai and Zechariah see in Zerubbabel the promised Davidic descendant, for Second Isaiah 'Yahweh's Anointed' is Cyrus, the non-Israelite, and the promise is interpreted 'in a dynamic-activistic sense: he prevents its becoming involved in the collapse of the Davidic dynasty and thus insures its permanent validity'. After a loud 'market-place' invitation — 'Ho, all who thirst, come to the waters...' — the proclamation comes: 'I will make with you an everlasting covenant (*berit 'olam*) *the inviolable promises of grace to David.* Behold I have made him a witness (*'ed*) to the peoples, a leader and commander for nations. Behold, you call nations that you know not and those who do not know you run to you because of Yahweh, your God, and of the Holy One of Israel, who glorifies you'. With lv 5 Yahweh turns to Israel promising, not authority over other peoples (as he formerly granted to David), but that He will glorify Israel in that 'Israel will henceforth call to herself many whom she did not formerly know, and that many who formerly knew nothing of Israel will hasten to her. ... With this promise, nothing is meant apart from that which stands elsewhere at the centre of the proclamation of Second Isaiah, particularly in the Servant Songs: that Israel, through her vicarious suffering and her silent witness, will convey to all the world the worship of Yahweh, finding grateful recognition on all sides in the fulfilment of this high calling'.[46]

It can be concluded that though Zion and David had not been parts of the ancient creed of Israel, their traditions were later fused with the early Israelite tradition and acquired a unique place in salvation history.

In pre-exilic Israel we can detect two attitudes towards David. That of the primary edition of the Deuteronomistic History (Dtr 1), which, though exalting David, offered little or no hope to either Jerusalem or the Davidids, the fate of Judah having been sealed by Manasseh's sin;[47] and that of the prophets, who, though

proclaiming the coming catastrophe, never abandoned their trust in
God's faithfulness to David and Zion. Exilic and post-exilic
prophecy strengthened the hopes of restoration, as we have seen, in
different accents. Second Isaiah saw the restoration in the glorious
Return; Third Isaiah projected the era of salvation outside history;
Haggai and Zechariah came back to earlier positions and put their
hopes in the rising new Davidid, Zerubbabel. With regard to
Jerusalem, on the other hand, prophets of all times were unanimous
about the final future glory of Yahweh's city. But again, exilic and
post-exilic prophecy spoke of it in the language of the old myth,
revealing through it the transcendent and universal meaning of
Zion. This is part of course of the general outlook after the close of
the monarchy.

Ezekiel and especially Jeremiah call the ideal prince of the future
'David', while never applying to him the title *masiah*. The prophets
did not speak of the 'coming of a Messiah' but of the restoration of
David's rule, according to the promises of Yahweh through Nathan.

In regard to the traditions of David and Jerusalem, therefore, it
would be a great mistake to call the prophets 'independent of the
tradition', and it would be misleading to call them interpreters of it.
They do not simply 'hold and proclaim eschatological beliefs which
were already extant, and in all essentials fully developed, in the
popular tradition', departing thence only in the question of their
application and its consequences;[48] and they do not simply
reinterpret an old tradition, which was not basic to their faith, 'so as
to be able with its help to express what they had to say'[49]. Both
these views take it for granted that the prophets ceased to believe in
the efficacy of the old salvific deeds of God, and in the light of what
we have seen we can declare them both absolutely wrong: prophetic
faith in Yahweh's old words and deeds remained unshaken, despite
all the historical vicissitudes of Israel. The prophets distinguished
between Zion and the Davidids and, as against 'official' ('divine
kingship' tendencies?) and 'popular' (Zion's inviolability) Canaanizing traditions, asserted Yahweh's supreme rule, sovereignty, and
liberty, and the primacy of His ethical demand. No unconditional
decree could be given by Yahweh to either his vassal, the king, or his
people. Such proud pretentions were anathema to prophecy. The
berit always kept for the prophets its basic meaning of pledge,
promise, obligation, and commitment. For Yahweh is 'a great God
which regardeth not persons, nor taketh reward' (Deut x 17). The
prophets safeguarded the uniqueness of Yahwism, and prepared
God's people for the reception of 'the day of its visitation'.

The new covenant
Walter Eichrodt was able to systematize the whole of Israel's
theology under the theme of the Covenant of Sinai as the source of
the grace and of the preference shown to Israel, the basis of Israel's
relation to Yahweh (the first table of the Decalogue), and of the

mutual obligations demanded by the solidarity of the human
partners in it one with another (the second table of the Decalogue).
Notwithstanding all the criticisms that one can make against the
idea of a theology of the Old Testament built as a 'system' around
the concept of covenant, or against Eichrodt's opinion that there is
only one theology of covenant, that of Sinai, his principle is
certainly sounder than von Rad's existentialism, springing as it
does from his sceptical dichotomy between the 'real' and the 'holy'
history of Israel.[50]

M. Noth's work made us realize that there are many kinds of
covenant and various types of covenant-making. God, for instance,
can be presented as a partner alongside the people, or (in later
times?) the One before whom the covenant is made through a
mediator, while the people just assent (cf. 2 Kings xxiii 3): which
means that God is not a contracting party.[51] G. Mendenhall[52]
showed how much Hittite treaties and their structure can contribute
to our understanding of the formulas and concepts used in the Old
Testament in connection with covenant, though later G. M. Tucker
pointed out that the term 'state treaty' is an inadequate modern-
ism.[53] The Hittites spoke of 'oaths', which they understood as
decrees of the king. Form and content, nevertheless, do not always
coincide and an authority such as Klaus Baltzer can assure us that
'the Israelite covenant is as far removed in content from the
international treaties as it is closely related in form. The historical
portions of the treaty formulary and the covenant formulary can be
compared on the basis of their form. The history that they record,
however, is incomparable and unique. The "antecedent history" of
the covenant formulary tells of God's acts among his people from
generation to generation — ultimately, in fact, from eternity. These
acts are saving acts, "demonstrations of Yahweh's righteousness".
Israel's loyalty to its Lord, its keeping of the commandments, is a
response to God's acts of grace in history'.[54] We realize that history
is of crucial importance in covenant as both inaugurating it and
witnessing to it. It is in history that the gift is given, and it is in
history that the answer to the gift is expected. Grace and Law,
promise and commandment meet in history as the forum of the
covenantal relationship, understood primarily as an obligation of
Israel to God.

What was the attitude of the prophets to the covenant, or better (as
there were more than one covenant) to the covenantal relationship
between Yahweh and Israel? R. E. Clements thought that the
prophets' primary role as the messengers of Yahweh was their
concern with this relationship. 'Their unique contribution to Israel's
faith', he wrote, 'was to have actualized the covenant tradition in
the days of its obscurity and loss'.[55] Others saw in the prophets the
preachers of the breaking of the covenant and of its end. Were they,
then, the saviours of the covenant, or the proclaimers of its
annulment?

It is always necessary to make distinctions and to approach the whole problem historically, i.e., taking into view the development that took place both in form and content. It is possible, for example, that the form of the treaty was adopted by the Deuteronomic school in order to express the heritage of prophets like Hosea. Each text must speak on its own. Yet, there is no doubt that the prophets criticized the traditional formulary of covenant. Isaiah xxviii 15, Amos v 14, Hosea viii 2, Micah iii 11, etc. are quite eloquent. But the prophetic criticism is directed not against the formulary as an expression of the relationship between God and man, but against presumptuous human misinterpretations of the tradition. What the prophets preached was Israel's breaching of the covenant through her sins of disobedience and lack of faith, and the inexorable coming punishment of this 'breaking of oaths'.[56]

Obviously, this refers mostly to pre-exilic prophecy, but it must not be thought that the motif is absent from the exilic or post-exilic prophecy. The prophetic word is not only prediction of the future, but also interpretation of the past. From Exodus to Second Isaiah and Deuteronomy 'God's deity is shown to be such by the continuity of His action in history'. Yahweh through his prophets both declares the things to come and tells 'the former things, what they were', in such a way that prospect and retrospect, proclamation and interpretation, meet (cf. the trial speech of Is xli 21-29). With the Exile the decisive change in Israel's lot has already taken place. The old guilt is cancelled and the dawn of the new day comes. This makes all the difference between pre-exilic and later prophecy. Let us compare Isaiah xlii 18-25 and xliii 1-7.[57]

The former oracle interprets in retrospect the catastrophe in the traditional technical language of lamentation. Yahweh proves that it was his people that was deaf and blind; they did not hearken to his *torah* and 'He poured upon them the heat of His anger'. As he says in the key-oracle of Isaiah xliii 22-28, 'Instead of being my *'ebed* (servant) you made me your *'ebed*'. This was the end of the covenantal relationship, and it explains the horrible past.

The oracle following immediately in Isaiah xliii 1-7 proclaims the imminent future. '*But now*: thus says Yahweh, who created you, Jacob, and founded you, Israel: Fear not, for I have redeemed you. . . . I, Yahweh, am your God, the Holy One of Israel, your Saviour (*mosia'*) . . . because you are precious in my eyes, and honoured, and I love you . . . I am with you'. A new hour has struck, and a new word comes from God ('but now'). He has redeemed Israel (*ga'al*, redeem by payment), and, as he once said to her father Abraham (Gen xv 1), he now says to her also: 'Fear not'. 'You are mine. I am your God. I am with you' — this is the covenant. The *realiter Aliter* (Holy One) is again with Israel, his precious, honoured and beloved elect. Election and covenant were rarely described in more beautiful and profound words. We notice, however, that the time-hallowed formulae express something which continues an intrinsic relationship between

Yahweh and Israel. Only the perfect 'I have redeemed you' indicates an act.

The only passage preaching a new act of covenant-making is Jeremiah xxxi 31-34:

Behold, days are coming — Yahweh's words — when I will seal a new covenant with the house of Israel and the house of Judah, not like the covenant that I made with their fathers on the day I took them by the hand to bring them out of the land of Egypt. For they violated my covenant and I had to proceed against them as befits a lord-husband — Yahweh's word. But this is the covenant which I will seal with the house of Israel after these days — Yahweh's word: I will give my law within them, and I will write it on their hearts; I will be their God, and they shall be my people. And no longer shall each man teach his neighbour and each his brother, saying, 'know Yahweh', for they shall all know me, from the least of them to the greatest — Yahweh's word; for I will forgive their iniquity, and I will remember their sin no more.

Though the final form of the oracle is perhaps to be ascribed to a disciple of Jeremiah, the content itself not only has a Jeremianic tone, but actually belongs to Jeremiah himself. It is part of what has been called 'The Book of Consolation' (Jer xxx-xxxi), prophecies of hope addressed mainly to northern Israel in the early career of Jeremiah together with later material, the whole having been subsequently expanded and supplemented in such a way as to apply Jeremiah's message more directly to the exiles in Babylon. Our oracle belongs to the prose portions of chapter xxxi, and more precisely, to a series of three pieces with the identical introductory formula: 'Behold, days are coming' (verses 27, 31, 38). In its present form it is addressed to Israel and Judah (v. 31), though the possibility that originally it was addressed to the northern tribes (cf. v. 38) cannot be excluded. However, it is such a high point in Jeremiah's message that I should be inclined to consider it as addressed to the whole of Israel, as God's community, whereas the nearly parallel promises of chapters xxiv 4-7 and xxxii 36-44 were certainly addressed to the exiles of Jerusalem of 598 and 587 B.C. respectively.

What makes this oracle a *locus classicus* is the promise of a new covenant — let it be noticed at once, not of a new *law* — to be ratified by Yahweh in the future, when he will 'reverse the fortunes' (xxx 3, *sub sebut*, turn the turning) of his people. After the exile this came to mean 'turn the captivity', but, still, whether or not we take 'after these days' (verse 33) as equivalent to 'behold, days are coming' (verse 31), the existence of an interim is not to be doubted. The very idea of a new covenant, however, is already found in Hosea, and here Jeremiah gives to it its classical expression. Hosea ii 16-23, for example, develops the theme in all its three oracles (16-17, 18-20, 21-23), reaching the climax in the third, where Jezreel is interpreted 'God sows', i.e., God sows again. The ancient promise will be

verified: I shall be your God, and you will be my people, and the
people answers now: 'My God!' — an individualisation and
deepening of the covenant. As for the law — a non-fixed entity in
Jeremiah's time — in the heart and soul, it is something very
Deuteronomic (cf. Deut vi 6; xi 18; xxx 14); and Ezekiel too speaks of
a new heart (Ezek xviii 31; xxxvi 26; xi 19, 'a heart of flesh'; cf. Jer
xxiv 7; xxxii 39), and a new spirit (Ezek xviii 31; xxxvi 26: an idea
absent from Jeremiah). But the greatest preacher of this future
conversion, or rather new creation, remains Hosea. In Hosea ii 14f,
just before the three oracles mentioned, we already have everything:
the new, which will follow the pattern of the old. 'Therefore, behold,
I will allure her; I will bring her into the wilderness, and I will speak
on her heart. And from there I will give her her vineyards, and the
Valley of Achor will be the Door of Hope; and there she shall
respond as in the days of her youth when she came out of the land of
Egypt'. Here is the famous prostitute wife and mother on the
children of prostitution all unexpectedly wooed again as a virgin by
her faithful husband after the terrible punishment. A new
honeymoon begins again exactly where the first was spent. Far
from her sinful friends she will again hear the words of her lover. He
will speak not only *to* her heart but *on* her heart (cf. Jer xxxi 31!). It
will be a marvellous re-beginning; her vineyards will be given back
to her again, and the Valley of Calamity (Josh vii 25) will become
the Door of Hope. At last she will respond joyously, giving herself to
her husband without reserve (*'anah*, cf. Ex xv 21; xxi 10). Renewal
of the election, new introduction into the land, new covenant, all
because Israel was dead, and is alive, she was lost, and is found.

What is unparalleled in Jeremiah, Hosea's spiritual disciple, is
that Yahweh will give his law to the heart of man as a gift, and that,
as a result of this, any need for religious instruction will be absent
(Jer xxxi 34).[58] 'What is characteristic of our passage', writes J.
Coppens, 'is not the gift of a renewed, or even new, heart, but the gift
of the divine law to the heart of man'.[59] This is a new promise,
different even from that of Jeremiah xxiv 7 or Hosea ii 14, where the
accent is on the intimacy and the tenderness between the two
partners. The two covenants, that of Sinai (verse 32) and the
promised one, are identical except on one decisive point: there will be
no mediation of a Moses, a priest, or a prophet, in the new one. By
implanting His law in the heart of the Israelites, Yahweh, in a
creative act, becomes certain of Israel's love. The effect of this act is
the close matrimonial union of the covenant and the knowledge of
God. The people are all promoted to the grace of prophetism (verse
34a), according to the original will of Yahweh (Ex xx 18ff [E], etc.).
The questions of Jeremiah v 1-9, 'How, and why, should I forgive
you?', are thus resolved, after the disastrous punishment, in the
announcement of a new covenant. Still, the partners are the same
and the new act is in continuance of their old relationship. The verbs
'forgive' and 'remember' in verse 34b are characteristic. It cannot

be an absolutely new beginning because Yahweh, at least, is the
same. It is a question of pardon and remission of sins that bring to
perfection the *means* used by God in order to assure the efficacy of
His covenant with Israel. After the old means proved insufficient, a
new means will be used, suppressing the old tension between written
law and word (cf. Jer viii 8f): the gift of a law implanted in the heart.
The same law, but put in the heart, a new heart indeed. A new
covenant between the old partners, graciously offered by the faithful
party to the treacherous.

I do not think that we can speak of a renewed covenant. The new
one will be decisively different and will have different effects. But it
can certainly be viewed as a renewal of the old promise in different
ways. Ezekiel, the historian prophet, will interpret with unprecedented boldness Israel's history as a history of sin and rebellious-
ness followed by judgement and renewal. A renewal not because of
any merit, real or hoped, of Israel, but because 'at the time when I
chose Israel and made myself known to the seed of the house of
Jacob in the land of Egypt, then I lifted my hand in an oath, saying,
I am Yahweh your God' (Ezek xx 5). This is the beginning, *the
election*.[60] Jeremiah knows as well as Ezekiel that Yahweh is above
Israel and his freedom absolute. Israel can break and overturn the
covenant that sprang out of God's election; she can never extinguish
the reason for this election: his love. And from it a new covenant
shall shoot forth for his name's sake. The sin of Judah can be
written with a pen of iron and engraved with a point of diamond on
Israel's heart (Jer xvii 1), still Yahweh will give a new heart
engraved with his law.

From the primeval chaos (Jer iv 23, the judgement as anti-
creation) a new creation will take place. God will triumph over death
at the same place where judgement was passed (Ezek xxxvii 1-10),
and a new Israel will be raised. For Exodus xix 6 (E?), Isaiah lxi 6,
and later for Qumran, the people will be promoted to the priestly
dignity; for Ezekiel the sign of the new Israel and the new covenant
of salvation will be Yahweh's 'sanctuary in the midst of them for
evermore' (Ezek xxxvii 26ff; xl-xlviii). For Jeremiah the people will
all become prophets, because their hearts will be the sanctuary of
Yahweh's law.

Jeremiah proclaims a future new covenant not because he does
not believe in the efficacy of Yahweh's old act, but because the old
covenant has been broken by the unfaithful Israel. God will record
his law on man's heart, and man will at last know his God. The new
covenant will be perfect and will inaugurate a new era of mutual
love and knowledge between God and his people.

Conclusion
The foregoing analysis reveals that to consider the prophets as
either dependent on, or independent of, tradition represents an
anthropocentric attitude, which cannot accord with what the

prophets themselves tell us about their own calling and message. Whether we see them as dependent on tradition or independent of it, we see them only as the prophets of Israel, and this is secondary; for, above all, they are *the prophets of Yahweh*. And here lies indeed the predicament of the historian, who 'knows only what he is told; he cannot penetrate the secret of the hearts'.[61] What is decisive, says Fohrer, is the secret experience of the prophet. But of this who can speak? 'Istarum visionum et divinationum causas et modos vestigare si quis potest, certoque comprehendere, cum magis audire vellem, quam de me expectari ut ipse dissererem'.[62] The commissioning of the prophet will always be a secret to those of us who have never undergone a similar experience. The little we know, we know from what *they* tell us. Those who speak of dependence or independence with regard to the tradition forget that they speak just of *the way* in which the message is delivered. And again, many of those who speak of the transmissions proper forget that not only Yahweh and the people are persons, but the prophet also is a person. The reception, the transmission, and the delivery of the word, are pre-eminently personal events.

G. von Rad marks the last and finest point of reaction against the Wellhausenian evolutionism. Prophecy is now seen not as revelation proper but as reflection, intellectual creativity of the first order. The reaction against seeing the prophets as radical innovators and rebels is good, but, as always, the truth cannot lie wholly in reaction. Fohrer tries to save what can be saved of Wellhausen. He is certainly right in reacting against tendencies to make of the prophets proclaimers of 'nothing new, nothing independent; like Jahve himself, they merely administer the Tora of Moses, mechanically predicting good or ill fortune, depending on whether the law has been faithfully kept or neglected'.[63] Von Rad would not agree, of course, with this caricature either. We must not forget that, besides the old election tradition, he recognizes other factors as well for the coming into being of the prophet's preaching: the new eschatological word of Yahweh to Israel and the personal situation of the prophet. He has answered his critics very well on the term 'eschatological' itself,[64] and we shall always be indebted to him for bringing to light one of the specific features of the Israelite prophetic hope, mamely the guarantee provided by the former acts and promises of God to Israel's future. 'We find a similar appeal to history and the traditions as guarantee of the future neither in Mesopotamia nor in Egypt, nor in the other of Israel's neighbours'.[65]

In all the three cases examined here we have seen the Old Testament prophets hovering in the tracks of two ages: the time of the Old demands the New. The fire of the seed, which must die in order to give life, is felt as the painful, agonizing pangs of childbirth.

True prophets are not tradition-inspired but God-inspired. Their judgement on the present or on the future is not pronounced in the

light of tradition, but in the light of God (cf. Jer xxiii 30: 'Behold, I
am against the prophets — Yahweh's word — who keep stealing my
words from one another' — a prostitution of the word). In a second
stage, they, their disciples, the historian, or the theologian, see the
link with the traditions, or the breach with them. This is inevitable.
The word falls from heaven, but not in a vacuum — though neither
in a plenum. Tradition certainly prepares initiatives, adaptations,
evolutions, but it is not enough to explain the new promises, the
promises of the new.

We always have to make fine distinctions. Each prophet and each
tradition must be examined minutely and individually. If we have to
generalize — as we do here — extreme cautiousness is needed. A new
David, a new Jerusalem, a new Conquest, a new allotment of the
Land, a new Temple, a new Covenant, the coming of the nations to
Zion, the end of the idols, are new elements in the prophetic
proclamation; yet, partly at least, they can be explained from
tradition. What is absolutely new is the prophets' proclamation of
the future re-creation of Israel by a mighty act of God as stupendous
as the first act of creation. A new Israel turned at last to God,
something beyond man's hope or power. Once a new Israel is
promised, all will be new and renewed; a new David, a new
Jerusalem, a new cult, a new covenant. And is it not as 'a light to
lighten the gentiles' that Israel had been created from the beginning
(cf. the oracle of Is xlii 5-9)? This new creation of Israel is the most
important part of the prophetic preaching, more important than the
unveiling of Israel's sin and the announcement of the ineluctable
punishment. *For though the latter could be derived from the
tradition, the former cannot be explained by it, it cannot be derived
from it.* It is revelation and knowledge of God. ('Approach your ear
and feel how, deep in the breast of a God, love is slow to die. ...')[66]
Neither literary genres nor traditions can equal this.

Between Israel's inconclusive moves from affirmation to denial
and God's demand, stands the gift of prophecy, beseeching God to be
patient and exhorting Israel to a proper attitude to the past, a
recognition of the present, and a resolve for the future. Once it is
realized that what is lost cannot be recovered, the dead past is left to
bury its dead, and God's proclamation of a new creation rises, a
promise that man's weakness will be absorbed by God's power. The
past can never be disowned, it lives within Israel. It is revived as a
reality as Israel understands its meaning, as it modifies the present,
and is modified by it. The future is built 'upon the real past.' In the
meantime, the people are neither the same people who left Egypt at
the beginning nor those who will arrive at the End which is to be a
Beginning.

The prophet's word does not proceed from tradition, though it is
born in the tradition, delivered with the help of tradition, received in
it, interpreted through it. It recalls tradition and commemorates it,
remembering it, reminding of it, celebrating it. But it aspires not to a

return but to a new creation. Future and past are not identical. The prophetic remembrance of the past is *epiphanic*, it makes present the event recalled, not for itself, but as revelation, guarantee, and foundation of the future. The past becomes a paradigm whilst remaining unique, irreducible, and unrepeatable. The future arises from God, not from the past, and is greater than the past. 'For that which was never told them they see, and that which they never heard they perceive' (Is lii 15b). We are in the sphere of the typological interpretation of history.

The word cannot be said to derive from the tradition, because it is not only a content, but the instrument also by means of which something is effected. That is why it has nothing to safeguard it: it does not rest on the past but on its own future fulfilment. Whether accepted or refused, God's immeasurable thought and plans shall be accomplished.

For the prophet true continuity consists in absolute obedience to God, even if it be in a series of absolute breakings with the past (as was the case with Israel from her beginning, when she broke with the ancestral polytheism [Josh xxiv], the sacrifice of the first-born child, the marriage with the half-sister, etc.). Traditions are not always Yahweh's traditions. Centuries before the Prophet from Galilee attacked the 'tradition of the elders' in the name of God's commandment (Mt xv 1ff., etc.), Jeremiah mocked 'the deceiving pen of the scribes' and their law in the name of the true word of Yahweh (viii 8ff). And the authoritative 'You have heard that it was said to the men of old . . . but I say to you' is prepared by Ezekiel xx 25: 'I gave them statutes that were not good and ordinances by which they could not have life' — a punishment permitted for their 'hardness of heart' (Mt xix 8). 1 Kings xiii ('the most expressive, rich, and comprehensive prophetical story of the O. T.', according to Karl Barth) demonstrates in an extraordinarily impressive way how man's sin and God's test work in the mystery of his inscrutable ways, and how impossible it is for man to judge.[67]

Prophecy ought never to be examined only in regard to tradition. Opposing prophets and tradition, or making of the prophets mere interpreters of the tradition, are absurd positions. With all due respect, it must be said that the great scholars associated with these interpretations fail to recognize the nature of both word and tradition. The first seem to ignore history and to identify tradition with repetition; the second seem to forget the timeless and to identify tradition with popular mythology. Fohrer's school tends to forget the identity of Yahweh; von Rad's school tends to conceal the 'novelty of the Spirit'. The former is too individualistic, and suffers from a lack of the sense of Israel as a community, the people of God; the latter tends to forget the person, ascribing to the community roles that only persons can have. The first is inclined to over-emphasise individual revelation; the second gravitates towards conceiving revelation only in terms of intellectual activity, thought, reflection.

Tradition in Israel is the sum of Yahweh's words. But a living sum of living *debarim*, 'words-acts', not a record of beloved dead voices. Tradition is the constant abiding of Yahweh in the midst of his people, not memory of past words. To continue the tradition means to have ears to hear. Prophecy can be turned to the future because it is historical, that is, lives 'in what is not merely the present, but the present moment of the past . . . is conscious not of what is dead, but of what is already living'.[68] True prophecy is in concord with the past, because free from the past as from some outward formal criterion. And it is free from it as from some outward formal criterion, because in concord with it. In the history of revelation Old Testament prophecy represents new revelation from God to his people in many respects. New revelation about the past, but preeminently new revelation about the future. The word of the Old Testament prophets coming from the Word testifies of things greater, 'the unspoken word, the Word unheard'.[69]

Chapter 2

ADVENTUS

Periodization in history is as necessary an evil as the division of a book into chapters. The only remedy I know against it is a very loose and vague title. For the time after the Exile and up to the Christian era I could find no better name than 'The Advent'. I realize that historians and theologians can raise many objections against such a heading. Yet, I still think that a Christian historian can legitimately name the period including the five centuries preceding Christ's nativity 'the Advent', without committing himself to any 'theocratic' or other historiography. Here I propose to examine the problem of Tradition and Prophecy in the Judaism of the Persian era, the Greek Oriental empires, the Maccabaean and Hasmonaean kingdoms, the age of the Roman Pompey and the Idumaean Herod the Great. Obviously the evolution and change are very great, astonishing though the continuity may be. A very general title was indispensable for this sequence of most unhomogeneous centuries.

The period starts with an astounding, but very understandable, break of generations. The Israel that emerged after the return from the Babylonian exile was no longer the Israel of the pre-exilic time. The horror and despair before the ghastly grimaces of history changed, and was still to change, the people of God in a very radical way. And the first casualty of this change was history itself, the idea of history. History as revelation was never again to be trusted in Judah as it once had been — with all that this means for the Jewish theology of that time and for our own theology and its ideas on 'biblical historicism'. This was to be the attitude of Judaism until very recent times, with short exceptions like the violent militancy inaugurated by Judas Maccabaeus and its fatal spiral of *Judaea armata, capta, resurgens*. The shift is now from action to contemplation, from history to eternity. We are on the way towards the synthesis in Christianity of Israel's historicism with the ontology of Greece, and it is shocking to see how little this has been noticed by biblical critics and theologians, who in their great admiration for the prophets tend to see Israel's history after the Exile as one of 'decline and fall', forgetting that the new situations, institutions, and beliefs of the intertestamental times are in no less degree a 'schoolmaster unto Christ'. Judaism in its totality is a most rich period in the history of God's people, and recent archaeological discoveries in the Judaean Desert and elsewhere in Palestine leave small room for caricatures and allow no illusions about the brilliance of that age.

The purpose of the present work is not history *sensu stricto* and I

do not propose to trace the history of post-exilic Judaism. Still,
matters of the greatest importance for our present pursuit pass
unmentioned in some standard histories of Israel. The problem of
language, for example: do biblical students really understand the
tremendous impact that a change of language has on a people? Yet,
it is common knowledge that the language of the people who
returned from the Exile was no longer exactly the same as the
language of the people who were exiled. The *sepat kena'an* or
yehudit (classical Hebrew) gives way to a more Aramaicized form of
the language, shortly to be supplanted by the *lingua franca* of the
whole Near East, Aramaic at first, Greek later. One often wonders
how deep a knowledge of the meaning of translation in Antiquity
some biblical scholars have. Is it always realized what the adoption
of the Aramaic alphabet instead of the so-called Palaeo-Hebrew,
and the ensuing transliteration of manuscript texts, meant for this
people — and means for us? A glance at the formidable work of
Kemal Ataturk and its repercussions on twentieth century Turkey
could give an idea of what such changes of alphabet could mean in
the fourth or third centuries B.C. The cleavage of generations and
the break with tradition that such actions generate can hardly be
overestimated. And this is very important for our subject. In the
period of the Advent, the Hebrew people passed through a whole
series of such momentous events and was shaken to the very core of
its existence: it changed foreign lords something like five times,
language twice, alphabet and calendar at least once, orthography
continually, and was dispersed in several countries. Under Simon
and Hyrcanus, the Zadokite priesthood itself gave place to new
parvenus as well, an event which recent Qumran and Samaritan
studies prove to have had the gravest consequences. The nation saw
resurgences of uncontrolled 'modernisms' and adaptations to
contemporary fashions and realities, as well as 'patriotic' revivals
of archaic styles, scripts, languages, customs, etc. (Not only the
Zadokites of Samaria or Qumran, but even Ben Kosibah in the early
second century A.D. resuscitated the Palaeo-Hebrew script.) The
people saved its identity through a tenacious particularism, but, at
the same time, the people became more receptive. Throughout this
period I see history with its fingers in Israel's ears, sighing and
saying to her in Aramaic (?), ' "EPHPHATHA", that is, "Be
opened" '.

From the time of the Return from exile to the Maccabaean revolt
we can delineate one period. The age that followed the Maccabaean
militancy is clearly different. However, for practical reasons the two
periods are here treated together. For this treatment many
justifications can, of course, be given. The process in the evolution of
God's people is the same in both periods. From a holy people Israel
tends, for example, to become a people of saints. This tendency can
be traced from the time of the Return, through Ezra, up to Qumran,
the early Church, and, beyond Jamnia, to the Second Revolt;

sometimes saving the people, sometimes degenerating into sectarianism. In a sense post-exilic Judaism is itself a sect tending to
exclude local Yahwists other than the Judahites. The gradual
estrangement from the Samaritans, which resulted in the final
schism in the Hasmonaean period, is a sad consequence of this
particularism.[1] Otherwise, an extreme cautiousness is needed in
applying the terms 'normative' and 'sectarian' to any 'Judaism' of
this age. In what follows I feel unable to use these distinctions as
proposed by the Christian scholar G. F. Moore, even after their
recent defence by such Jewish scholars as G. Vermes or S. Lowy.

The first Jewish encyclopaedism

The period from the Restoration to the Maccabaean revolt starts
with the feverish expectations of the last exilic and the first post-
exilic days and continues with a long disappointment which finds
its climax in the anguish of the days of the Seleucid Antiochus IV
Epiphanes (175-164 B.C.). Scholars have often stressed this
psychological climate of frustration. Yet, this is not all. There is
another face of post-exilic Judaism and it must be seen as well. I do
not know any short description of the age between the Exile and the
rise of the Maccabees better than that given by L. Grollenberg:
'Years of silent reflection and hopes, when Israel meditated the
whole previous action of Yahweh: she read and re-read what was
left of the traditions of Moses and the great prophets. . . . During the
centuries that elapsed between the completion of the Temple and the
revolt of the Maccabees the Jewish people stays, with its priests,
gathered around the altar of Yahweh, more than ever people of God,
separated from the pagan world, outside the great politics'. A silent
period of seclusion when the people reflects on its past with a broken
heart, producing the grandiose recital of the benefactions of God
and the continuous infidelity of His people which is the Old
Testament we know.[2]

This sober aspect of post-exilic Judaism must not be obscured by
any overemphasis on disappointment. Frustration from 'inexact'
prophecies would be characteristic of a static religion, but this is not
the case with Yahwism. Religion after all is not a brute and material
fact of the order of the 'strictly exact'. The Old Testament that we
have is the work of precisely this sober and reflecting Judaism, and
not of any depressive anxieties or frantic rages.

The early post-exilic period saw the appearance of what I propose
to call *the first Jewish encyclopaedism* (the second would be the
period of the Mishnah and the Talmud). Though there was nothing
like an effort to establish a classification and a summa of learning,
yet the interest in preserving the types of the past is unmistakable in
the work of the Chronicler, the Pentateuch, the edition(s) of the
prophetic books, especially in the work of the 'inspired scribes' and
the whole sapiential literature that they produced. In the case of the
collection of proverbs, fables and allegories, and of regulations for

correct social behaviour, we are confronted with a real encyclo-
paedia of learning and *savoir vivre*. Two phases can be distinguished within this encyclopaedism falling *mutatis mutandis* in the early
Persian and the late Persian and Greek periods respectively. In its
initial soaring the first Jewish encyclopaedism produced the
Pentateuch, the prophetical books more or less as we know them,
and the history of the Chronicles. At the beginning of the same
period we witness 'the last flicker of the old prophetic spirit which
briefly flared when Zerubbabel rose up as pretender to the royal
office',[3] and before the second (exilic) edition of the Deuteronomistic
history, Deuteronomy itself, and the Priestly work. These late exilic
works are highly original historical compositions and interpretations, written (especially P) along with Ezek xl-xlviii in preparation for, and in hope of, the restoration of Israel. But the edition
of the Law, with all the additions, rearrangements, and reorient-
ations that it necessitated, the edition of the Prophetical books as we
now understand it, and the Chronicles, are no less original works.
Recent studies show that the Chronicler for example did not intend
to rewrite the history of Judah or to gather what had not been
covered by his predecessors, but to teach his people through history,
especially concerning the legitimate Israel and the true worship and
its legitimate place and ministers. Findings from Qumran like the
4QSamb, 4QSamc, and 4QSama, show that the Chronicler utilized
for Samuel-Kings an Old Palestinian text type, i.e. a different one
from the Masoretic. These facts force us to change radically our
views on his supposed personality and his work.[4] These re-
interpretations or re-editions of past history for present situations
are the beginnings of what will later be examined as the 're-
reading of the Bible'. Though they are not prophecy *sensu stricto*
they show how the tradition was conceived and how the previous
word of God was becoming living and actual again in completely
new situations. Moreover, we are dealing not only with the old word
actualized, but, in many cases, with a new word. We encounter
prophecy again, a prophecy no less daring, active, and contemporary than the classical prophecy. I would not hesitate to call those
unknown inspired scribes and editors 'the later prophets'.... To this,
however, I shall come back later. Here I must again underline how
original, sensitive and alive was this initial soaring of what I called
the first Jewish encyclopaedism. Beyond rediscovering, recovering
and safeguarding, it remained always ready to adapt and progress.
It gives the impression of a world open and penetrated by the living
reality. It is an encyclopaedism with a soul, turned not only to the
past but also to the present and to the future, for which it has a
programme.

During its second phase, things change. Judah was already a
theocracy centred round the Temple, the Law, and the Priest. The
institution of a preserved zone protected from any dangerous
assimilation, change, and innovation is to be expected from a small

and impotent theocratic state enjoying a certain amount of independence in the framework of a decentralized world empire like the Persian. The flourishing of the sapiential literature does not mean that this literature appears in Israel first at this time. Its origins are centuries older and its proper *Sitz-im-Leben* was the royal court. What we now witness is primarily an encyclopaedic collection of older wisdom, and the resulting creation of compendia. Evidently we are encountering bibliophile erudites and moralist preachers rather than wise royal counsellors or humanists. Books like Ecclesiastes and Sirach show, nevertheless, how profoundly these scribes could be influenced by their time, and how they too wanted to answer contemporary questions. Wisdom was by its very nature international and in Israel it created a kind of natural theology based on traditions such as those embodied in the first nine chapters of Genesis. The 'inspired scribes' reveal to us Israel as a thinking people, a fact too often forgotten. With them the age of the first Jewish encyclopaedism finds its close. It started in the late exile in Babylon, and, as far as we can see through the history of the biblical text, it never acquired a centre, but kept developing in different centres, often in isolation. As the political situation changes again, apocalyptic, until then a clandestine religious attitude, comes to the foreground.

The flowering of apocalyptic

The Judaism of the age that we are studying is a very complex phenomenon. Its diversity is as amazing as its unity. If I avoid speaking of 'the period of apocalyptic', it is because this period (second century B.C.-first century A.D.) was in no way the monopoly of the apocalyptists. Apocalyptic had appeared centuries before, and in the period between the second century B.C. and the first century A.D. it flourished; always along with other theological and religious attitudes and movements. To give just one example, the scribes continued their work in this period also, and it is precisely at this period that the son of Sirach composed his hymn of the ideal scribe, who applies his heart to the study of the law, wisdom, and the prophecies (Sir xxxix 1-11; note the three parts of the Old Testament). It is true though that in this period 'to some extent all minds in Israel are coloured by Apocalyptic'.[5]

The origins of apocalyptic are still debated. On the whole there are two schools, that which derives apocalyptic from Wisdom, with G. von Rad at its head, and that which affirms the prophetic origins of apocalyptic, with G. Fohrer, F. M. Cross, S. Amsler, R. North, D. S. Russell and D. N. Freedman as its most noted representatives. The history of the investigation of the problems around apocalyptic has been told by J. M. Schmidt[6] and, more popularly, by K. Koch.[7] G. von Rad denies any primary connection between prophecy and apocalyptic. Instead, he affirms that the mother of apocalyptic is Wisdom; that apocalyptic is an eschatologizing of Wisdom notions,

ideas and interests; there is in it a unity of history.[8] G. Fohrer finds
that apocalyptic is a younger and more modern form of eschatology
of the type found in Zechariah.[9] Zechariah's relations with
apocalyptic have been examined with positive results by S. Amsler
and R. North.[10] Further research is needed on the pattern of F. M.
Cross's essays in his *Canaanite Myth and Hebrew Epic*, especially
those on 'The Divine Warrior' and 'The Song of the Sea and
Canaanite Myth'.[11] The 'Note on the Study of Apocalyptic Origins'
that he appends to the book is a good directive. 'History and myth,
the wisdom tradition and the prophetic tradition', he says very
justly, 'coalesced in the late sixth century never fully to separate
again'. Apocalyptic is the final stage of that transformation from
epic tradition by way of prophecy that occurred in the late exilic and
early post-exilic literature as a resurgence of old Canaanite
mythical lore, always it seems living underground in Israel.[12]
Apocalyptic, thus, appears as a more complex and ancient
phenomenon than was previously supposed. G. L. Davenport's
warning that 'we must be reluctant to burden any single movement
or tradition with sole responsibility for the rise of a later
phenomenon' is always timely.[13]

The question of apocalyptic belongs to the more general problem
of eschatology and its transformations in Judaism. The vexatious
ambiguity of the term 'eschatology' is well known to every vigilant
student of the Bible.[14] It has been said that only that which has no
history can be defined. Apocalyptic has a long history, and a closer
study of it shows, I think, that there are not one, but many
apocalyptics. I would only say that it is not a literature (the name
Apocalypses would suffice for that), but an attitude of mind and
soul, and a special feeling born out of the great contrast between the
ideal and reality. An attitude of non-fatalistic withdrawal from
history, and expectation of a regained paradise, born out of history's
more and more tragic, absurd, and burlesque, character at some
special moments. The flowering of apocalyptic coincides with the
oppression of Antiochus IV, the tradition of military resistance
inaugurated by the Maccabees, their assumption of the high-
priestly dignity, and the subsequent Roman occupation, the two
great unsuccessful risings, and the final fall. It is as a response to
these awe-inspiring events that the flowering of apocalyptic must
be seen. It is not characterized by the violence of Maccabaeus, but
neither is it characterized by the long-suffering gentleness of the
scribe Eleazar. Apocalyptic is a loss of patience, and the ensuing
nervousness, which, though not losing the will to oppose, opposes,
but with something future, in the future. It has little to say about the
past and less about the present, although it considers them as far
from meaningless: they invite the desired future. The apocalyptist
was a pious Jew for whom his contemporary national situation
(external oppression *and* internal unfaithfulness) stands under the
sign of unsuccess, not because he had no hope, but because his hope

had not been realized. Life thus appeared tedious, an impossible impasse — though never an illusion. The apocalyptist's fancies seem to us grotesque, but his answer would be that of Montherlant's Don Juan: *'Il n'y a pas de fantastique: c'est la realite qui est le fantastique'*.

I am not one of those who think that apocalyptic is of perennial value, although it is easy to see why people of the present age are attracted to it. It undervalues history, and though (often by) asserting God's sovereignty over history, it separates in an ominous way salvation history from history at large. Its individualism favoured sectarianism and struck a blow at the concept of 'Israel' itself by continually disintegrating it into smaller and smaller groups of select, pious, and, finally, perfect men. To its narrowness is due in great part the fact that Israel lost some of the most precious prophetic insights concerning the fate of the Gentiles, their final conversion and salvation. And no one can fail to see in it the seeds of Jewish proto-gnosis. Daniel, the only apocalyptic book of the canonical Old Testament, belongs to the beginnings of the period of the flowering of apocalyptic and comes from a milieu of orthodox Hasidim. Compared with later apocalypses it is undeniably a most sober book. I would not hesitate to call it proto-apocalyptic: it is a very primitive apocalypse, and the earliest of the known ones. Qumran is an apocalyptic community, but it must be remembered that the covenanters of Qumran believed that they were the ones entrusted with the preparation of His way in the wilderness (1QS viii 12-16; ix 19-20), and this, as well as the person and the mission of the Teacher of Righteousness, gives them a quite specific colour. Recent studies, moreover, show that in the texts which could be qualified as official the air is much more sober than in the works which do not belong to the principal current. 1QpHab vii 1-2, for example, asserts that the exact time of the end is not known; 1QH vi 10-13 (especially if we reconstruct verse 12 following A. Dupont-Sommer and M. Delcor) leaves a door of hope open to the nations — even if under stereotyped Old Testament phrases; and speculations about figures such as *Milki-sedeq* and *Milki-resa'* are, as J. Milik has shown, marginal in Qumran, their source being the pre-Essenian Aramaic Visions of Amram.[15] These are warnings to be cautious. G. L. Davenport has argued for three different editions of the Jubilees, the first to be dated in the latter part of the third century, or the early part of the second century B.C. M. Testuz showed that the Essene authors of the book do not belong to the classical party as we know it from Qumran and Josephus, and are not yet separated from the Pharisees and the Sadducees. It is to be hoped that very few would now be eager to attribute the whole of the apocalyptic literature to the Essenes *tout court*, or, even worse, to the community of Qumran. What is of interest, however, in this study is the hermeneutical method of apocalyptic, and to this aspect we shall shortly return. At this stage it is safe to conclude by saying that apocalyptic is not prophecy, but — and this is very important — it does presuppose a living contact with the spirit of God. This contact being a fiction rather than a reality, we are before a *sui generis* pseudo-prophecy. In the history of revelation the importance of apocalyptic lies in its very appearance and in the fact of its existence rather than in its content.

Until an accredited prophet shall arise

The period of the Advent opened with three prophets, but there is no doubt that it was primarily the period of the scribes. Scholars have spoken of it as 'the period of the silence of the prophets' or 'the period of the quenched spirit'. Both opinions are old and in a sense date from the very period we are examining. But discrimination is needed here too. For these attitudes seem to presuppose that the only way for the Spirit to act is through prophecy. This is fundamentally mistaken as far as Israel is concerned. King, priest, prophet, wise man, institution and event, are always thought of in Israel as the area of the Spirit. The second presupposition is that a 'normative' Judaism has been in existence ever since post-exilic times. I have said earlier what I think of this idea. The plain fact is that some Jews of the period under discussion maintained these beliefs of a prophetic silence and a quenched spirit, whereas others not only opposed them, but indeed believed themselves endowed with the spirit and the prophetic gift. Now what we, as scholars or Christians, are to do with these beliefs is another question.

J. Jeremias gives all the important instances of the doctrine of the quenched spirit in later Judaism.[16] It seems to me that the recognition of the presence of God's spirit among his people depended not only on religious reasons, but, sometimes perhaps primarily, on political and party considerations and interests. There is no doubt that for later Pharisaism and the Tannaitic rabbis law, spirit, and prophets were one, the prophets being the inspired transmitters of the law after Moses, Joshua and the elders, and before the men of the Great Synagogue (*Abhoth* i 1). The three post-exilic prophets were considered especially important as the links with the Great Synagogue, and Malachi was identified with Ezra, Ezra being the disciple of Baruch son of Neriah, the disciple and amanuensis of Jeremiah (*bMeg.* 15a; 16b). R. Abdimi of Haifa (A.D. 279-320) said: 'From the day whereon the Temple was laid waste, prophecy was taken from the prophets and given to the sages'.[17]

This saying of R. Abdimi comes very close to what the sages were thinking of themselves. The ideal scribe in Sirach xxxix 6 is 'filled with the spirit of intelligence', and Wisdom ix 17 presents the possession of God's holy spirit as the prerequisite, along with His wisdom, to the knowledge of His will. Obviously, the sage, whose archetype is Solomon, has both. Recent studies of sapiential literature show unmistakably how far wisdom was assimilated and identified with the spirit, all whose traditional functions she

assumes (cf. Wis vii 11-viii 1 and Is xi 2ffff — note the twenty-one
attributes of the wisdom, three times seven, and the seven gifts of
the spirit in Is xi, 2 LXX). If the reality is the same, we must not be
deceived by a change of names. This evolution in the wisdom
literature has to be accounted for in all studies on tradition and
prophecy in the intertestamental period. Not only did the scribes
and sages consider themselves as inspired by God's spirit, but both
the Synagogue and the Church recognized them as such by
receiving their works and their editions of the Law and the Prophets
in their respective canons.

There is no doubt that apocalyptic believed in the presence and
work of the spirit of God among his chosen. Its proper character as
'revelation' is eloquent enough: for the revealer is God. And it must
be noticed that the apocalyptist believed himself to possess a
revelation higher than that given to the prophets, sometimes even
higher than that given to Moses himself. For the Jubilees, for
example, the supreme code of Judaism is the book itself. 'The
revelation of the divine law', wrote M. Testuz, 'is progressive: the
patriarchs transmit to their descendants, as a testimony, the
precepts of the Law that they know; then the angel wrote for Moses
the Book of the First Law; finally, perfect formulation of the Law,
the faithful possesses this book of the Jubilees'.[18] 'For until that
time [of Jacob and Reuben] there had not been revealed the
ordinance and the judgement and law in its completeness for all, but
in the days (it has been revealed) as a law of seasons and of days,
and an everlasting law for the everlasting generations' (Jub xxx 16).
I need hardly say that this holds true for Qumran as a whole.
Though the Teacher of Righteousness is never called a prophet, in
the *Hodayoth* he claims many prophetic titles, and in passages such
as 1QpHab vii 4-8 he assumes that the prophets have neither said
all nor known everything. His knowledge completes the prophetic
revelation: 'That he who reads may read it speedily' (Hab ii 1b). Its
interpretation concerns the Teacher of Righteousness to whom God
made known all the mysteries of the words of His servants the
Prophets. 'For there shall be yet another vision concerning the
appointed time. It shall tell of the end and shall not lie' (Hab ii 3a).
Its interpretation: the final age shall be prolonged, and shall exceed
all that the Prophets have said; for the mysteries of God are
astounding'. The 'community psalms' of the *Hodayoth* show that
this was not an exclusive privilege of the Teacher (see 1QH xiii 19f;
xvi 11, etc.).[19] After all, the presence of the spirit is of the essence of
the Qumranic *peser*, to which we shall shortly return.

The earliest references that I know to a complete absence of the
spirit come from the Christian era. *tSot* xiii 3: 'When the elders came
to the house of Gadia in Jericho, a heavenly voice proclaimed to
them: There is a man among you worthy of the holy spirit, but this
generation is unfit for it. They fixed their eyes on Hillel the Elder' (fl.
c.30 B.C.-A.D. 10); *bSanh* 65b: When R. Akiba (c. A.D. 50-132)

reached Deut xviii 11 ('or that consulteth the dead') he wept: 'If one
who starves himself that an unclean spirit may rest upon him has
his wish granted, he who fasts that the pure spirit [the Divine
Presence] may rest upon him, how much more should his desire be
fulfilled! But alas! our sins have driven it away from us, as it is
written,But your iniquities have separated between you and your
God' (Is lix 2).

Concerning the absence of prophets and the disappearance of
prophecy, the following points must be made:

1. As has been already said, the holy spirit is not necessarily
always the spirit of prophecy, even if the terms are interchangeable
in the Targumim.

2. Though sage, scribe, and apocalyptist, claim prophetical titles,
they are not expressly called prophets.

3. The disappearance of the office of the prophet does not mean the
end of prophetism itself. We have seen that certain quarters claimed
a knowledge and a revelation completing the Prophets, or even
higher than the Mosaic one.

4. Psalm lxxiv 9 usually adduced as a 'proof text' for the
disappearance of prophecy does not say all that much. The psalm is
a lament and uses stereotyped lament language. The destruction of
the Temple that it bewails can be that of 587 B.C. or the Temple
desecration of 168 B.C. Though the present tense is usually used in
translating verse 9, such an eminent commentator as A. Weiser uses
the past tense throughout, translating: 'We did not see our signs;
there was no longer any prophet; and there was none among us who
knew which way to turn.' The first part of Psalm lxxvii is a lament
too and verse 8b(9) expresses, I think, the personal anguish of the
psalmist, who cannot discern God's answer in conditions of national
affliction about which we are in the dark. This crisis in the
psalmist's own faith is characteristic but must not be absolutized in
a general belief that prophetic word was silent. Both passages can
be compared with Lamentations ii 9b: 'The law is no more, and her
[Jerusalem's] prophets obtain no vision from Yahweh', or Ezekiel
vii 26b: 'They will demand a vision from the prophet, teaching will
perish from the priest, counsel from the elders', which referred to the
coming disaster. All these texts have their setting in a time of
nationwide affliction when men feel abandoned by God. Psalms
lxxiv 9 and lxxvii 8 must be understood in this sense.

5. Daniel iii 38 belongs to the same category as the passages just
mentioned and refers (again in stereotyped Old Testament phrases)
to the condition of the exiles: 'There is no more at this time prince or
prophet, or leader, or burnt offerings, or sacrifice, or oblation, or
incense, or place to offer before Thee and to find mercy'. This is not
the image of the author's times.

6. Zechariah xiii 2ff belongs to Second Zechariah and must be
understood as a polemic against cicatrized ecstatic nebi'im in the
line of the oracles of Jeremiah xxiii and Ezekiel xiii. It announces

the purification of the land, idolatry and corrupted prophecy, the
quintessence of the 'impurity', being swept out. Nehemiah vi 12-14
gives us a possible background for such post-exilic pseudo-
prophets.

7. The only canonical book from this period that clearly expresses
the idea that prophets have disappeared is 1 Maccabees. 1 Macc iv
46 and xiv 41 show how the 'blameless priests' that Judas
Maccabaeus chose, and 'the Jews and the priests who were all
pleased that Simon should be their leader and high priest for ever'
(hereditarily), decreed on at least two important occasions that, as it
was impossible to know God's true will, their decrees were to remain
valid until God decreed otherwise: until the coming of 'an accredited
prophet'.[20] We know very well how grave was the second decision,
to break finally the succession of the Zadokite high-priesthood and
to inaugurate the new Hasmonaean high-priestly dynasty. I cannot
avoid thinking that this belief about the disappearance of prophecy
and the impossibility of knowing God's will was adopted and used
by the Maccabees and their party for their political interests. 1
Maccabees ix 27 proves that the author of the book himself (a
Sadducee?) believed that the non-prophetic era had started long
before: 'And there was great tribulation in Israel, such as was not
since the time that a prophet appeared unto them'.

Josephus, in the first century A.D., holds a similar view (cf.
Contra Apionem i 41) and it has been shown that this was the
rabbinical belief as well. Ezra ii 63 (Neh vii 65) indicates that the
priests — under whose inspiration 'His Excellency' obviously acts
— held practically the same opinion with regard to 'priestly
divination'. In religious affairs their decisions were to be valid 'until
there should be a priest to consult Urim and Thummim'. (The
Talmud testifies, in fact, that the second Temple did not have the
sacred lots.) So hesitancy about God's real will was an early feature
of a certain post-exilic Judaism. As far as I can understand, it must
have been the opinion prevailing in priestly circles. Our sources
witness to this from the times of Ezra ii 63 to Josephus, 'a priest
himself and of priestly descent'. The reason why this was so we can
detect quite easily. It was the general spirit of the conservatively
minded Jerusalem priesthood, which strove to preserve the people as
a religious community rather than as an independent nation.
'Apocalyptic frenzies' were considered a danger from the days of
Ezra to the Sadducean Caiaphas (Jn xi 47-53) and Ananus and
Jesus, the last high priests, murdered by the Zealots in the winter of
A.D. 67-68. If any prophets were to be recognized, these were the
priests themselves, and especially the high priest (Jn xi 51).
Josephus could not agree more: the only 'prophets' he recognized
were priests, the Essenes (a priestly sect) and himself. One cannot
avoid suspecting a professional note in all these assertions. Philo,
after all, would not be an exception: he never doubted his own
inspiration — even though *de Somniis* ii 252 translated from the

Greek frame of reference could point to poetical inspiration rather
than to prophecy.

I assume, thus, that in the period we are examining, the belief in
the disappearance of prophecy was coloured by political considerations; but this is not to say that those believing in the presence of
the prophetic spirit were necessarily politically engaged or rev-
olutionary: the covenanters of Qumran and the apocalyptists in
general are obvious examples to the contrary. Strictly speaking only
1 Maccabees ix 27 asserts a disappearance of prophecy, whereas iv
46 and xiv 41, though they probably presuppose it, do not declare it
expressis verbis.[21]

To recognize the presence of the prophetic spirit did not preclude
the expectation of a greater measure of it in the new age. And vice
versa, to expect the coming of the eschatological Prophet, for
example, did not mean belief in the disappearance of prophecy. In a
certain sense post-exilic Judaism never thought of itself in terms
other than of an interim. All decisions and all decrees were viewed
as interim regulations, until the new age should come. 1QS ix 10f
and CD vi 10f, xii 23f, xix 10-11, etc. indicate that the apocalyptic
community of Qumran was no exception to the general rule. Far
from accepting any novelty the members 'shall be ruled according
to the first precepts by which the men of the community from the
very beginning have been instructed, until there shall come a
Prophet and the Anointed ones of Aaron and Israel'; 'until he comes
who shall teach righteousness at the end of days'. Statutes are to be
followed 'in the age of wickedness until the coming of the Anointed
of Aaron and Israel'.[22] Obviously, the awaited Prophet shall teach
the will of God in matters of *halakhah* (be he a precursor of the two
Messiahs or a simultaneous eschatological office-bearer — it must
always be borne in mind that the term is very flexible).[23] Until then,
in accordance with the Ezekielian directives, 'the sons of Aaron
alone shall command in matters of justice and property, and every
rule concerning the men of the community shall be determined
according to their work' (1QS ix 7-8).[24] We must assume that, as
with the rabbis, their judgement was based not on new revelation,
but on tradition and reason. It is well known that not even the *Bath
Qol* (the heavenly 'voice' of God) was allowed by the rabbis any
authority in matters relating to *halakhah*.[25] Its verdict was
formally admitted only in matters of personal holiness or divine
commands. I do not think that it can in any way be considered as a
substitute of prophecy in our period, even if this is frequently
asserted by scholars seduced by later ideas, like that of *tSot* xiii 2,[26]
or legends, like those about John Hyrcanus related first by Josephus
(*Ant* xiii 282f). Returning to Qumran, I conclude that the texts we
have seen say that until the time of the eschatological Prophet,
when the 'final precepts' will be given, jurisprudence belongs to the
sons of Aaron alone, and they do not speak about, or presuppose
any, disappearance of prophecy.

From what has already been examined it can be seen that a great
many nuances are necessary. Tannaitic or Amoraitic beliefs do not
necessarily express the opinions held at the period we are
examining. A great diversity of views is revealed all the time. The
view that prophecy had simply disappeared is not attested more
convincingly than its opposite. A general absence of the spirit is
never, to my knowledge, affirmed. Prophetic consciousness and
belief in the possession of the spirit are met among sages, scribes,
priests apocalyptists, and especially at Qumran. What must be
noted is a devaluation of the concept of prophecy and of the
corresponding terminology. Both Philo and Josephus witness to
this. They think and write of prophecy more and more exclusively in
terms of divination, prediction, foreseeing, prognostication, or
oneiromancy. This is not a survival of the 'intellectual' aspect of
prophecy, but just the opposite,a real impoverishment of its concept
through a shift to its irrational aspect only.[27] Philo tends indeed to
be more 'intellectual' when speaking of inspiration (is not the
'spirit' of *de Somniis* ii 252 the Greek Muse? And what about the
famous passage of *Vita Mosis* ii 37 on the seventy-two translators?),
but prophecy is for him too primarily an insight into the future,
which, moreover, comes (he appears to say) because of a wise, good
and just life (*Rer. Div. Her.* 259ff). The popular idea of prophets, as
far as we can infer it from our sources, seems to have been more and
more one of miracleworkers and charismatic healers. It must not be
forgotten, however, that devaluation of terminology does not mean
devaluation of reality itself. It has been shown above that wisdom,
for example, was in many respects assimilated with the spirit and
replaced it. And, in my view, the greatest and most genuine
manifestation of the prophetic spirit in the period under examination 'the Advent' period was the inspired activity of Bible re-
reading. This is certainly so if prophecy is the announcement of the
divine will at a certain historical moment; God's message for a
special time; his living word to living persons.

Textus vivus

In Israel the word of God was never merely handed down: it was
always creatively applied. This was so, is, and shall be so, as long as
there will be a people of God that lives 'by every word that proceeds
from the mouth of God'. 'The Old Testament awareness of history
as the sphere of divine activity is to be found', writes P.R. Ackroyd,
'not only in the way in which a prophetic word belongs in a historic
setting, but in the way also in which a prophecy or a law or a psalm
may be seen to illuminate some new moments of history.... For the
message delivered from God to man cannot be of merely limited
application; it belongs to the divine will, however much its
expression is conditioned by the human agent through whom it
comes and the historical moment to which it belongs. The element of
truth within it cannot but be of enduring value',[28] (the same as the

saving event). The impetus to this process is given by the prophet himself: 'Bind up a testimony, seal an instruction in the heart of my disciples' (Is viii 16).

But the disciples of the prophets are not always prophets themselves. They can be scribes, like Baruch, the disciple of Jeremiah who appears as the archetype of the scribe-successor of the prophet in post-exilic Judaism. The inspired scribes succeeded the prophets of Yahweh. To them fell the call to preserve alive the word of the prophets and to reveal God's message to their contemporaries. I have already described the process of reflection and creative handling of the word by these scribes, priests, and sages. It must not be forgotten that prophecy and wisdom 'coalesced in the late sixth century never fully to separate again'. Law, counsel, and word proceed now out of the same lips. Ezekiel is, here also, the father of Judaism. The re-reading of the Bible was not the work of a special class of men; the inspired scribe of Judaism could be a priest or a layman, a sage or an apocalyptist, a pro-Maccabaean hasmodaean or a hellenizing sadducee, a Palestinian Jew or a Babylonian or Alexandrian one, an editor, or a translator, or a simple pious reader; and he could think of himself as an adaptor or as a corrector. I do not for a moment say that all this exegesis is inspired and a fruit of the prophetic spirit. I do not think, for example, that the various 'decent' *tiqqune sopherim* (corrections of the scribes) are inspired, even if they are found in the Masoretic text, or (more rarely) in the LXX. And I should not hold that an extra-biblical midrash or pesher are Spirit-guided; although, along with the early Church, I shall not deny divine assistance to what we call the Septuagint. The whole exegesis, however, of the post-exilic era is a work of the people of God, and so it is significant for the historical revelation, even when (along with much Christian exegesis) it lacks the assistance of the Spirit and is not part of the divine dispensation. 'New beliefs' of inter-testamental Judaism, even if scarcely witnessed in the Old Testament, could be true revelation from God, and Jesus himself embraced those that were true and reproved the 'conservative' sadducees (and through them a certain type of Old Testament scholar?). The inspired re-reading of the Bible is that re-reading and re-writing and editing which produced our Bible, lives in our Bible, *is* our Bible.

The whole activity could be described as midrashic, if the term midrash is taken in its broad sense or definition (implicit, or covert midrash). It is in this sense that R. Bloch writes of God's word as a midrash: 'revealed at a given moment of history ... addresses itself, nevertheless, to men of all times. But, then, it is bound to stay infinitely open to all the developments of the meaning of the message, to all the legitimate adaptations, to all the new situations. ... So long as there will be a people of God considering the Bible as living Word of God, midrash will always exist and it is only the name that will change'.[29] If every actualization of the text is midrash, A. Robert's 'anthological style' is, of course, midrashic. For, as he defined it, this style, so frequently employed by the prophets, among others, is 'reemploying literally or equivalently words or formulas of previous Scriptures', developing, of course, enriching, and transposing their primitive message.[30]

A very quick look at the main exegetical procedures of the period we are examining would perhaps be necessary. I shall not enter into the discussion of what midrash exactly is, or is not. If midrash, beyond being a genre, is an activity, then every re-reading of previous Scriptures is part of it. For my part, I would prefer to see the term midrash used only for the literary kind. I think that R. Bloch recognized the difficulty inherent in her above-mentioned definition, when towards the end of her article, she tried to distinguish between midrash and apocalyptic. For they have indeed to be distinguished. The midrash is a work of tradition and reflection turned towards the past, even if thinking of the present, whereas apocalyptic is turned towards the future, even if studying the past. In the end both are interpretation, but I should like to think that not every interpretation is midrash. The specificity of the Qumran pesher, for example, lies in its eschatological perspective and in its expressing the tenets of the sect, not in its being 'interpretation'. Still, some would like to see it as a special Essene type of midrash.

That the midrash has deep biblical roots has long been demonstrated. Ezekiel xvi and xxiii are not just parables. These symbolic histories of Jerusalem and Samaria are 'perfect examples of the midrashic process in the Bible'.[31] Wisdom x-xix is an inspired midrashic re-reading of the book of Exodus. The author has his own philosophy of history and tries to present his thesis so as to edify and to explain. This is the most typical biblical midrash before the rabbinical midrashim. A different procedure is that of the *De viris illustribus* of Ben Sirach (xliv-l 24), where rhetoric is used for encomiastic purposes, though in the midst of all these eulogies the author meditates seriously on the history of his nation.[32] In comparing these two works we can perhaps understand better what it is that differentiates the midrash from other Scriptural meditations or expositions. A good extra-biblical example of the midrashic process in our period is the book of Jubilees, which is otherwise called The Little Genesis, an 'implicit midrash' or a 'midrash haggadah'. Its author endeavoured to answer 'practically every question any skeptic has put to the Book of Genesis', as W.H. Brownlee put it.[33] If Moses wrote Genesis, where did he get his information? When did God create the angels? When did God make Eden? How does this story of creation in chapter ii of Genesis fit into the account of chapter i? Why does Genesis i represent the creation of the human race, both male and female, taking place on the sixth day, whereas Genesis ii indicates that Adam lived for a time without wife?

The pesher *sensu stricto* is not found in the Bible, except in Daniel perhaps and in the pesher-type midrashim found in the New Testament.[34] According to the definition of J. Carmignac it is 'a literary genre which turns to Biblical texts, considered as announcements or prophecies of future realities, and interprets them as a consequence of these realities, showing how the various details of the Biblical texts apply to such person, to such event, or to such circumstance'. The same author has distinguished two great categories of *pesarim*: the continuous (line by line, e.g. 1QpHab) and the thematic (e.g. 11QMelch).[35] The pesher-exegesis which flourished in Qumran in this period is peculiar in that it considers the message of God as consisting of two halves, the 'mystery' and its 'interpretation', either of which is given to a different person in a different time; so that the message is not understood until the time of the 'interpreter', i.e. the present time of the 'clearing of the way'. The Zadokite apocalyptists of Qumran believe, thus, that prophecy is comprehensible only in the community; for all the mysteries were revealed to the Founder (1QpHab viii 4-5), who declares open the era of the New Covenant. Biblical exegesis is the *Instrumentum* of the 'perfect way', and this interpretation is sometimes rightly called fulfilment-interpretation. Elieser Slomovic reminds us, nevertheless, that the traditional methods and rules of exegesis were used by the Qumran people no less than by others.[36]

It must be underlined that in Qumran we have no dreams, visions, voices, or similar apocalyptic revelatory fictions: the new revelation is discovered in the old scriptural text itself, and the main work of the covenanters is studying the sacred text, copying it, reading it, interpreting it, and being ready for its final fulfilment. The Founder is primarily the teacher, the instructor. According to the *Serekh* the *derek Yahweh* is the *midras hattorah*: ' "In the wilderness prepare the way of . . . . , in the Arabah make straight a highway for our God" (Is xl 3). This is the study of the Law which He commanded by the hand of Moses, to act according to all that is revealed from age to age, and according to what the Prophets revealed by His holy spirit' (1QS viii 15-16). How much prophecy is at the heart of the Qumran covenanters, need not, I hope, be reemphasised. As far as Qumran goes, to speak of a 'silence of prophecy' in the Advent would be absurd. As 11QMelch puts it, interpreting Is lii 7 ('upon the mountains are the feet of the herald proclaiming peace. . . .'), 'Its interpretation is: the mountains [are] the prophet[s], they wh[ose words are "the Feet", (the words) that] they prophe[sied] to all [those who listen to God]. And "the Herald' i[s] the Anointed with the Spiri[t], of whom Dan[iel] spoke (Dan ix 25)'.[37] Khirbet Qumran and its texts radiate still this exaltation before those 'beautiful Feet', the Prophets.[38]

Much work has been done on apocalyptic as re-reading of prophecy.[39] Daniel ix, to mention just one notorious example, is a meditation on the prophecy of Jeremiah xxv 12ff and xxix 10 that the exile of the Jews to the land of the Chaldeans would last for

seventy years. The imperfect fulfilment of the prophecy about the
destruction of Babylon and the return from the exile annoys the
author. Zechariah i 12 and 2 Chronicles xxxvi 21 show how literally
this number was taken. In relating this last reference to Leviticus
xxvi 34 and xxvi 18 the author of Daniel ix arrives at his
interpretation, namely, that Jeremiah was speaking of seventy
sabbatical years (seven times seventy), or that Jeremiah's ten
sabbatical years are, in fact, ten jubileal years (seven times seven
times ten).[40] This is a perfect example of biblical actualization of an
older scriptural passage, and the author admits it openly.

A different expression of Scriptural exegesis and re-reading in our
period is the scribal glosses. They fulfil different purposes and J.
Weingreen has defined four categories of them: i) explanatory; ii)
extensions of themes; iii) variant readings; iv) Masoretic-type
notes.[41] Some of them appear in the LXX and so are clearly early
post-exilic; generally they are found only in the Masorah. G. R.
Driver remarks that the primary purpose of glosses is 'to obviate
difficulties whether by simplifying the construction of the sentence
or by interpreting obscure or unknown words; a secondary purpose
is to present varying readings or draw attention to parallel
passages. Glosses are also inserted in the text to explain historical
allusions or even to put right what the glossator regards as false
history. Others are added to enhance or mitigate the force of the
original text or to give vent to feelings, chiefly of indignation, or to
utter warnings which the reader or scribe may think appropriate.
There are also glosses expressing theological opinions, and, what
are exceptionally important, liturgical glosses'.[42]

In Psalm lv 16c we read: 'for evil is in their dwelling place, in their
midst'. 'In their midst' is, we must suppose, a variant reading gloss.
The words 'and the snow' in Isaiah lv 10, a text originally composed
in Babylonia, represent perhaps an extensional gloss. Jeremiah
xxiii 18 could be a pious exclamation from a sceptical reader
wondering how true and false prophecy can be distinguished at all.
But it need not be so. It can very well be an introduction to verses 19-
20. Deciding what is a gloss or not is very difficult. In Isaiah xxxv 8b
the words 'and it is a processional way' are sometimes regarded as a
gloss. But certainly Isaiah xxxv 7-8 is a corrupted text. How can one
know what is a gloss and what is not? Those who consider this
clause a gloss pronounce a gloss their emendation, of course. Verses
18-19 of Psalm li are a good example of an addition by a pious reader
anxious to see the cult restored in Jerusalem. It is a liturgical gloss,
and some scholars would even regard the mention of 'burnt
offerings and whole oblations' as a second liturgical gloss in the
gloss. We see how a reader of the times of Haggai and Zechariah
adjusts the pre-exilic ideas of the Psalmist to the imperative of his
own time. I do not think that he misunderstood the psalm. Sacrifices
are obviously offered in Jerusalem. The glossator prays for the
blessing of Zion and the reconstruction of her walls. First he applied

this individual psalm of penitence to the nation. He now prays for Jerusalem, the head of the nation, that her bones, which God has broken, may rejoice again. Then she shall offer Him her sacrifices on her altar. The penitent is different, his way of giving thanks for his forgiveness will also be different. I do not see here any dark ritualism. The pre-exilic writer speaks for himself, for his own situation before God. The post-exilic glossator prays for the nation and its capital. His prayers join those of all the pious Israelites of the post-exilic age that the prophecies about Zion may be fulfilled. 'Mayest thou attain to everlasting righteousness; and the blessings of the notables mayest thou receive. Accept a vision bespoken of thee, and dreams of prophets mayest thou receive....' (*Hymn to Zion* in 11QPsa 16-17).[43] Verses 18-19 can be said indeed to bear the influence of Jeremiah xxxiii 6-11.

It is supposed that a great many of these glosses come from the Levitical circles. Scholars have for a long time seen in some Levitical circles the successors of the prophets and the teachers of the law. In Nehemiah viii 7-8 (M) the Chronicler presents the Levites as helping the people to understand the law, translating or interpreting it 'clearly' (*mprs*): 'And they gave the sense so that the people understood the reading'. In 1 Chronicles xxv 7 the Levites, who 'should prophesy with lyres' (verse 1), are presented as *mebinim* (men with understanding), precursors, as it were, of the *maskilim* of Daniel and Qumran. And the LXX (and AV) understood the injunction (to) of the Temple-singers in Psalm xlvii 7 in a characteristic way: 'Sing ye praises with understanding (*maskil*)'.[44]

Re-reading of the Bible is yet more important and significant when earlier teaching is recast in the light of later doctrine. Later beliefs concerning the covenant, the law, God's word, the messiah, the national destinies, the angels, resurrection, immortality and the future life, were inserted in the biblical text when the earlier tradition came to be reedited.[45] Much work remains to be done on lines similar to those traced by R. Tournay. Israel's faith was a living faith overflowing into the text itself, registering on it the development of the Revelation, the elan of which 'went beyond the material content of the texts. And these latter were not considered as dead documents, fixed once for all; they always remained open to eventual enrichment'.[46] Tournay thinks that this re-reading of the Hebrew Bible started in Maccabaean times within the pietist circles. I believe that it had started much earlier, with the exile itself.

If we are to believe E. Lipinski — and we have very good reasons to do so — the celebrated name of Isaiah's son was not *se 'ar yasub*, but *se 'er yasub*, i.e. not 'a remnant will return', but 'the blood will fall back'.[47] In chapter vii Isaiah reassures Ahaz that the coalition of Razon and Pekah will not succeed. Judah's blood will be visited on the heads of Damascus and Samaria (vv.8-9): 'the blood will fall back (*scil.* on the kings of Damascus and Israel)'. In Isaiah x 20ff,

the exilic, or post-exilic, exegesis reads: 'a remnant will return' —
God's message for Israel at that moment.

If I may give a second example of E. Lipinski's work on the
biblical text, I should like to draw attention to his article 'De la
reforme d'Esdras au regne aschatologique de Dieu (Is iv 3-5a)',
where he demonstrates in a very clear way how 1QIs re-read Is iv 3-
5a eschatologically — a process we find in the LXX and the Targum
as well.[48] Here are both texts, along with the LXX and the Targum:

Isaiah iv 3-5a: 'And it comes to pass that he who was left in Zion
and remained in Jerusalem can be called holy: every one who has
been recorded for life in Jerusalem. When His Lordship washed
away the filth of the daughters of Zion so that he rinsed the
bloodstains of Jerusalem from its midst in a spirit of judgment and
in a spirit of cauterization, Yahweh created over the whole site of
mount Zion and over her assembly a cloud by day, and smoke and
the shining of a flaming fire by night.'

'His Lordship' in verse 4 is Ezra. The same title, *'adonay* is given
to him in Ezra x 3 (cf *Monseigneur; Milord*). The text speaks of the
reforms of Ezra ix-x, when Ezra 'excommunicated' all who refused
to break their marriages with foreign women. 'Holy' are those of
pure blood.

1QIsa: 'And it shall come to pass that he who will be left in Zion
and who will remain in Jerusalem will be fit to be called holy: every
one who will be recorded for life in Jerusalem. When the Lord will
have washed away the filth of the daughters of Zion, so that He will
have rinsed the bloodstains of Jerusalem from its midst by a breath
of judgment and by a breath of tempest, Yahweh will create over the
whole site of mount Zion and over her assembly a cloud by day
against the heat, and for a refuge and shelter from the storm and
rain'.

This is clearly a reinterpretation relegating the text to the
eschatological future, when God will rule in Zion over the Rest of the
people. *'adonay* is now Yahweh, the Lord; 'holy' is the rest purified
by God; the end of verse 5 and the beginning of verse 6 fall away
intentionally perhaps, for in the new Jerusalem there shall be no
night (cf. Rev xxi 25; xxii 5; Midrash Rabbah on Ex xviii [81a]) —
though the possibility of a scribal error because of the homoioteleut-
on *ywmym* of verses 5b-6a must not be excluded.

LXX: 'And it shall come to pass that what will be left in Sion and
what will remain in Jerusalem they shall be called holy: all who
have been recorded for life in Jerusalem. For the Lord shall wash
away the filth of the sons and daughters of Sion and shall purge out
the blood from their midst in a spirit of judgment and a spirit of
burning. And He shall come, and it shall be with regard to every site
of mount Sion and all the region round about it shall a cloud
overshadow by day, and there shall be as it were the smoke and light
of fire burning by night.'

The Septagintal re-reading is in many respects more theological

than that of 1QIsa. The neuters of verse 3 underline the theology of
the remnant, and the addition of 'the sons' in verse 4 betrays a
complete oblivion, or rather disregard, of the original historical
setting. The 'menstrual flows' become in the same verse the
'(innocent) blood'. A theophany and the installation of God on the
holy mount is promised, and the word 'overshadow' refers, of
course, to the divine Shekinah. Verse 5a is translated in a very
equivocal way so that — if I understand the Greek of the passage
correctly — the mention of night is quite artistically concealed.

Targum[49]: 'And it shall come to pass that he that shall be left
shall return to Zion, and he that hath kept the law shall be
established in Jerusalem, holy shall he be called; everyone that is
written down for eternal life shall see the consolation of Jerusalem:
when the Lord (*yhwh*) shall have removed the pollution of the
daughters of Zion, and carried off from the midst of her the spillers
of innocent blood that are in Jerusalem, by the word (*mymr*) of
judgment and by the word of *his* final decree. And the Lord (*yhwh*)
shall create over the whole sanctuary of Mount Zion, and over the
house of the Shekinah, a cloud of glory. It shall be a covering over it
by day, and thick darkness, and brightness like flaming fire by
night.'

Obviously the theological retouching continues in Targumic lines.

Editorial work should not be overlooked either. W. H. Brownlee has
shown how interpretative, creative indeed, is the text of the great
Isaiah Scroll from Qumran. Paragraphs, gaps, orthographic
peculiarities, etc. play an important role in exegesis and bear
witness to the way the editor, or the scribe, interpreted a particular
passage or the book as a whole.[50] The prophetic books are another
case. It is not only the additions of 'extra-prophecies', glosses, and
other interpolations, that reinterpret the original message. The
object of the prophetic books is to preserve the eternal truth of the
word of God for the editor's contemporaries and for the future,
because '*Verbum ... Dei nostri manet in aeternum*'. This disting-
uishes a prophetic book from the detached oracle, uttered in an
actual situation. To a great extent the original context of particular
oracles has been forgotten for the sake of the collection. The unit of a
prophetic book is not the oracle of the prophet, but 'the word of
Yahweh', always the same, unique and identical, through the
manifold variety of prophecies. These collections of prophecies
began, of course, in pre-exilic prophetical schools (e.g., Is viii 16-17;
[xxviii 9-10]; l 4), but they took their actual form in post-exilic times
in scribal schools.[51] And even 'purely editorial habits', such as the
bisection of a book into two scrolls, beyond giving clues to the
structure and outline of the material, may have an exegetical
significance. The gap between chapters xxxiii and xxxiv of Isaiah in
1QIsa, for example, could mean perhaps that the book of Second
Isaiah begins at chapter xxxiv and not at chapter xl as it is usually
supposed.

A more important editorial retouching is the final appendix to the
book of Malachi which also concludes — in the Pharisaic canon —
the whole prophetic literature. For the final redactor of Malachi — a
man versed in the Deuteronomistic tradition — the mission of the
prophets was to remind the people of 'the Law of Moses', certainly
the 'law' recently promulgated by Ezra. To the observance of this
Law he calls his contemporaries, reminding them of 'the great and
terrible Day of Yahweh', and promising, at once, a ministry of
reconciliation through the fiery figure of Elijah, with whom the
collection of the prophets appropriately closes. The LXX tradition
moves verse 22 to the end (LXX iv 6) closing the prophets on a
legalistic note of 'statutes and ordinances'. It is difficult to say
which of the two arrangements is the original, but each one is
important in its own right, whether it represents the original
sequence, or — still more significantly — a later rearrangement.

The books of the prophets were continually searched, interpreted
and re-read in this period because of their special interest with
regard to the future. We have seen how profound indeed was the
concern of all in Israel with the future of the nation and of the world.
But we must not suppose that interest in the prophets was directed
exclusively to their eschatology. Their ethical teaching was also
studied, interpreted (especially when it appeared to contradict the
Law), and re-read. The book of the Psalms, as well as the Qumranic
Hodayoth, testify to this influence of the prophets in the spiritual
life and doctrine of post-exilic Judaism. It is enough just to name the
psalms celebrating the re-establishment of Israel and the evident
influence on them of Second Isaiah and his disciple(s) and
predecessors. In other psalms the prophetic message and hope were
transformed into prayer; individual or Levitical Temple-prayer. The
mistakes, however, of H. Gunkel and J. Begrich ought not to be
repeated now: the ethic of the prophets is in many respects based on
the ethic of the wisdom, and not the other way round.[52] The wisdom
'murmuring in every people and so eloquent in Israel' is very much
older than post-exilic Judaism. In 1960 P. E. Bonnard demonstrated
the literary and spiritual influence of Jeremiah alone on thirty three
psalms of the canonical Psalter.[53] To pick just one example, the first
Psalm, *Beatus vir*, though it can be said to draw on the wisdom of
Amen-em-opet vi 1-12,[54] most probably draws on Jeremiah xvii 5-
8, a piece of wisdom poetry itself. But in many a psalm we can speak
indeed of a Yahwistic re-reading of heathen holy Scriptures....[55]

That the Greek version of the Old Testament is part of exegetical
literature can hardly be overstressed. On the occasion of the
appearance of the New English Bible translation of the Old
Testament S. P. Brock reminded us in an excellent study of the
tremendous importance of this undertaking, unique in Antiquity, of
translating into a foreign language a whole collection of books.[56]
The Greek Pentateuch was indeed an event totally without
precedent in the Hellenistic world. It came in an age when the

Hebrew text was still *in via* and ideas of inspiration were still developing. We know that the earliest translations are freer than the later. Ideas of inspiration applied still to the *sensus* and not to the *verbum*, but they were already moving in this second direction. Things changed radically with the triumph of Pharisaism and the school of Hillel, but in the period we are examining we are still in the age of the 'living text'. The 'egyptianisms' of biblical Greek indicate more strongly than its 'hebraisms' how wide, many-sided, and difficult, was the undertaking: a translation of numerous Hebrew texts of different ages and kinds (legal, historical, sapiential, etc.) into Greek by Egyptian Jews of the early Ptolemaic times. Their work became the foundation of the religious Judeo-Hellenistic culture and created the idiom of Philo, of the New Testament, and of the Greek Fathers. With cases such as Luke we can almost speak of literary 'sub-languages' emerging from the LXX. Beyond undertones and nuances, whole new theological notions came immediately into being, that of the *Nomos* being not the least important.[57]

The whole theology and exegesis of the period is mirrored in this translation: the emerging new anthropology; the accent on monotheism, on creation and on the idea of eternity; the tendency to eliminate anthropomorphisms and images, to attribute to the angels what the Hebrew text attributes to God, to underline the doctrine of resurrection, to read the Bible messianically; the endeavour to smooth the text and to adapt it to the hellenistic culture, while, at the same time, eliminating dangers of misinterpreting it in a pagan sense.

Here are some examples, taken at random, of translations stressing the transcendence of God:

Exodus iv 24 becomes in the LXX: 'And it came to pass that the Angel of the Lord met him by the way in the inn, and sought to slay him'. For the 'Yahweh' of the original the Greek version substitutes 'the Angel of the Lord' in order to eliminate any possibility of injury to the glory of God. For a similar reason the ancient LXX (Genesis, Job) attenuates the expression 'sons of God' into 'angels of God', whereas the Psalms preserve *'huioi'*.

Exodus xxiv 10a is rendered: 'And they saw the place where the God of Israel stood'. It was not the God that the elders of Israel saw (M), but the place (*ton topon*) where he stood.

Exodus xxv 22 LXX reads: 'And I will make myself known to you from thence, and I will speak to you above the propitiatory between the two cherubs'. God speaks 'above' and not 'from above' the mercy seat.

Deuteronomy viii 3 is translated with the precision *rhema* ('Man does not live by bread alone, but by every word that proceeds from the mouth of God') in order to eliminate the danger of speculation about emanations and births out of the mouth of God — something to be found among the Gentiles, and later among the Gnostics.

The text of Isaiah vi 9-10 is smoothed in the LXX to a considerable degree (cf 1QIsa!)

The doctrine of the resurrection of the dead is underlined in passages such as Isaiah xxvi 19, where the LXX translates: 'The dead shall rise, and those who are in the graves shall be raised, and the dwellers in the earth shall rejoice'. God's dead, the exiles of Babylon, have now become 'the dead' in general.

These are not peculiarities of the Diaspora. Recent studies have shown that the opposition between the Diaspora and Palestine must not be forced. The primacy of Palestine is incontestable, from the fact of the Temple, the High Priest, the Sanhedrin, the doctors, the schools of the scribes, later the rabbis. It is the Promised Land. But it always follows (with a certain delay), if not all, most of the initiatives of the more receptive Diaspora. There was no fundamental divergency.[58] The LXX, though the work of Alexandrian Jews, belongs to the general stream of the Judaism of the time. It is the last actualization of the Torah before the Pentecost, the word of Yahweh in the language of the *goyim*. Its heir was to be the Church.[59]

A final word on chronology. We have seen that the process of the re-reading of the Scriptures appeared with the exile and began to flourish after the restoration. The study of the fragments of Qumran, of the LXX, and of the *tiqqune sopherim*, can help us to define the time when this activity was brought to an end. The 'corrections of the scribes' were examined in a magisterial study by D. Barthelemy.[60] They are corrections made in the text by different scribes in order to eliminate any possibility of desecration of God's name, honour, and glory. Sometimes, however, they could have much more serious results than the suppression of a letter here and there. Barthelemy gives an example in the series of corrections and other adaptations and suppressions that resulted in the Masoretic text because of the *tiqqun* of Deuteronomy xxxii 8, where 'the sons of God (or gods)' were changed into 'the sons of Israel' in order to avoid the fatal expression, and to create also a parallelism with the hebdomecontad of the list of the peoples, instead of the ancient Canaanite hebdomecontad of the 'sons of God'. The consequence was that the number in Exodus i 5 was corrected accordingly, as it was also in three related passages of Genesis, where, moreover, almost a whole verse was suppressed and another rearranged. Both the Qumran fragments and the LXX ignore these alterations, whereas they are found in the Samaritan Pentateuch, and the Jubilees (xliv 33-34) betray their knowledge of the old uncorrected tradition and try to justify the new one. Evidently the *azinu* and the Priestly tradition were corrected by the sacerdotal and pietist circles that surrounded the Hasmonaean dynasty at its beginning, after the first years of the principate of Simon (143/2-135/4 B.C.), when the schism of Qumran most probably occurred. This activity came to an end with the hegemony of the Pharisees after 75 B.C. Their attitude was that of a minute respect for the text and for its

unification on the basis of 'copies of good tradition'. The Sadducean
liberal approach to the text during the Maccabaean age ended once
and for all, and with it the whole post-exilic attitude to the
Scriptures changed, leaving the way open to the new Pharisaic
fundamentalism. The Pharisees were to become henceforward the
faithful keepers of a text which they inherited, and for the actual
form of which they had no direct responsibility. Scholars should be
grateful to them for putting an end to the indiscreet theological
corrections of the Hebrew text of the Bible, and for preserving it as
pure as they found it; though we cannot help regretting their
transforming the 'living text' of the Scripture into a 'written word'.
By the time of the Second Jewish Revolt the Hebrew textual
tradition found its conclusion in the Rabbinic recension. By then the
Old Testament revelation had achieved its end and perfection a
century before, in God's Incarnate Word.[61]

Conclusion

Though a part of the material examined in this chapter does not
belong to the inspired canonical Scriptures, it nevertheless belongs
to the whole process of the *praeparatio evangelica*, uncovering *its
sensus plenior*, if not that of the text of the Old Testament.[62]

It can now be concluded that to speak of the period between the
return from exile and the coming of Christ which we have called
'The Advent' in terms of 'silence of prophecy' is unjustified.
Classical prophecy was still speaking, and God's word and
revelation were ever flowing out of the living Scriptural text,
through it, upon it. Tradition was in no way an empty shell. It was
living and growing; evolving towards its accomplishment. Creativity was at its height and the age saw as many reforms in institutions
and teachings as any previous period. What seems to many a silence
could, in fact, be called 'living in the word'. Post-exilic times are
times of interiorization, meditation, and reflection. A period of
expectation for the fulfilment of the word.

As the fulness of time approaches, everybody in Israel seems to
feel it, except those in seats of authority, who become more and more
preoccupied with themselves; some with their power; some with their
piety and traditions; all with their prerogatives. But the pangs of
childbirth are felt everywhere in Judaism. Apocalyptic gives the
impression of puerperal fevers accompanied with delirium; a
feverish state with incoherent speech, restlessness, and frenzied
excitement. And we know how much of the subconscious and the
unconscious these delirious words reveal.

Bible re-reading introduces us into a much more sober world, full
of patience, and indeed of joy. The musical atmosphere of the work
of the Chronicler, the praise of Yahweh in the Psalter, the joy of the
servants of God in the Temple or in the Synagogue, the sweetness of
his commandments and of their study, are also features of this age,
though this is often forgotten. In chapter viii of Nehemiah we read

how the hearing of the law made all the people weep, but the Scribe
said to them: 'Do not be grieved, for the joy of Yahweh is your
stronghold'. Even the anxiety of the apocalyptist is not left without
consolation: 'O Daniel ... I am come to show thee; for thou art
greatly beloved' (Dan ix 22f).

The great work of post-exilic Judaism was the establishment of
the Old Testament as an inspired, canonical corpus of holy
scriptures — the *torah se-biktab*. By the first century B.C. all Jews
accepted besides it the *torah se-be-'al-peh*, the oral torah. But the
Pharisaic oral torah was not the same as the Sadducean or the
Essene. Oral tradition did not exist in intertestamental Judaism;
what did exist was the principle of oral tradition and many
particular traditions. *The* oral tradition appears only after Jamnia
and the triumph of the Rabbis. Then *the* Bible appears also. In the
'Advent' every party has *its* Bible[63] and *its* tradition, in great part
identical indeed with the Bible and the tradition of the second
century A.D., but considerably larger. The canon will be established
by a process of exclusion. But I would not call the period of the
emergence of the Old Testament a period of 'the quenched spirit', or
of 'the silence of prophecy'.

The work of the 'Secretaries of the holy Ghost in penning the
books of Scriptures'[64] throughout the period of the Advent produced
a treasure and a mirror. It was a conclusion and a balance-sheet;
but also the gathering of new forces in view of the future. The
transfer of every finality, of every hope to the *beyond* condemned
any *this side* to a state of vanity at worst, at best a state of
preparation. The treasure was open to contemplation, yet the mirror
demanded vindication.

Chapter 3

ECCE

If the Old Testament could be summed up in the cry 'Hear, O Israel!', the New Testament could be summed up in the 'Behold!' — the peace-making 'Behold' of the *Ave* and the *Fiat*, the trembling 'Behold' of the Baptist, the inviting 'Behold' of the parable, the flaming 'Behold' of the Tomb, the incandescent 'Behold' of the End. The New Testament transcends hearing into vision, being the theophany par excellence, the Incarnation of God. 'Verbum caro factum est et habitavit in nobis; et vidimus gloriam quasi Unigeniti a Patre, plenum gratiae et veritatis' (Jn i 14). This is no longer the eternal and sovereign presence of God among his people; this is the personal and human entry of God into the time of men. 'At that moment he opens in his human present all his human past and future. Consequently, he is set as the fulfilment of all the past, making from it his preparation; he is set as the starting point of all the future, making from it his own development; and it is the radical novelty of the Incarnation to be founding at the same time the before and the after, and to be, indissolubly, conclusion, realization, and anticipation. But because this is the irruption of the eternal in time and the rooting of the incarnate word in the *Verbum incarnandum*, behold! in the midst of the new, of the irreducible, of the unique, even in the midst of the *ephapax*, there is absolute continuity of plan, of exemplarity, of finality, between that which precedes and that which follows the Incarnation'.[1]

That is why a chapter on 'new and old' in the New Testament can be written, even though the event of Christ fulfils, ends and, in a certain sense, abolishes both prophecy and tradition: because, being the end, it is also the beginning and brings the coming of the ultimate, the coming of the Kingdom which is to come. Christ is conclusion, beginning, restoration, anticipation and inauguration, because he is not an historical accident or an intruder and a stranger in the world, man, time and history: he is the Word — the Beginning, the Principle, the Fulness, the Alpha and Omega of all. The event of Christ is rooted in the historical testimony of Israel and the apostolic generation recognizes in Christ the 'Word made flesh'. 'This novelty', comments P. Ricoeur, 'does not purely and simply substitute the ancient letter, but stands in an ambiguous relation to it: it abolishes it and it accomplishes it; it changes its letter into spirit, as the water into wine. The Christian reality then understands itself by operating a mutation of sense inside the old scripture. The first Christian hermeneutics is this mutation; it is all

contained in this relation between the letter, the history (these words
are synonyms) of the old Covenant, and the spiritual sense revealed
after the event by the Gospel. .... The event becomes an advent: in
taking time, it takes meaning'.[2]

> Then came, at a predetermined moment, a moment in time and
> of time,
> A moment not out of time, but in time, in what we call
> history: transecting, bisecting the world of time, a moment
> in time but not like a moment of time,
> A moment in time but time was made through that moment:
> for without the meaning there is no time, and that moment
> of time gave the meaning.[3]

With John the Baptist we encounter a renaissance of Old
Testament prophecy. It was my contention in the last chapter that
the spirit of prophecy was never quenched in the period between the
exile and the coming of Christ. Yet we have nothing similar to the
great figures of the classical era of prophecy until John the Baptist
starts his preaching of the good news of the Kingdom. I shall not
repeat what has been said many times already. In the fiery words
and life of John even non-Christian Jews would have recognized
Israel's prophetic voice, had he not linked himself with Jesus.[4] Yet it
is precisely this link that differentiates John from the ancient
prophets and apocalyptists. John not only called to repentance in
view of the imminence of God's salvific judgement (prophets), not
only prepared the way by baptizing (many apocalyptists), he
pointed to the Messiah and introduced him to Israel: he was 'the
friend of the Bridegroom'. With the announcement of Jesus John
fulfilled himself and the whole of the old dispensation. Becoming
'the beginning of the gospel', he became 'the end of the law' and
'the seal of the prophets'. God's rule had been inaugurated.

But this was the God of Israel, and not of human desires. His rule
proved to be the kingdom of a lamb rather than of a lion, and its
announcer was soon dying at the hands of the Idumaean, Herod.
Once again the Yahweh of the prophets was to be 'who he would be',
beyond any human expectation, prediction, or conception; by the
Cross defeating the old hope, in the Resurrection surpassing it, with
the delay of the Parousia upsetting it. 'The Lord is King!' — and
nowhere more so than in his own Kingdom.

The new order of God is opened with the disorder of the
resurrection narratives. After Easter there can be no word of either
tradition or prophecy; yet neither tradition nor prophecy had ever
been more meaningful and alive and in place than after Easter. For
the early Church the jubilant news was not only the fulfilment of the
Scriptures, but also their narration, their exegesis and their
interpretation. With Pentecost the first Palestinian community
began a unique work of Scriptural re-reading.

One thing can be safely asserted: that the early Church read her
Old Testament as a 'sacrament of Christ', whereas the rabbis were

reading it as 'law', and the apocalyptists as 'secret'. Where the rabbis read the prophets as a commentary to the law, the Christians read the law itself as prophecy, for, as Melito of Sardis wrote later, they believed that 'the Law became Word'.[5] This new attitude started with Jesus himself. 'It was Jesus himself who shook the foundations of the ancient people of God. His criticism of the *Torah*, coupled with his announcement of the end of the cult; his rejection of the *Halakah* and his claim to announce the final will of God, were the decisive occasion for the action of the leaders of the people against him. ... They took Jesus to be a false prophet. This accusation brought him to the cross' — thus J. Jeremias summarizes his conclusions of Jesus' attitude to the old dispensation.[6] And for the change of the word 'criticism' to 'sublimation' (in the sense of 'elevation to a higher plane of existence') I would agree with him. Three days after Jesus' death, the first disciples believed that he was raised to life eternal, and, having received the gift of the Spirit on the fiftieth day after Easter, they began Christian theology by discovering prophetic texts that would fit the crucifixion and resurrection. Soon came the sapiential texts, through which Wisdom and Word ideas were applied to Jesus, and the Church became aware in the Spirit that God's agent in the redemption was also his agent in creation.[7]

The Easter experience is the key to the whole subsequent 'phenomenon of Christianity', its 'biological' continuity with Judaism, its remarkably wise absorption of elements from its Hellenistic environment, its astonishing power of creativity in ideas, institutions, and language. For however hard one tries to find the 'sources' of different Christian realities, at the end one will always find oneself before the newness of a *tertium genus*. And, vice versa, however hard one tries to assert as genuine only what is completely new (the notorious 'dissimilarity criterion'), one will always be defeated by life, the life of this world and the life of God, One and the Same, creator of all, as well as God of Israel and Father of Christ and of those of Christ's. (The sectarian smell of this criterion can hardly deceive a catholic nose. ... Scientifically the whole thing is utterly indefensible.)

New Testament Christianity is new *(kaine)* and at the same time rooted in the Old Testament. It comes after the Old, in succession to it; if not from it, still from the same Author. The New is the Old's end: goal, limit, fulfilment, and perfection. In fulfilling it, it supersedes it, but does not destroy it; for the Old Testament as history cannot be undone, and as revelation cannot be despised, it can only be consummated (cf Rom iii 3). The final, radical, decisive, and lasting intervention of God into history threw new light on the old interventions, gave to each one of them a new value, and it so happened that the new valuation paid greater honour to the prophets and a smaller or qualified honour to the law (the final, but by no means the original, challenge for this was the conversion of the Gentiles). If, as it was maintained in the first chapter, the prophets were a further step in God's progressive revelation to Israel this was only natural and just. Through the prophets, and in them, Christianity found and maintained its organic link with the old dispensation. As for the apocalyptic, far from being 'the mother of all Christian theology' (E. Kasemann), it was little more than a piece of actual 'language traffic'. Even in their most febrile apocalyptic moments Paul and the primitive Church of the Acts never seem to preoccupied with the length of the times as with the depth of their experience of Christ 'everyday, as long as it is called "today" ' (Heb iii 13). For them there was not so much a 'decisive event', as a decisive person, Jesus Christ. And this person was not future or past, but a present loving person.[8] Beyond abstract ideas of time, there was this Person; beyond the encounter with him (about which we have heard so much in the recent decades), there was life with him, in him.

In the New Testament documents how final does the revelation of Jesus appear, the revelation in him and about him? This is basically the question of this chapter. Essentially we are concerned with the relation of Christ and the Spirit in the New Testament. I shall start by saying that at the end of my research I fully embrace the words of H. de Lubac that, 'Il y a deux manieres egalement mortelles de separer le Christ de son Esprit: en revant d'un regne de l'Esprit qui conduirait au-dela du Christ, en imaginant un Christ qui ramenerait toujours en deca de l'Esprit'.[9]

The synoptic tradition: Matthew

W. O. Chadwick said in the Centenary Lecture of the Cambridge University Faculty of Divinity in 1971 that, 'Before Baur the early Christians were part of the history of the New Testament. After him the New Testament was part of the history of the early Christians'. Later I read J. Lebreton's warning in 1931: the hypotheses of these protestant historians tend to join 'nos theses traditionnelles en rattachant les evangiles a l'Eglise; elles s'en separent en detachant l'Eglise de Jesus-Christ'.[10] In the years after 1931 it became evident that for some people Jesus was not Christ and for others Christ was not Jesus.[11]

These regions are a real *topos tes anomoiotetos* to the Church, 'locum ubi floret spiritus sanctus'.[12] There is very little to be said. The 'riddle of the New Testament' can never be solved except in the Holy Spirit. It is an historical fact that these documents claim to be incomprehensible outside the light of the Spirit, and this is the predicament of the New Testament historian. 'Non dicit: "quia ad scholas ivi, quia a doctis didici," sed: *quia mandata tua quaesivi* (Ps cxviii 45). . . .'[13]

To the eighth-century iconoclasts protesting that it is impossible to have an icon of Christ, because either his human nature is painted, and this is ebionism, or his divine, and this is blasphemy and madness, the Church answered by confessing that she paints neither the human nature nor the divine, but the one hypostasis of the one Christ; neither a naturalistic portrait nor a representation of the absolutely unrepresentable, but the image of the Incarnate *eis hypomnesin kai didachen*. This is also, I think, the image of Jesus Christ that the early Church painted in the gospels: a verbal condensation of the intersection of history by Eternity 'for remembrance and teaching'. For teaching: a catechetical and mystagogical representation; for remembrance: a historical loving testimony, *ktema es to parachrema*, 'until He comes'.

Catechetical aims and the post-Easter situation of the early Church raise immediately the question of the authenticity of the purported sayings of the earthly Jesus and of their place in the life and theology of the early communities. The story of modern research in this field has been told many times and will not be repeated here. Bultmann and his school consider Jesus' preaching as a preliminary, and so secondary, factor in New Testament theology. J. Jeremias considers it as the indispensable first volume of every New Testament theology. The Church has always followed it as the rule of Christian life.

Following the path of R. Bultmann's celebrated *History of the Synoptic Tradition* and the no less celebrated *Parables of Jesus*, by J. Jeremias, recent New Testament scholars have devised four criteria for testing the authenticity of the primary stratum of the tradition (dissimilarity, multiple attestation, coherence, linguistic and environmental tests[14]), and we witness an attempt to analyze the very *psyche* of the New Testament. 'The famous *Sitz-im-Leben*', writes A. Malet, perhaps Bultmann's finest interpreter, 'derives in part from the unconscious: the morals, customs, institutions, and laws of the primitive Christian community as well as the un-literary genres or the literary ones (apophthegms, tales, and legends) which translate them, depend in a large measure on the unconscious'. And a little later: 'On the whole it can be maintained without fear of error that in a large part the *History of the Synoptic Tradition* draws its scientific value from the fact that it is a study of the unconscious of primitive Christianity, although it goes without saying that it would be a nonsense (in regard to Bultmann as well as to Levi-Strauss) to believe that only the unconscious exists'.[15] Two facts remain, however: i) that we are more or less asked to believe that the Christian (what is sometimes called the modern) category of historicity and temporality was born out of some books produced by the mythopoeic collective unconscious of certain first-century communities; ii) that Christianity has always claimed to be a matter neither of thought nor of feeling, but of revelation. Its experience ultimately belongs not to the experimental (experiments, tests, counter-tests, and checks, ordered towards the discovery of a truth and the establishment of a fact or law), but to the experiential (immediate knowledge of the concrete linked with life).

No one would deny that the early Church modified the sayings of Jesus according to her post-Easter situation and to her belief that they were not dead letters but 'spirit and life'. New applications were made, new theological deepenings were reached in the light of Easter and Pentecost. But that the early Church was a wretched community of deluded forgers or a family of oafs unable to distinguish between the earthly Jesus and the exalted Lord, is not, I believe, established; and all the existing evidence points to the contrary. Most, if not all, assertions about the so-called 'Prozess der Neubildung solcher Herrenworte' are unfounded and uncritically dogmatic.[16]

I will examine the process of the handing down of the 'Jesus tradition' in the early Church through two examples. The first is a radical case of a logion whose authenticity is almost universally rejected.

Mt xviii 20: 'Where two or three are gathered in my name, there am I in the midst of them'. To make the case even more radical I shall start with the comments of a fairly conservative scholar, F. W. Beare: 'It is perfectly clear', he wrote, 'that during the lifetime of Jesus, there were no small (or large) groups meeting"in his name", and that if there were, he could not be present with them. So long as he was living the life of man on earth, he was subject to the same limitations of place as anyone else. At any given moment, he was in a particular locality — a house in Capernaum, a roadside in Galilee, a porch of the Temple, a boat on the lake. He could not be present wherever his followers should meet in his name until after the resurrection. Not this one verse alone, but the whole passage from verse 15 to verse 20, and in a certain degree the entire chapter, presupposes the organized Church of the apostolic age'. At this point another conservative scholar was quoted by Professor Beare: 'In the words of T. W. Manson, "The speaker is the risen and glorified Christ whose presence is a reality in the community of his followers" '.[17]

The saying reappears in different forms in later tradition, in *Thomas* (logion 30); POxy i 2-6; Clem. Alex., *Stromata* iii 10, 68; Ephraem, *Evangelii concordantis expositio* xiv 24 (cf Ign., *ad Ephesios* v 2). There can be no doubt that Matthew xviii 20 is the original source of all these variations.[18] This fact, however, cannot, and must not, prejudice our judgement concerning the authenticity of the saying, as happens with Bultmann.[19] First he classifies it among 'legal sayings and Church rules', then under the ' "I"-sayings'. In it the risen Lord speaks of his person, but actually it is a Christian prophet filled by the Spirit who speaks in the name of the ascended Lord. Our saying comes from Jewish tradition, i.e. it belongs to the Palestinian Church, though, in general, the ' "I"-sayings' were predominantly the work of the Hellenistic Churches. For this enthralling detective story little or no evidence is given to the reader. Matthew xviii 20 or xviii 19f seems to be a number in a list of sayings rather than a verse of the Gospel of Matthew. The factor Matthew or Jesus is really non-existent.

We must suppose that the saying is ascribed to the Palestinian Church because of *Abhoth* iii 2(3) and 7(8). In actual fact, valuable as these rabbinic sayings may be for our understanding of the Gospel logion, they are attributed by the *Abhoth* to R. Hanina b. Teradion (died A.D. 135) and R. Halaphta of Cephar Hanania (second half of the second century), i.e. they are much later than even the 'later strata' of Matthew. Before resorting to the Mishnah we should first examine the saying for its own sake, as a Gospel saying, as a Matthean saying.

Matthew xviii 20 belongs to a series of lessons on the life of the community, life in community. The purpose of the grouping is catechetical and the organization follows the numeric principle of mnemotechnics. The logion is appended to a series of disparate sayings of different origin containing the words 'one' (Mt xviii 12, 14), or 'two or three' (Mt xviii 16), or 'two' (Mt xviii 19). Jesus says that where two or three are gathered in his name (*eis to emon onoma* in the same sense as *epi to onomati mou* in Mt xviii 5), there will he be in the midst of them. The first question is whether Jesus could speak of an 'assembly' (*ekklesia*) gathered by him in his name. Could Jesus expect an 'assembly' instead of the kingdom? Even more, an 'assembly' before which lawsuit cases should be brought (Mt xviii 16f)? On the answer we give to this question depends half of our answer to the question about the authenticity of Matthew xviii 20. I am one of those who believe that Jesus could, and did in fact, envisage a congregation gathered by him in his name. The reasons have been given in summary by J. Jeremias in his *Theology*.[20] In speaking of his *ekklesia* Jesus meant his eschatological *'eda*, the eschatological congregation of the people of God in his name. In Matthew xviii 17ff we should more appropriately translate 'people of God', rather than 'church'. Having said this, we can now turn to the Jewish background of the logion — if there is one.

An attentive reading of the relevant Mishnaic passages in a good edition — P. Blackman's *Mishnayoth*, for example — will show that Jesus is here defining the *minyan* of his congregation, the requisite number of faithful for congregational worship. From *Sanh.* i 6 par. we see that pharisaic Judaism, like the Zadokites of Qumran (1QS vi 3), deduced this to be ten (ten adult males) from Numbers xiv 27 (twelve minus Joshua and Caleb leaves ten). In Matthew xviii 16 Jesus, distinguishing between fraternal and judicial corrections differentiates between the 'congregation' and the 'two or three'. Final decision belongs only to the plenary assembly. In Matthew xviii 20 he defines the requisite number for congregational worship as 'two or three'. To the petitions of this congregation he promises the answer of the heavenly Fathers because of his own presence in

the midst of it. The transmission from the judgement to the
numerically akin prayer sayings is supplied, conceptually and
verbally (through the catch-words 'earth' and 'heaven'), by verse
18. It must also be noted that the expression 'there am I in the midst
of them' is preeminently Matthean. Matthew begins his Gospel with
Emmanuel, God-with-us, and closes it with the promise 'Lo, I am
with you always, to the end of the age'.

Could then Jesus utter the substance of Matthew xviii 20 during
his lifetime, or should we fall back to the *deus ex machina*, the
Spirit-filled prophet of the early Church? The first and fundamental
objection that Jesus could not speak this language, because during
his lifetime he was under the limitations of space, can be dismissed
at once by the historian of religion as being irrelevant. Religious
realities are not bound by Newton's or Einstein's laws. (And even in
scientific terms, 'the life of man on earth', about which F. W. Beare
speaks, far from being a simple and well known thing, still remains
the awe-inspiring secret of Oedipus's riddler). If Paul could say:
'For though absent in body I am present in spirit', or 'In the name
of the Lord Jesus you and my spirit, having been assembled with the
power of our Lord Jesus, we are to deliver this individual, etc'. (1 Cor
v 3ff), I do not see why Jesus, hardly twenty years before, could not
speak a similar language.[21] The best gospel parallel to Matthew
xviii 20 that we can find is John xvi 23-24: 'In that day ... truly,
truly, I say to you, if you ask anything of the Father, he will give it to
you in my name. Hitherto you have asked nothing in my name; ask
and you will receive. . . .' John gives us perhaps the original setting of
the dominical saying. Jesus before his departure from this life
promises to be in the midst of the worshipping congregation of his
followers, made up of even two or three disciples assembled 'in his
name', i.e. as members of the eschatological community of salvation
that he gathered.

These facts, and the fact that Jesus, according to the whole of the
Gospel tradition, always expected to have a very small number of
followers, a 'little flock', make the probability that he reduced the
minyan of his congregation more than plausible. Before entering
with the many the 'wide and the easy gate' of 'the early Christian
prophets', the New Testament scholar should always spend a
minute or two trying to hear what the particular saying is, first of
all, saying, then what the evangelist says, and what Jesus says.
This is a duty to honest and conscientious science.

I am now coming to my second example of how the 'Jesus
tradition' was prophetically handed down in the early Church: the
Matthean dominical sayings about false prophets. This case is little
less radical than the first, but we are fortunate enough to have a
study from the pen of E. Cothenet, 'Les prophetes chretiens dans
l'Evangile selon Matthieu'.[22]

According to the school of Bultmann, Matthew vii 22-23 and the
warnings of Matthew vii 15ff and Matthew xxiv 5, 11, 23, 24, against

false prophets, are a creation either of the early Christian prophets or of the Christian 'establishment', as against the prophets. After detailed and painful research Cothenet comes to the conclusion that the essential of these sayings goes back, beyond Easter, to Jesus of Nazareth. Contrary to the opinions of Bultmann and Kasemann, authority in the early Church lies not with the 'pneumatics' as such, but in the sayings of the Lord, transmitted and applied according to the needs of the communities. The ultimate criterion for discernment of the spirits is the word of Jesus as preached by the Twelve.

But could Jesus preach against false prophets? Are not the pseudo-prophets a reality of the Church? Pseudo-prophecy was, and still is, a permanent and constant reality in the midst of the people of God. Jesus could call pseudo-prophets any and all groups that opposed his teaching and, so, taught error. In fact Cothenet gives good evidence, arguing that Jesus had in mind the Zealots of his time, what we should rather call 'the party of Judas of Galilee'.[23] Jesus warned his disciples against an ideology of violence which sinned against the heart of his teaching, the law of love. In the true prophetic spirit of the Old Testament Jesus proclaims the sovereignty of God, and, beyond this, preaches the new law of non-resistance (Mt v 39ff) and love of enemies (Mt v 43ff). These are the 'fruits by which false prophets can be discerned (Mt vii 16,20). Using this criterion Matthew reformulates Jesus' sayings in view of the 'spirituals' of his community, who while making 'signs' in the name of the Lord (Mt viii 22), contribute to the proliferation of lawlessness (Mt vii 23, xxiv 12), and by their 'sectarian' attitude and violence cool the *agape* of the community.[24]

In 1 Corinthians xii-xiv Paul will apply the same criteria when judging in the midst of the Corinthian Church. In every case it is the sovereignty of the Lord's teaching that judges and discriminates. The dominical sayings are transmitted not as museum pieces or list numbers, but as the truth which enlightens the life of the disciples, elucidates the problems of the Church, and preserves the faithful vigilant. Matthew is neither for nor against abstract notions of 'prophecy'; he is preaching Jesus Christ, the Law and the Wisdom of God.

Paul

Our second trial run will be directed through the Pauline corpus.[25] In his monumental *Theology of the New Testament*[26] R. Bultmann asserted that 'the teaching of the historical Jesus plays no role or practically none in Paul.... In fact, his letters barely show any traces of the influence of the Palestinian tradition concerning the history and preaching of Jesus'. The great German exegete was building not only upon his own previous work, but also upon the work of many predecessors, especially W. Bousset and W. Heitmuller. In 1930 A. Schweitzer wrote in his controversial *Die Mystik des Apostels Paulus*: 'If we had to rely on Paul, we should not know that Jesus taught in parables, had delivered the Sermon on the Mount, and had taught his disciples the "Our Father". Even where they are specially relevant Paul passes over words of the Lord.'[27]

James Robinson defended Bultmann's opinions at the centenary meeting of the Society of Biblical Literature in 1964. In his paper 'Kerygma and History in the New Testament'[28] he quoted with approval D. Georgi's statement to the effect that, 'Paul developed his christology in complete ignorance of the contents and tendencies of the developing traditions about Jesus. Rather he knew about them and clearly rejected a motivation that at least at times clearly asserts itself, namely the objective of using a certain form of presentation to make of the life of Jesus an unambiguous manifestation of the divine, to cover over the offence of the cross and the humanness of Jesus in general and to replace the eschatological revelations of God with historically ascertainable "proofs of God" '.[29] I wonder whether the canonical Jesus tradition had these objectives at any time, and whether Georgi or Robinson would have known anything much about the 'offence of the cross' without the gospel Jesus traditions. I hope that I do not need to repeat here what D.L. Dungan and other scholars have said very well. I will just remark that it is anachronistic to ask Paul to cite sayings of the Lord. It must be remembered that the first to give explicit citations of Jesus' sayings are Irenaeus and Tertullian. The usual way of the ancients was allusiveness, not careful citation. This, of course, does not mean that the fantasies of those who see everywhere in Paul allusions to sayings of Jesus are to be followed. Without the gospels, however, we would never guess that Paul refers to express sayings of Jesus in 1 Thessalonians v 1-11, for instance. But the problem is more general. We must remember that in Paul's times no Christian documents were yet canonical. Then, no spiritual teacher or letter-writer of Paul's stature makes citations in his writings: no saint or mystic claiming that 'Christ is speaking in me' (2 Cor xiii 3) will then fill his writings with quotations. Paul, like Jesus and the great Fathers of the Church, speaks as one who has authority, and not as a scribe (cf. Mt vii 29).

In 1971 C.F.D. Moule reminded us of the importance of the circumstantial and situational nature of the Pauline corpus in any discussion of the *Jesusuberlieferung* in Paul.[30] What we have are letters of a pastoral nature and purpose. We have none of Paul's sermons, and knowledge of Jesus is presupposed in every letter that we possess. To this I should add that these letters are addressed to Churches founded by Paul himself, the only exception being Romans, where Paul addresses a community unknown to him. Now it has been noted many times that there is an unusual concentration of allusions to dominical sayings in the paraenetic sections of this letter (Rom xii 14, 17; xiii 8ff; xiv 13, 14; xvi 19). This is not accidental, but on the contrary very significant, I believe. My own research leads me to subscribe heartily to D. L. Dungan's conclusion:

'At least this much may be agreed upon: the alleged contrast between Pauline Christianity and that branch of the early Church which preserved the Palestinian Jesus-tradition that finally ended up in the Synoptic gospels is a figment of the imagination. In fact, they were one and the same branch.'[31]

Let us now come to 2 Corinthians v 16: *Hoste hemeis apo tou nun oudena oidamen kata sarka ei kai egnokamen kata sarka Christon, alla nun ouketi ginoskomen*. In 1932 Bultmann interpreted *Christos kata sarka* as an expression for the 'historische Jesus', opting for the adjectival reading of the phrase.[32] In his *Theology*[33] he opted for the adverbial reading, noting, however: 'A Christ known *kata sarka* is precisely what a Christ *kata sarka* is'. Elsewhere he argued that 'Christ according to the flesh' refers to Jesus as a miracle worker, a view dear to the Gnostics.[34] On these lines (though in the first case in the opposite direction) W. Schmithals argued that 2 Corinthians v 16 is a gnostic gloss, parallel to the 'Jesus be anathema' of 1 Corinthians xii 3,[35] and D. Georgi that the 'Christ according to the flesh' is 'the divine man Jesus', viz. the Jesus of Paul's opponents in 2 Corinthians .[36] As against these interpretations, C. F.D. Moule, in his already mentioned essay on 'Jesus in New Testament Kerygma', saw *kata sarka* as a moral or religious term. To know Christ 'according to the flesh' would mean an assessment of Christ in human terms, 'a stance belonging to a world which the apostle has renounced'. Similarly, W. G. Kummel has argued that in 2 Corinthians v 16 Paul does not deny any interest in the earthly Jesus, but 'pushes aside as unimportant for the Christian a purely human, intra-worldly relation to Jesus'.[37]

Now, I do not think that 2 Corinthians v 16 can be taken in isolation. The first thing for us is to know *the question* which Paul tried to answer in this letter in general and in this specific section in particular. Need I repeat that Paul was not writing as a systematic theologian? That Paul's 'theological reflection' arises from his missionary work can never be overemphasised. 'Wenn Kasemann', wrote Martin Hengel, 'betonte, dass "die Apokalyptik ... die Mutter aller christlichen Theologie gewesen" sei, so konnte man dies noch in dem Sinne naher definieren, dass die durch die Auferstenhungserscheinungen ausgeloste *eschatologische Mission* der Urgemeinde, "*die Mutter der christologischen Reflexion*" und damit der *fruhchristlichen Theologie uberhaupt wurde*.'[38]

I believe that Georgi was in principle right when he advocated a difference in nuance between the centre of opposition in 1 Corinthians and that in 2 Corinthians. I am inclined to think that Paul's opponents in 2 Corinthians were Judaizers, probably 'coming from or having come into contact with esoteric Judaism' (A. D. Nock), and glorying in their descent and noble religious past.[39] 2 Corinthians v is addressed to those who 'pride themselves on externals and not on inward reality' (2 Cor v 12b),[40] and is, I believe, a defence of the Gentile Christians who do not observe the

Law. Having Christ, they cannot lack anything, and in no way can
they be considered as a danger or as inferior. (Did the 'Qumranic'
fragment of 2 Cor vi 14-vii 1 come from the opposition and become
confused with Paul's letter in the archives of the Church of
Corinth?) Paul exhibits his missionary glory not, as he says, in
order to commend himself — as his opponents do (2 Cor iii 1) — but
in order to make the Corinthians aware of the riches of his calling, of
God's work through him. Whatever he does, he does it under the
overwhelming pressure of Christ's love, convinced that Christ died
for all men, and so in him died all, irrespective of position, race, or
descent. It must be noted that when in Romans iii 11 Paul underlines
again the fact that God 'admires no face of man' (Deut x 7; cf. Acts x
34), he does it in relation to Jew and Greek. Those who boast their
prosopon are always the Jews.

Now in 2 Corinthians v 14-15 we see an allusion to the Pauline
metaphor about the relationship between the Christian and the
risen Lord as of one between wife and husband.[41] The soul of the
Christian is bound to the resurrected Christ as a bride to her
bridegroom, even as a widowed bride to her leviratic new
bridegroom (cf 2 Cor xi 2-3; Rom vii 1-4). Verse 16 must be
understood in this context. I take the phrase *kata sarka* adverbially,
and the protasis in the second half of the verse as introducing not an
unreal condition. If Christ died for all, reasons Paul, and not only for
some 'elect ones', and if all died in Christ and are risen to a new life
for him, and not for themselves, 'Consequently we do not know
anyone according to the flesh', i.e. as Christians we are not bound to
anyone according to the flesh. 'Even though we once did know
Christ according to the flesh, we know him thus no longer': Even
though we Jewish Christians were bound to the Christ by the blood
bond, we can claim exclusiveness on him no longer. *Oida* and
ginosko are used here 'hebraistically': they denote not an intellectual knowledge, but an intimate relationship, even in the sense of the
carnal connection of male and female.[42] 'According to the flesh'
means literally 'according to the flesh', and not 'from a human
point of view', etc. If after Christ's death and resurrection those who
are in Christ live a new life, for Christ and not for themselves (verse
15), 'Consequently from now on we are related to no one according
to the flesh; even though we once were related with the Christ
according to the flesh, we are related to him thus no longer'. In the
words of the pre-Pauline text of Romans i 3-4, Jesus did descend
from David according to the flesh, but he was proclaimed Son of God
in power according to the Spirit of holiness by his resurrection from
the dead. And again, Romans ix 5: 'of their [the Israelites'] race,
according to the flesh, is Christ, who is above all, God blessed for
ever'.[43] The Messiah is from the Jews, and they are related to him
by blood. But the Risen One died and was raised for all, and with
him there can be no blood relation: he is 'according to the Spirit'.[44]

'Therefore', continues Paul, 'if any one is in Christ, he is a new

creation; the old has passed away, behold, the new has come' (2 Cor
v 17). The expression 'new creation' is taken from the Jewish
theology of proselytism.[45] The new event in Christ is a new creation
into union with Christ. Those who died 'with Christ' were raised
into a new existence; they have nothing to do with their previous life
'according to the flesh', now they are 'in Christ'. And in Christ
there is no Jew or Greek, for in him God reconciled to himself the
whole world and entrusted to Paul the ministry of reconciliation
(verse 19ff). A new age has dawned, 'Behold, now is the acceptable
time; behold, now is the day of salvation. We put no obstacle in any
one's way. . . .' (2 Cor vi 2ff).

It can be concluded that in 2 Corinthians v 16 what Paul says is
that a purely human, racial relation to Jesus belongs to the old age
and has no existence in the new. Here as everywhere the mother of
Paul's Christological reflection is his mission. Is the verse relevant
to the modern Protestant discussions on 'the Jesus of history and
the Christ of faith'? If it is, not in the way Bultmann thought. What
Paul says is that Jews cannot claim any privileges from their blood
relation with the Messiah. The relationship with the risen Christ is
not 'by blood', but 'by marriage'. Paul does not think in terms of two
realities, an 'earthly Jesus' and an 'exalted Lord', but in terms of
one, unique person, the pre-existing Son of God who emptied
himself, became man, died for man's sin, and was raised for man's
justification, inheriting the 'name which is above every name' (Phil
ii 6ff; Rom iv 25). For Paul, as for the Church always, the conclusive
fact is not the teaching of Galilee. What enflames Paul is the light of
the road to Damascus, 'When he who had chosen me while I was
still in my mother's womb, called me through his grace and deigned
to reveal his Son in me, so that I might announce him among the
Gentiles' (Gal i 16).[46] Paul lives in the new creation of God in Christ,
he lives *in* Christ Jesus, the new Adam. He is not just following the
preaching of Jesus, he preaches Jesus. Paul sees the world and God
through the pierced hand of the crucified and risen Jesus that
covered his eyes once and for all on the road to Damascus. It is
absurd to speak of a development from Jesus to Paul: there is no
development; Paul lives in a new world. In the grave matters of law,
of the Gentiles, etc., Paul, and the whole early Church, are not
following the teaching of the earthly Jesus — probably there was no
teaching on these points at all. Paul could not think in Bultmann's
terms, because for him the Incarnation was not mythology and he
never spoke of Jesus as a historian, or a psychologist. Paul speaks
about Jesus from within the Church, so, in the Spirit.

What is Paul's attitude to Christian prophecy? First a survey of
modern research about early Christian prophecy.[47] The idea that
charism and regular Church organization were and always are in a
state of war is a sad legacy of the pietism of the brilliant but
superficial and over-systematic eighteenth-century Church historian Gottfried Arnold.[48] The whole question is intrinsically linked

with the perennial struggles of Western Christendom with the concept of authority. I have the impression that somehow a certain element in the West tends to treat the Holy Spirit not as a person, but as a 'gift'. The Giver is confused with his gifts, which again are confused with the psyche and with psychic phenomena, whereas Paul sees the Spirit as inhabiting and addressing the *pneuma-nous*, and not the feeling (the 'sensible' and 'pathetic' soul: desire and imagination). It is characteristic also that B. Rigaux noted once that the index of W. G. Kummel's monumental *The New Testament: The History of the Investigation of its Problems* gives only four references for the Holy Spirit, and no reference at all for pneumatology.

Two special scholars bear a particular responsibility for the confusion over the Spirit still reigning in the minds of many New Testament students: Adolf Harnack and Rudolf Sohm. The first by creating in the Prolegomena of his edition of the *Didache*[49] perhaps the most nefarious neologism in New Testament studies, *Charismatiker*; the second by creating in his *Kirchenrecht* [50] an image of the early Church as a 'charismatic anarchy'. The ugly coinage of the first survived, unfortunately, the collapse of the edifice of the second, and is treated by most, if not all, scholars as an original and undisputed New Testament word. Yet in the first years of this century hardly anybody would know it outside Germany. Harnack spoiled once and for all, and in all Western languages, the Greek word 'charisma'; he specialized it, made it unrecognizable to any Greek, abominable, a perennial source of outrageous confusion. Would that British scholars had heeded the timely warnings of J. Armitage Robinson! 'St Paul uses "charisma",' he was writing in the second decade of this century, 'of any and every manifestation of grace (*charis*) in the members of the Christian Church, whether it be the great gift of prophecy or the humble gift of "shewing mercy with cheerfulness". There is a "charisma" in virtue of which a man is able to refrain from marriage, and a "charisma" in virtue of which another exercises due self-restraint in a married life. He who presides has a "charisma" which enables him to rule with an earnest diligence; he who shares his good things with another has a "charisma" which enables him to act liberally and with a single mind. In face of this it seems extraordinary that the word "charisma" should have been specialized in modern discussions of the history of the Christian Ministry, so that the office of an Apostle, a Prophet, or a Teacher should be described as "charismatic" in contrast with the office of a Bishop, a Presbyter, or a Deacon. Can we imagine that St Paul would have spoken of his apostolate as a "charisma", or described it as "charismatic" (if there had been such a word as *charismatikos* in the Greek language)?'[51]

I consider it superfluous to offer yet one more detailed discussion of 1 Corinthians xii-xiv. Basically Paul offers us a clear summary of his judgement on the matters he discusses in these chapters in

Romans xii 3ff: the different 'charismata' are manifestations in the various parts of the grace given to the whole. 'Every function of the Body, any power whatever of helping the whole, is a "charisma", a manifestation of that grace (*charis*) with which the Body is endowed.'[52] What makes their use Christian is the presence of the Christian basis, humility: 'Do not think of yourself more highly than you ought to think, but think with a sober judgment' (Rom xii 3). What Paul wants the disciples to see is not the speciality of each gift, but their mutual interdependence and the uniqueness of the Giver. Nothing is given to individuals *qua* individuals; whatever is given to them is given to them *qua* members of Christ: so the gift's value is to be judged according to its contribution to the 'edification' of the Church. Whatever weakens the 'bond of perfection' among the members of Christ, and destroys their concord, sins against the first fruit of the Spirit (Gal v 22) and cannot be esteemed as good. Similarly, whatever dissociates the unity of man by excluding one of his faculties from participation (in the present case the *nous*, mind, 1 Cor xiv 13ff) cannot be good either, for it threatens the irreducibility of the human person, and so, inevitably, the communion of the Church.

Paul starts his discussion, however, by giving the fundamental criterion for the discernment of spirits: 'I declare to you: no one speaking in tongues by the Spirit of God calls Jesus cursed and no one can say "Jesus is Lord" except by the Holy Spirit' (1 Cor xii 3).[53] The exegesis of this verse is notoriously difficult,[54] but I cannot accept the emendations proposed by W. F. Albright and C. S. Mann.[55] *Plus interpretationis eget Paulus quam emendationis.* W. Schmithals's theory, that Gnostic Christians would cry in their worship services 'Cursed be Jesus' in order to give expression to their faith in the 'heavenly' Christ and not in the earthly Jesus, is grotesque.[56] The verse must be understood in the general frame of 1 Corinthians and the problem of Paul's opponents to it. I have already said what I think on this point in relation to 2 Corinthians.

It is my firm opinion, nevertheless, that when Paul comes to the subject of 'spiritual manifestations',[57] he is not answering only his 'opponents', but is teaching the whole Church of Corinth. It is evident that not only the vanity of the 'spirituals', but also the simplicity of the many was captivated by the gift of tongues. He poses immediately the corner-stone of everything; only the confession of the faith of the Church is from the Spirit of God; if anyone utters pronouncements contrary to it, he is not inspired by God's Holy Spirit. Paul of course is not speaking of a pure verbal confession of Christ as the Lord, but presupposes the obedient and faithful following of him as Lord. Whether the cursing of Jesus is an ad hoc construction or whether there were indeed some Christians who, while believing themselves 'filled with the Spirit', were in fact 'demon-ridden' and in moments of possession cursed Jesus in full Church, one thing is obvious: Paul's key to the discernment of spirits is the faith they confess.[58] The Spirit confesses Christ as Lord. The question of 1 Corinthians xiv 36: 'What! Did the word of God originate with you, or are you the only ones it has reached?', elucidates Paul's mind. No prophet or 'spiritual' or ecstatic is the originator of God's word: there is only one word, only one gospel, that which came out (*exelthen*) of Palestine, the general faith of the saints ('are you the only ones that it has reached?' — the principle of the *consensus fidelium*. Compare verses 33b: 'as in all the churches of the saints' and xi 16 'this is not our way, nor that of the churches of God'). The truth is the authentic message that the apostle delivers with certainty from the Lord (1 Cor xiv 37 [I do not read *entole*]) who speaks in him (2 Cor xiii 3).

We stand before the sacrament of the *apostolicity* of the Church, founded on the apostles and on their preaching. In the question 'or are you the only ones that it has reached?' we encounter the Church's *catholicity*, excluding every self-assertion, drift, particularism, oblivion of the brother; and manifesting concord, brotherhood, union and love in the fulness of Christ. The first question, 'did the word of God originate with you?', controls the second, 'are you the only ones?', and the second is founded on the first. Paul judges not according to any democratic principle of the majority, but according to his apostolic authority and the catholic ecclesial *consensio* in the truth of the Holy Spirit of God, which animates the Body of Christ. We see that for Paul the Corinthian question is not a question of tradition or prophecy, but of truth and love — God's truth in Christ manifested in the love of those who in the Spirit are made members of Christ.

'So it is with Christ ... in one Spirit we were all baptized into one Body' (1 Cor xii 13). The major mistake of the modern discussion of 1 Corinthians xii-xiv is that they take these chapters in isolation from chapter xi. *Yet it is absolutely clear that Paul discusses the charismata in the context of the Eucharistic assembly* . The gifts of the Holy Spirit are ecclesial realities, outpourings of the Spirit around the Cup of the New Covenant. Charismata and order are seen by Paul in this context, the context of the eschatological gathering of the Church of God at the Lord's Supper. Most contemporary discussions of 'charisma', order, and ministry in the New Testament fail, precisely because they do not place Church charismata, order, and ministry there where they belong and whence they spring: in the Pentecostal assembly of the Eucharist, the place where the Body of Christ, full of the fervour of the Holy Spirit, is *literally* built, realized, and gloriously manifested — the one Body ('totus Christus, caput et corpus') into which all faithful were baptized in one Spirit. We can summarize our brief discussion of 1 Corinthians xii-xiv by saying that for Paul there can be no *en Pneumati* without *eis Christon*, as there can be no *eis Christon* without *en Pneumati*.

Paul's usage of the word 'spirit' is specifically Christian, but ambivalent. It can mean either 'God's power,[59] grace, and gift in Christ' (and in this sense it is equated with the grace, power and operations of the risen Christ present in his Church), or the Holy Spirit as the divine person sent by the Father to the Church after Christ's exaltation. In this second sense the Spirit is known as the witness, and announcer, and bringer of the filial adoption of the Christian by God in Christ — 'The proof that you are sons is that God has sent the Spirit of his Son into our hearts, crying, "Abba! Father!"' (Gal iv 6).[60] Because of this ambivalence, and the ensuing ambivalence in the language used by Paul about the Spirit, it is sometimes claimed that Paul does not think of the Spirit as of a person. This is not the place to answer these fallacious affirmations. I will just say that the arguments brought forward are usually very shaky indeed. When a scholar of the stature of W. Kummel, for instance, writes that Paul does not think of the Spirit as of a person, because he speaks of 'having' and 'receiving' the Spirit, I am not certain that I follow him, for Paul speaks of Christ in similarly 'impersonal' language (e.g. Gal iii 27). And when Kummel says again that Paul speaks of 'quenching' the Spirit, and so the Spirit cannot be a person, his argument is unclear. For certainly Paul in 1 Thessalonians v 19 uses the word 'spirit' in its first sense of power and grace. In 2 Corinthians xiii 14, the *koinonia* of the Holy Spirit, is then deployed. But is it really impossible to use the genitive in the case of a person 'participated in'? Does not Paul use the same construction for Jesus in 1 Corinthians i 9 and for the Eucharistic 'participation in' Jesus in 1 Corinthians x 16? After all, is not this 'participation in' a person a specifically Christian notion? And, anyway, what is the exact meaning of '*the koinonia* of the Holy Spirit' in 2 Corinthians xiii 14? Could it not be that, in the words of a contemporary commentator, 'l' Esprit est en meme temps celui qui cree la communion, le fait meme de cette communion, et le resultat de cette communion.'[61] I am afraid that on this occasion Kummel is a victim of that disposition which modern language analysts know as *asymboly*, the incapacity to perceive or handle symbols, i.e. coexistences of meanings. After all, what about those Pauline passages, like 1 Corinthians xii 4-6, where the Spirit is in parallel with God and the Lord? And if the Risen Lord and the Spirit are identical, what is the reason of Paul's consistent distinction of prepositions when he speaks of Baptism as being *eis Christon en Pneumati?*

2 Corinthians iii 17a is sometimes considered as the final proof of the identity of the Spirit with the Lord in Paul. Recent studies of the verse, however, return to the exegesis of Chrysostom and other Greek Fathers who took it as an interpretation of the biblical quotation in verse 16, of Exodus xxxiv 34.[62] In 2 Cor iii 4-iv 6 Paul defends the legitimacy of his apostleship through a midrashic development of Exodus xxxiv in combination with Genesis i 27. 2 Corinthians iii 17a is a perfect example of the *pesher* technique as

we know it from Qumran and other Pauline passages (1 Cor x 4; Gal
iii 16).[63] 'The Lord' in verses 17-18, when substantive, is the
Yahweh of verse 16 — though there are Christological connotations
as well (cf. 1 Cor ii 8, where Yahweh's title 'the Lord of glory' is
given to Jesus...).

Our exegesis of 2 Corinthians iii 17 will always depend, of course,
on our interpretation of verse 18. I would like to start by saying that:
i) I believe that the verb *katoptrizesthai* means to behold, to
contemplate, and not to reflect;[64] ii) 2 Corinthians iv 4-6 is
indispensable for a right understanding of 2 Corinthians iii 18. The
whole passage iii 18-iv 6 is a Christological interpretation of the
Exodus and Genesis passages already mentioned with the help of
Wisdom vii 25-26. Paul's thought and terminology are parallel to
Hebrews i 3 and the Johannine Prologue (Christ as the *Eikon,* and
Logos, revelation, glory, reflection, of the Father). I dare to offer the
following translation: 'But to this day ... *every time he turns to the
Lord, the veil is removed. The Lord* is the spirit; and where the Spirit
of the Lord is, there is freedom. And we all, with unveiled face,
beholding as in a mirror the glory of the Lord, are being transformed
into the same likeness, from glory to glory; inasmuch as this is from
the Spirit, which is Lord.'[65]

Paul's vocabulary is polyvalent and we have to respect this. In
saying 'every time he turns to the Lord' he means both the Moses of
the Exodus text which he is quoting, the Moses of verse 15 which
means 'the Torah' ('the letter'), and the Jewish reader of Moses. So
the verb 'turn' preserves both its historical, local, meaning (Moses
'going in before the Lord'; this is a rule of the pesher exegesis), and
its religious sense of conversion, turning to God (for the sake of
which it was chosen instead of 'going in'). 'Paul, like any Jewish
exegete,' writes D. M. Derrett in another context, 'revels in
significant ambiguities, and will take advantage of double meanings, puns, which are hardly to our modern taste.'[66] *To pneuma* in 2
Corinthians iii 17 is also purposely ambivalent, I believe.[67] But it
does not mean as yet the Holy Spirit as person, but, primarily, the
'spirit' of which Paul has been talking since v.4: the Grace, the new
order of the Spirit, in contradistinction and relation to the old order,
the letter[68] (the starting point of the discussion being, let us
remember, the *letters* of Paul's opponents, v. 1). We are concerned
with the Pauline antithesis of law and gospel. Immediately there
rises Paul's cry of liberty: 'where the Spirit of the Lord is there is
freedom'. This exclamation is invited by the image of the removed
veil-callus (*porosis*, verse 14 — note that *noemata* here and in iv 4 is
eqivalent to *kardia* in verse 15). The Holy Spirit is the gentle breeze
blowing (or the awesome wind sweeping) in the direction of Christ.
Turned towards Christ, the Jew is healed from his *porosis*
(hardening) — *perosis* (blinding) and sees at last the glory of God
shining not passingly on the face of Moses, but unfading in the face
of Christ (2 Cor iv 6), mirror and image of God (2 Cor iii 18; iv 4).[69]

Contemplating God's likeness, the Christian is being transfigured into that same Image, from glory to glory; inasmuch as this comes from the Spirit, which is Lord.[70]

The passage is certainly one of the summits of Paul's theology and self-revelation (cf 2 Cor iv 6 with its Damascus overtones, expressed in a hieratic baptismal language). But it cannot be claimed in support of the identity of the Spirit with the risen Lord in Paul. 2 Corinthians iii 17a is a pesher of Exodus xxxiv 34 and the 'spirit' there denotes the reality of the New Covenant, in contrast to the *gramma* of the Old, its imperfect prefiguration. Confidence, boldness and glory (i.e. filial status, dignity and freedom) can be given, says Paul, only by the New Covenant of the law-Spirit in the heart, as promised by the prophets and realized in Christ, 'qui est Imago Dei'. Paul has no need of human recommendations or underhand ways: his ministry is to manifest God's open truth (2 Cor iv 1-2). 2 Corinthians iii 17a has no intention whatsoever of asserting the identity of Christ and the Spirit.

The Pauline experience of the Spirit is the experience of a second divine messenger 'from the Father', who, coming after Christ, seals Christ's work, testifying to the adoption of the Christian, and being the first-fruits of the eternal blessings. The Holy Spirit is the interiorization of the invisible presence of Christ and of the powerful continuity of God's action in, and by, him. 'The Spirit gives life' (2 Cor iii 6) means for Paul: 'the Spirit gives Christ'. The Holy Spirit, 'poured' in the Christian's heart, does not give any new revelation, does not lead beyond Christ. There is no other foundation than that which is laid, Jesus Christ (1 Cor iii 11). No one, be it Paul himself or an angel from heaven, can preach a gospel different from that which was received (Gal i 8-9): there is no 'other' and no 'beyond', no 'higher', no 'deeper', no 'broader'. Christ is the *eschatos*, the last, the final, and the ultimate — the 'limitless limit'. 'For all the promises of God find their "Yes" in him; and so through him also is our "Amen" to God, to his glory. And he who strengthens us ... in Christ and has anointed us, is God; he who also has sealed us and given the pledge of his Spirit in our hearts' (2 Cor i 20-22). From whence it rises to the Christian's tongue to cry, again, 'Abba! Father!' (Rom viii 15ff.).

John

Our last trial run will be traced through the Gospel of John. I do not intend to offer an essay on 'the Spirit Paraclete in the Gospel of John', and I hope that what follows is not another 'additional note on the Paraclete'. My objective is much humbler: to examine the Paraclete's relation to Jesus.

Following R. E. Brown who saw John vi as a commentary on the words 'This is my body; this is my blood', A. Lacomara called the Farewell Discourse, 'a commentary on the words "of the new covenant" '. He did this at the end of an essay in which he tried to

show that the Discourse is deeply in debt to the form and contents of
Deuteronomy.[71] Without adopting Lacomara's views, I still feel that
there is a kinship between the testament and last ode of Moses and
Jesus' testament and farewell prayer in John. One could go so far as
to say that the Johannine Paraclete represents the Mosaic 'prophet-
like-me'. This, however, would not be true in every sense. For the
Paraclete is not promised as one from among the brethren in whose
mouth God will put his words, but is described as that very voice of
God which the Israelite was afraid to hear on Horeb, 'lest he die'. On
Sinai Israel begged to be spared the necessity of hearing the divine
voice directly, and so Yahweh instituted the prophetic office of
mediator (Deut v 24ff; Ex xx 19ff), which, before his death, Moses
promised would never fail Israel (Deut xviii 15ff). In John the
Incarnate Word before his death and exaltation promises never to
become 'too wondrous', or remote or inaccessible, never to go 'far
off'. [72] The Word shall remain very near the disciples, in their mouth
and in their heart, 'so that they can do it' (Deut xxx 11-14). This will
be fulfilled through the indwelling of the Paraclete in the believers'
heart; the interiorization of God's voice within man, 'so that he can
live'.

I believe that the Johannine term *parakletos* is irreducible.
Scholars should accept the fact that the word is not found outside
John in the Johannine meaning. Not even in the Dead Sea Scrolls.
To say that God is the Paraclete of Israel, or that the Right Teacher
is a Paraclete *par excellence*, is to deprive the word of any and every
meaning: in this way everybody and everything can be called a
'helper', every religious person an 'intercessor', every angel an
'interpreter', every messenger of God a 'spokesman', every god a
'comforter', and so on. It is a common *topos* that early Christianity
created in a striking way a radically new vocabulary, renewing and
modifying old language patterns. And then we must respect the
genius of the Greek language, always opposing specialization of
words; always respectful of the mysterious essence of the reality
which lies in the word; always preserving both the original meaning
and the acquired special sense; always in ecstasy before names (and
every word is a name for the Greek).[73]

Could not the Spirit of the new tongues take a new name for itself
as well? Though I believe that Jewish contacts exist (especially in
Jewish angelology), I do not believe that there should be any talk
about possible 'sources'. Whether this new name of the Spirit
originated with John, with his community, or with Jesus himself, is
not very important, and perhaps we shall never know. (And one
wonders what is meant by 'community' in such cases, anyhow.) The
important thing is the reality denoted by the word, and this comes
both from Jesus, John, and the Johannine community. My own
research has brought me to the conclusion that the primary
meaning of the word *parakletos* in John is comforter. This, however,
does not affect my exposition here.[74]

If then we are to avoid what Whitehead used to call 'the fallacy of the misplaced concreteness', we must remember that *parakletos* is the name, or perhaps still the symbolical designation, of a person, and so not expect it to be interpreted every time it turns up. In fact, as things stand now in John, every saying in which the name is encountered (with the possible exception of the first occurrence, Jn xiv 15 — and this is very eloquent!) reveals an aspect of the function and mission of the person signified. The evangelist speaks of the Paraclete as of a well-known person and it never occurs to him that one of his readers might not have been introduced to this person. Even if he thought of this possibility he obviously chose not to make the introductions. This is one more reason why the present writer believes that the Paraclete sayings cannot be isolated from their natural context, which is the Farewell Discourse: they belong organically to the Farewell Discourse, and outside it they are completely unintelligible, despite the noble efforts of many exegetes. Here, as in every other part of the gospel, the great classical scholar's verdict is true: 'It is impossible to distinguish between "discourses source" and the actual text of John, for John *rewrites the discourses* and whether he speaks himself (Prologue) or makes John the Baptist [Jn iii 31-36] or Jesus speak, it is always the same language, the same style, the same proceedings of style (parallelism, antithesis, etc.)'.[75] There is only one way: that of the evangelist.

In John xiv 15ff we hear nothing of the Paraclete *qua* 'paraclete', though we hear that he is 'another (*allos*) Paraclete', the first one obviously being Jesus himself. The saying is, however, most important, for it portrays the Paraclete as a divine person in union with the Father and the Son. Verse 17 links the Paraclete promise with John vii 37-39 and, by affirming that 'he dwells with you', with John i 32ff In this way (and later through Jn xix 34ff.) the gift of the Paraclete 'in the disciple' ('and he will be in you') is shown to be organically related with the Incarnate's endowment with the Spirit (as against W. G. Kummel and others). The Paraclete Spirit of Truth who will come from the Father through the intercession of the Son is no one else than the Spirit that remains (*menei*) on the Incarnate, and so already dwells with the disciples (*par'humin menei*, Jn xiv 17), with whom the Incarnate dwells (*menon par'humin*, Jn xiv 25). But as the world cannot see or receive the Son or the Father (Jn i 10; viii 19, etc.), so it cannot either see or receive the Spirit of truth, visible only to the believers. When some interpreters, deceived by their prejudices about the origins and meaning of the word *parakletos*, present the Paraclete as *ad mundum*, they miss the point and certainly are in grave error: for the Paraclete is unknown and unacceptable to the world. In John the Spirit's coming has nothing of the spectacular character of the event of Acts ii, no mention of the great cosmic event prophesied by Joel is made, no external manifestations are foretold. For John the coming of the Spirit Paraclete will pass unnoticed by the world

(John xiv 17). As we shall see when we come to John xv 26-27, the
Paraclete could be said to deal with the world only through the
Apostles, the apostolic witness of the Church to the world.
Exclusively 'functional' Christologies and Pneumatologies tend to
present the Son and the Paraclete as living *dia ton kosmon*, because,
and for, the world. This neo-Arian view, however, on closer scrutiny
can be seen to lack any biblical support. For John the Paraclete, like
the Son, comes, lives and acts in the world *dia ton Patera* (cf Jn vi
57), because of, and for, the Father, whose word and work he
accomplishes in the believer's heart. This becomes evident as soon
as we see John xiv 15-17 in its context, and not in isolation.

The saying is just a 'variation of a theme'. The musical way of
'Theme and variations' is a common feature of John's style. In this
case the 'theme' is My lover (*ho agapon me*), and we have three
variations: i) My lover will keep my commandments; and I will ask
the Father to give him another Paraclete to dwell in him (15-17). ii)
My lover is he that keeps my commandments;and my Father will
love him, and I will love him and manifest myself to him (v.21). iii)
My lover will keep my word; and my Father will love him, and we
will come to him and make our home with him (23). At the end of
each variation comes as a shadow-refrain the problem of the world;
the world cannot receive the indwelling of the Paraclete, because it
neither sees nor knows him (17a); 'How is it that you will manifest
yourself to us, and not to the world?' (22); 'He who does not love me,
does not keep my word' (24). The second half of each variation is the
key to the world's predicament: knowledge of God is the reward of
love. And love's proof is the keeping of the commandments (cf Wi vi
18). The coming and indwelling of the Paraclete is parallel to the
manifestation of Jesus, and his coming with the Father to the
believer's heart. The Paraclete will be God's manifestation in the
heart of the believer, the Spirit-knowledge of God in the heart of
God's people of the New Covenant (cf Jer xxxi 31ff; Ezek xxxvi
26f).[76]

Verse 26 forms the conclusion: 'The Paraclete, the Holy Spirit,
whom the Father will send in my name, he will teach you all things,
and bring to your remembrance all that I have said to you'. The
Spirit will teach, comment, and keep alive in the believer's memory
God's word through Jesus. This *hupomnesis* is not the intellectual or
Platonic *anamnesis*, but rather the dynamic biblical remembrance
(*zkr*), which makes alive, re-confirms and gives anew the things
remembered. The believer will not remember his origins, his divine
past, or anything in relation to himself. He will be reminded of
Jesus' words (cf Jn xvi 4; ii 22); he will be reminded of Jesus'
commandments which he must keep. A unique commandment in
fact, the new commandment of the brother's love in the image of the
Son's love for the disciples and the Father's love for the Son. The
Paraclete, love's reward ('if you love me...'), will thus assist the
believer to remain in the love of Jesus, and, so, in the Father's love.

Following the Paraclete, the Father and the Son will come to the believer; he will receive them in himself, he will become their abode, he will share their life. The believer will enter the pre-eternal (Jn xvii 5) circulation of love and glory between the Father, the Son, and the Spirit.

The Paraclete ,then, is introduced in the Farewell Discourse as a promised reward for loyalty and love. The setting is covenantal. The loyalty and love of the disciples is already there and they are already Christ's (Jn xvii 6-10), but the reward is not unconditional. The keeping of Jesus' commandments, the manifestation of their love for him, is necessary. The paradox is that it is that very gift which will help them to remain in Jesus' love. As in the ancient oriental and Old Testament grants, Jesus promises to his loyal friends (Jn xv 14) 'land' and 'house' (family). 'In my Father's house are many mansions ... I go to prepare a place for you' (Jn xiv 2-3); 'We will come to him and make our home with him' (Jn xiv 23); 'And he will give you another Paraclete to be with you for ever' (Jn xiv 16). The reward is 'for ever', *'ad 'olam*. There is no question here of the Paraclete substituting, or not, the Parousia. The gift of the Lord's benevolence is 'for ever', as the whole covenant is. Is he not the God 'who keeps his gracious promise to those who love him and guard his commandments' (*bmr hbryt whhsd l'hwy wlsmry mswtw,* Deut vii 9)? And is there any thought anywhere in the New Testament that the Christian will be separated from the Spirit in the kingdom? (Not even in modern post-Dibelian Luke, as far as I know). By reminding the believer of Jesus' commandments, the Paraclete teaches him how to keep them: the art of 'abiding in the Son' (Jn xv 1ff). The Paraclete is the inward teacher of the life in Christ: this is the 'everything' of John xiv 26.

'When the Paraclete comes, whom I shall send to you from the Father, even the Spirit of truth, who proceeds from the Father, he will bear witness to me; and you also are witnesses, because you have been with me from the beginning' (Jn xv 26-27). The third logion about the Paraclete brings further revelation about the Spirit and its work. After speaking of the Father's love for him and the disciples, Jesus contrasts to it the world's hatred (Jn xv 18ff). The world hates the Father, Jesus, and the disciples, with a sinful hatred without reason (Jn xv 24-25). This hatred will not stop with Jesus' death. The disciples also will appear before the tribunals of the world, and, as we shall see in chapter xiv, the world will appear before the tribunal of the heart of the Christians. The great work of the witness to Jesus will be assumed by the Paraclete, the Spirit of truth. 'He will bear witness to me': the Paraclete as the first and great *'martyr'* of Christ. Verse 26 cannot be properly understood except through the following verse: 'and you also are witnesses, because you have been with me from the beginning'. Evidently the witness is about the identity of the earthly Jesus, the Galilean (cf Jn vii). Those who have been with him from the beginning of his

ministry, his disciples and apostles, can bear witness to him, for
they have seen and known who he is: 'You have the words of eternal
life; and we have believed and have come to know, that you are the
Holy One of God' (Jn vi 66ff). This knowledge the Paraclete has not
only 'from the beginning' (cf the *arche* of Jn ii 11), when he came
and remained on Jesus (Jn i 32ff), but 'in the beginning' (cf Jn i 1):
for the Paraclete 'proceeds from the Father' and comes from him,
the same as Jesus. He knows heaven, because he too descends from
heaven (cf Jn iii 13). But, as will become evident later, verse 27
speaks of a witness different from that of verse 26; or rather of the
same witness given in different judgements: the Spirit's witness is
given in the heart of the believers; the apostolic witness of the
Church is that very same inward witness of the Spirit translated in
the mouths of the faithful before the tribunals of the world. As
Augustine says, 'Ille testimonium perhibebit de me et vos
testimonium perhibebitis. Utique quia ille perhibebit, etiam vos
perhibebitis: ille in cordibus vestris, vos in vocibus, ille inspirando;
vos sonando.'[77]

With the beginning of chapter xvi Jesus comes back to the
warnings of John xv 20 and starts explaining at greater length the
hatred of the world against himself and the disciples. Those who
finally reject him will always try to kill him. While he is on earth,
they will try to kill him in his body, when he is exalted they will try
to kill him in his 'little children'. Chapter xvi presupposes a
religious world and from verse 2a we can see that the people
immediately meant are the Jews, the people of the Old Covenant as
symbol of the rebellious world.

These sad things about future persecutions were not said to the
disciples from the beginning, because Jesus was with them and
could bear the burden himself (cf Jn xviii 8). Now he is going back to
him that sent him, and so he must prepare them for the future. But
they must not let their hearts be filled with sorrow. The deep truth is
different, a cause of joy for them, not of sorrow.

'I tell you the truth: it is to your advantage that I go away, for if I
do not go, the Paracelete will not come to you; but if I depart,[78] I will
send him to you. And when he comes, he will confute the world in the
matter[79] of sin, and in the matter of justice, and in the matter of
judgement: in the matter of sin, because they do not believe in me; in
the matter of justice, because I [have overcome the world and] go to
the Father,[80] and so[81] you see me no more; in the matter of
judgement, because it is the prince of this world who is condemned.[82] I have yet many things to say to you, but you cannot bear them
now. But when he comes, the Spirit of truth, he will guide you into[83]
all the truth; for he will not speak from himself, but whatever he will
hear he will speak, and[84] he will announce to you the things that are
to come. He will glorify me,[85] for it is from what is mine that he will
take what he will announce to you. All that the Father has is mine;
that is why I said that[86] it is from what is mine that he will take

what he will announce to you' (Jn xvi 7-15).

The Paraclete cannot come unless Jesus has gone to the Father, i.e. the Spirit cannot be given unless Jesus is glorified (Jn vii 39). The Spirit of constancy can conquer only in the sign of the Cross. It cannot come to the world unless the prince of the world is cast out. And this can be achieved only by the Incarnate's voluntary death. Only love unto death can destroy the power of death and grant life eternal (cf. Jn iii 16). 'And this is eternal life, that they know thee the only true God, and Jesus Christ whom thou hast sent' (Jn xvii 3). But only through the witness of the Spirit of truth can man know Jesus as him that God has sent (Jn xv 26). For besides truth there is for John not just error, but perversity, the lie, and the false witness (cf especially Jn viii),[87] the darkness trying to suffocate the light (Jn i 5). In this gigantic battle between truth and lie the faithful need not only constant help and guidance, but also continual assurance and proof. In John xvi 7ff the Paraclete is presented precisely as the Spirit of truth, defender of the truth and reprover of lies, on the one hand (Jn xvi 8-11), revealer of the truth, on the other (Jn xvi 12-15). Both missions are inseparable. Both take place in the believer's heart. In both the Paraclete is the believer's helper and counsellor, but in the first instance as his comforter in the face of his condemnation by the world, in the second as his guide along the way of truth, leading to the Father's bosom. In the first the Paraclete is Jesus' advocate in the face of his condemnation by the world, in the second the Paraclete is the Christian's teacher and sustainer. In both missions he glorifies Jesus by preserving his disciples firm in their faith. Let me repeat once again that the 'trial of Jesus' about which John is speaking here is not a trial before the tribunal of eternity (God has already passed his judgement); it is not a cosmic trial, etc., as several modern exegetes thought. Theo Preiss's brilliant theories[88] have been corrected a long time ago by M.-F. Berrouard: the judgement happens on earth, but in the conscience of those to whom the Spirit has been sent. The Paraclete acts only in the souls of the faithful, bringing before their conscience nothing less than the point of view of God.[89]

In verses 8-11 we see the Paraclete defending Christ before the Christian's conscience not only by accusing the world, as Moses accuses the Jews (Jn v 45), but by proving it to be in sin, and by demonstrating its shame and condemnation. Pointing to Jesus exalted 'with the Father', he proves that Jesus has overcome the world. In condemning Jesus the world unknowingly committed parricide: for in reality it condemned not Jesus, but its own 'murderer father' (Jn viii 44; xii 31f.). A lifeless corpse awaiting its complete extinction, the world still refuses to believe, for it loves darkness rather than light, and does not come to the light, lest its deeds should be exposed (Jn iii 19f). The lovers of light shall never lack, however. For them the Spirit will be a 'lamp to their feet and a light to their path', his testimonies their delight and their counsellors (cf Ps cxix).

In John xv 15 Jesus declared that, 'whatever I have heard from
my Father I have reported it (*egnorisa*) to you'. In John xvi 12f he
says that, 'I have yet many things to say to you, but you cannot
bear them now', and promises that the Spirit will guide the disciples
'into all the truth'. The Spirit will lead the disciples along the way of
all truth. This means that it will keep them in Christ, who is 'the
way and the truth, and the life' (Jn xiv 6). 'Guidance along the way
of truth', says R. E. Brown, 'is guidance to the mystery of Jesus who
is the truth'.[90] The Paraclete will be the *Hodegos* along the *Hodos* —
Christ.

'For he will not speak of himself, but whatever he will hear he will
speak' (Jn xvi 13). The Spirit's work will be a continuation of Jesus'
work, as we saw it in Jn xv 15: he will keep the disciples in the
intimacy of the Father's family. As Jesus' friends they will be told
the Father's mind and the Spirit will communicate to them the
counsel of the Father and the Son (14-15). The Paraclete will not
give the disciples a new Revelation of God. The revelation of the
Father is the only Son who is in the bosom of the Father and has
described him to them (Jn i 18).[91] There is no other description of the
Father except the Son, and the Son discloses the Father in showing
himself: 'He who has seen me has seen the Father' (Jn xiv 9) — this
is 'the very definition of the Fourth Gospel' (A.-J. Festugiere). What
Jesus says about the Spirit is that its guidance of the believer will be
from God; not just an inspired guidance, but a divine guidance.
Through the Spirit of God the Church does not possess just an
inspired teaching, but God's teaching. Thus, the truth of the Church
is not just a particle of truth but the whole truth, all truth, the entire
truth: because God's truth. What these verses desire to underline is
not, I believe, so much the continuity of the word of Jesus, as the fact
that, despite Jesus' bodily absence, the Church will always possess
God's truth, the fulness of truth.

The disciples will lack nothing of what they enjoyed when Jesus
was bodily among them. Even that supernatural prophetic knowledge that he always unfolded (Jn i 48; xi 11-15, etc.) will continue to
be with them. The Spirit will bring them word even about the things
to come. This particular promise is already comprised in the general
promise of guidance into all the truth. In John xvi 13c it is only
brought out more emphatically. For how can one avoid going astray,
if he does not know what is lying in front of him? Exegetes seem
unwilling to adopt this obvious interpretation because of pre-
conceived ideas of what the author *ought* to have meant. The right
way, nevertheless, is to see what the evangelist's words indicate.
When Brown says that Bultmann's view seems most reasonable
'since it would fit within the Johannine emphasis on realized
eschatology', he shows that he is biased.[92] I will not answer
Bultmann's argument in detail. I will just say that I think that it is
very strange indeed to say that, 'the future will not be unveiled in a

knowledge imparted before it happens, but it will be illuminated again and again by the word that is at work in the community' (Bultmann, *in loc.*), by saying, *ta erchomena anangelei humin*. If this is Greek, then . . . *es sind mir bohmische Dorfer*.

Studies of the meaning of the verb *anangellein* in the apocalyptic literature have shown that it denotes interpretation of (mysterious) knowledge *already communicated* in dreams and visions. The verb in this technical sense means: to unveil, disclose, interpret already imparted secrets. This can never be the case here. The knowledge that the Spirit will communicate to the disciples is not a knowledge or interpretation of truths that they have already been given. It is not they that are said to have already heard it; it is the Spirit that is said to hear it first and then communicate it to them. I believe that in the verses under discussion the verb preserves its usual Hellenistic meaning and is synonymous to the Attic *apangellein*: to bring word, report, announce what one has heard. P. Jouon, in his 'Le verbe *anangello* dans saint Jean'[93] should be the starting point for any right assessment of the meaning of John xvi 14-15. Jesus says that the Paraclete will speak whatever he will hear, and, in particular, he will transmit to the disciples whatever he will hear about the things to come. This should not mean exclusively apocalyptic prophecy, but the prophetic gift of foreknowledge in general.[94]

The phrase can be said to come nearly word by word from Isaiah xliv 7 LXX (cf Is xlviii 14). Commenting on the Isaiah verse, C. Westermann wrote: 'Deity or divinity is proved according as, over a long period of time, the god concerned guides a community's history by means of proclamations whose fulfilment allows the community to know that this god can be relied on to guide'.[95] This is a common ancient motive in Babylon, Egypt, and Israel. What John means is that, despite the bodily absence of their teacher, the disciples will walk in the fulness of truth, because they will be guided by God himself. Thus they will possess even knowledge of the future, a thing divine *par excellence* (cf Jn i 48-49: the proof of Jesus' divinity is his miraculous knowledge; Jn xviii 4: Jesus knows *ta erchomena ep' auton*).[96] I do not see why one should deny to John a belief shared by Paul, Luke, and the entire early Church, and which is the very essence of the second major component of the Johannine literature, the Revelation, and is recognized in 1 John iv 1ff (cf the technical term 'test the spirits'). What is more significant, however, is that the Fourth Gospel sees prophecy as a demonstration of the Paraclete's divinity, the fact that he 'proceeds from the Father' and will come from him: the Church can rely on him as on an infallible guide to the Truth, along the way of Truth.

'He will glorify me, for it is from what is mine that he will take what he will announce to you. All that the Father has is mine; that is why I said that it is from what is mine that he will take what he will announce to you' (Jn xvi 14-15). The Spirit will glorify Jesus,

because it will receive the truth and power that it will communicate
to the disciples from Jesus, from the common knowledge and power
of the Father and the Son. If the Paraclete is the Spirit of truth,
Christ is Truth and his Father is the True One (Jn xiv 6; vii 28; xvii
3). The glory of Jesus will be the manifestation of his divine power
as Son and envoy of God (a Johannine theme *par excellence*)
through the Spirit's inerrant guidance of the Church. The Church's
progress along the way of truth will be a manifestation of the 'works
of God' in her. The Spirit's mission will be the credentials of Christ,
not to the unbelievers (something that he consistently refused to
give them: Jn ii 18; vi 30), but to those who have already accepted
him. Prophecy, being for John part of the Church's general
possession of the truth, is one more aspect of the Spirit's witness to
Jesus' divine Sonship, mission and authority. This is a constant
feature of the theology of Christian prophecy in the Apocalypse and
in 1 John also. 'Worship God: for he that bears witness to Jesus is
the Spirit of prophecy' (Rev xix 10), i.e. God's Spirit.[97]

The above analysis makes it impossible for me to accept such
statements as: 'Thus the Spirit-Paraclete is basically none other
than the exalted Christ' (G. Bornkamm); or: 'The Paraclete is ... the
word ... the living word ... the word which is spoken by the
community itself' (R. Bultmann); or: 'Whatever is said about the
Paraclete is said elsewhere in the Gospel about Jesus' (R. E. Brown);
or: 'The Paraclete continues the work of God in Jesus, he is the
representative of the exalted Christ until the promise becomes
fulfilment' (W. G. Kummel).

Bornkamm falls into a grave logical error in identifying two
persons because their work is described in the same language, and
we can see the same error at work in Brown's mind. The terms used
are the same, the work they describe is *not* the same. The Father's
work is described in the same terms also as Jesus' work, but this
does not mean that the Father is identical with Jesus, or that his
work is the same as Jesus' work. No one, to my knowledge, has said,
for instance, that since the Father bears witness to Jesus (Jn viii 18),
he is none other than the visible Incarnate, who is also said to bear
witness to himself (Jn viii 14). Why then should the Paraclete be
identified with the exalted Christ because he is said to bear witness
to Jesus? What is said of Jesus is that he bears witness to himself;
what is said of the Paraclete is that he bears witness to Jesus. I am
afraid that some of the above-mentioned scholars were more
anxious to answer questions than to examine them. Their
paradoxes/muddles arise from an illegitimate 'identification' of
utterly different uses of tokens like (to continue with our example)
the word 'witness', 'to bear witness'. Arguments like Bornkamm's
amount to syllogisms like, 'If the shepherd bears witness to himself
and the dairymaid bears witness to the shepherd, then the
dairymaid is the shepherd'. Now this is a further step beyond
Brown's assertion, which is of the type: 'If the *Times* says that the

shepherd bears witness to himself and that the dairymaid bears witness to the shepherd, then the same thing is said by the *Times* of the shepherd and the dairymaid'. Which is nonsense, of course, because the *Times* does not say that the dairymaid bears witness to herself. 'To bear witness' is being used interchangeably by Bornkamm and Brown within vastly different logical areas. Bultmann's reasoning I acknowledge that I do not understand. His final conclusion sounds to me like the assertion that, 'The dairymaid is the word which is spoken by the Jury itself'.

With regard to Kummel's judgement, I will say that my analysis of the Paraclete sayings in John does not authorize me in any way to speak of the Paraclete as of 'the representative of the exalted Christ until the promise becomes fulfilment'. With his Passion the Incarnate accomplished *in perfection* the work that the Father gave him to do (Jn xvii 4), and John xix 28-30 makes it clear that for the evangelist the work of Christ, gift of the Father, is consummated, and there remains nothing to be added.[98] The Paraclete's mission is to bear witness to this, and to help man to appropriate it in its fulness. In the believer's heart the Paraclete will become 'a fountain of water springing up into eternal life' (Jn iv 14).

The Paraclete sayings cannot be understood in isolation from the rest of the Gospel, especially the key sayings of John vii 37-39, xix 34 and xx 21.[99] The one to whom God has given the Spirit without measure (Jn iii 34) is his incarnate Son. It is he who is the source of the Spirit for his Church (Jn vii 37), and only out of the glorious mystery of his Cross can the Spirit be poured (Jn vii 39; xix 34), only he can breathe it on the disciples (Jn xx 21). The Spirit is the proof that the victory belongs to Jesus; the coming of the Spirit *is* the victory. Christ overcame the world by founding his Church, which lives for him and is strong in her faith in him and her knowledge of him through the indwelling of the Paraclete in her.

To interpret the Paraclete as a *locum tenens* of the absent Christ, to think of him as 'post-Christic', or to expect him as 'meta-Christic', are sheer misunderstandings. The promise of the Paraclete is inseparable from the promise of the continuous presence of the glorified Jesus. The Paraclete will not reveal new truths transcending the revelation of Jesus; he will give new apprehensions of Jesus' truth. His gift will be the perfection in the knowledge of the Incarnate only begotten Son, 'full of grace and truth'.

Conclusion

It would be easy to conclude that the New Testament does not offer a clear criterion for the discernment of the spirits. But this would be wrong. Rather let us say that the New Testament does not know of a Spirit which ignores Christ and the apostolic message; as it does not know of a Christ who ignores the Spirit and the Church. For the same God the Father has sent his Son, and, through him, given his Spirit, his Son's witness, revealer, and teacher. The idea of a new kingdom of the Spirit is equally strange to the New Testament as Christomonism. To know the grace of the Holy Spirit is to know God through Christ; and this is what makes Christianity different from Judaism as well as from the other religions, even different from a knowledge of God through the Scriptures.

Afterword

SPONSA

When Jeremiah was promising the Jerusalemites that God would do them no harm if they would turn from their evil ways (Jer xxv 3ff), far away, at Megiddo, Israel's most pious king, Josiah, was being slain by Pharaoh Necho of Egypt (609 B.C.). 'Before him there was no king like him, who turned to Yahweh with all his heart and with all his soul and with all his might, according to all the law of Moses; nor did any like him arise after him' (2 Kings xxiii 25). These two remarkable Old Testament figures mark the ambiguity of Old Testament prophecy. Josiah, the king according to Yahweh's heart, perished at the hands of Pharaoh in the very land of the Promise. And Jeremiah, God's prophet, died some years later in the land of Egypt, the house of servitude.

The failure of the prophets' historical messianism was repeated with Wisdom. The sage's insensibility to the divine event ended in the boredom of the Ecclesiastes. 'The end of the matter; all has been heard'.

With apocalyptic the close was no better. Haunted by visions of a world laid like a minefield with the snares of apostasy and abomination, the apocalyptist beat a retreat to an otherworldly 'future', where the frenzied passions of his heart found refuge.

By the end of the era before Christ, the people of God was miserably torn between the idealism of its dreams and the frustration of the reality. Having failed to enter into a real dialogue with the nations, it found no other consolation for its political oppression and religious failure except in a wretched legalism and a still more wretched trust in revolution. The nightmare of Herod's despotism was already matched by the rising nightmare of the imposed Pharisaic piety, in the same way as the Maccabaean physical violence was twinned with the mental violence of the apocalyptist.

Thus, when at last God's long-awaited response came unexpectedly in Jesus, needless to say, the leaders of the nation rejected it,

Having prayed for a Rabbi or an armed Messiah
And found the Son of God.[1]

But in his Church also Jesus Christ was to remain a stumbling-block. His claim to uniqueness seemed to some of his followers excessive in view of the holiness of the past; as his claim to eschatological finality seemed to others unjustified in view of the ongoing miserable reality of the world. Judaizing Christians were ready to accept Jesus only as one of God's emissaries to his people — perhaps the greatest but still only one of them. Gnosticizing

Christians 'advanced beyond the doctrine of Christ' (2 Jn ix), seeking a higher knowledge.

The legendary Simon the Magus claimed, it seems, to be a new 'face' of God, appearing for the nations as Holy Spirit, as he appeared to the Samaritans as Father, and to the Jews as Son.[2] Certain Jewish Christians turned to a Christology according to which Christ was continually reappearing through the ages.[3] For the Valentinians it was Paul who came 'in the image of the Paraclete'[4] (basically a view they still share with some Protestant New Testament scholars). And in A.D. 156-7, in an age which has been called 'pathologically traditionalist', the world witnessed the outbreak of the 'New Prophecy' in Phrygia, with the Paraclete offering hopes of change, and Christ (dressed as a woman) giving all good Christians an appointment at Pepuza. The original Trio (Montanus, Prisca and Maximilla) do not appear to have preached that they were the Paraclete, but soon their followers acclaimed Montanus to have been the Paraclete. If a Tertullian could write that, 'iustitia ... primo fuit in rudimentis ... dehinc per legem et prophetas promovit in infantiam, dehinc per evangelium efferbuit in iuventutem, nunc per Paracletum componitur in maturitatem' (*De virg. vel.* i), no wonder in the fourth century a certain 'Flabius Anus domesticus' could begin his inscription, 'in nomine Patris et Filii [et] domini Montani'.[5]

But in the meantime (and after the appointment at Pepuza was indefinitely postponed) in A.D. 240-1 the Parthian Mani, 'by the providence of God the Father Apostle of Jesus Christ', received his birth from the Spirit and became the bodily manifestation of the Johannine Paraclete, his divine *suzugos*. A son of the Elkesaites,[6] he intended to supersede Christianity in what still remains the only premeditated universal religion in the history of thought. By the seventh century the religion of the Persian Paraclete was the greatest in the world spreading from northern Spain to Peking.

Yet the Paraclete was not to stop his exotic tours. In A.D. 610 eight hundred miles to the south of the Byzantine frontier, in Mecca, the Prophet Muhammad was called to restore primitive authenticity, after Christianity's corruption. Kur'an lxi 6 makes Jesus announce to Israel the future coming of one 'more worthy of praise', *Ahmad*. Muslim theologians, under the inspiration, it has been suggested, of Christian converts, soon identified Muhammad to the promised Paraclete, *al-Ahmad*, the *laudatissimus*. But even he, though acclaimed by all his devotees as the *Al-'Akib* (the last one) and the *Khatim al-anbiya'* (the seal of the prophets), he was not to be accepted by all as the Seal of the *walayat* (friendship, 'Initiation'): for the Twelver Shi'is the eschatological initiation and life will be given with the revelation of the hidden Twelfth Imam, *al-Faraklit*, the Imam-Paraclete, *al-Ka'im*, the Imam of the Resurrection. He who will give the final initiation into the *Nur al-Kalam*, the Light of the Word.[7] In the East 'Paracletism' is an amplification of the

Judaeo-Christian theme of the *Verus Propheta*, the true prophet who 'hastens from prophet to prophet till the place of his rest', always a new prophet.

In the West the prevalent theme is that of the Third Covenant, the Covenant of the Paraclete. In the late middle ages the Calabrian Abbot Joachim of Flora shook the foundations of Western Christendom with his prophecies about the imminent coming of the Kingdom of the Spirit, prepared already by St. Benedict, the Patriarch of the monks. In 1254 a young Franciscan published in Paris his *Introduction to the Eternal Gospel* where he treated Joachim's works as the gospel of the Third Kingdom, which would supersede the two previous Kingdoms of the Old and the New Testaments. Soon the movement was joined by the Spiritual Franciscans, who in Joachim's new Elias recognized St. Francis. Had it not been for the grim face of the rising Aristotle, Joachimitism could very well have swept from Europe Christ's New Testament. For as a Joachimite Minorite put it to a sceptical Preacher in a recorded discussion, 'You believe in the Prophets? Then why not in Joachim?'

For all their *naivete*, however, Joachimitism and similar movements in Christendom pose to the Church a real question, because they express a real need and a real thirst. The theologian who has not forgotten the Holy Spirit (if there can ever be a theologian without the Holy Spirit) can understand these needs, even if he cannot accept the answers that are given. The nostalgia of a new Pentecost can be only too well understood in a Church where God's revelation has become a system, a conformance, or a professional non-conformity; where the eternally young Word and Bread of life has been alienated into a sclerotic formula, or has become a philosophy of morals, or mere sociological dust.

Our essay has not produced an easily grasped picture of the way in which the new is understood in terms of the old, and the old is deepened in the process rather than discarded. But the student of prophecy and tradition in the Bible can estimate what is lost when, instead of turning to the always true experience of the saints, the Church turns to human opinion and ideas, abandoning herself to the flutterings of the imagination, the passionate desires of the heart, or the devices of the mind. Then, whatever her message to her children or to the world may be, it is a message of man to man, not the message of God to man. Amid the turmoil of the restless world and the uneasy soul, the Holy Spirit leads the Christian not along the lengths of the times, past, present or future, but along the depths of the Above, 'where Christ sitteth on the right hand of God': an exaltation through humiliation, the point of the intersection of the horizons with the sources.

NOTES

INTRODUCTION: *VERBUM*

1. St Gregory of Nyssa, *De pauperibus amandis Or II; In Eccl* vii. *Opera*, ed W. Jaeger, ix, 112; v, 400.
2. A phrase by I. L. Seeligmann quoted by M. Weinfeld in *Deuteronomy and the Deuteronomic School* (Oxford, 1972) 15.
3. L. Durr, *Die Wertung des gottlichen Wortes im Alten Testament und im antiken Orient* (Leipzig, 1938).
4. E. Lipinski, *Essais sur la Revelation et la Bible* (Paris, 1970) 19.
5. Nikolai Velimirovich of Ochrid at the first Faith and Order Conference in Lausanne (1927). Cited by N. Zernov in R. Rouse and S. C. Neill eds, *A History of the Ecumenical Movement 1517-1948* (London, 1967) 655.
6. F. M. Cross, *Canaanite Myth and Hebrew Epic* (Cambridge, Mass, 1973).
7. A. Ohler, *Mythologische Elemente im Alten Testament: eine motivgeschichtliche Untersuchung* (Dusseldorf, 1969) 218: 'As mere poetic decoration the myths are no longer taken seriously .... The myths are detached from their real context and robbed of their original meaning by becoming metaphors for God's actions in history.' Cited by H. W. Wolff, *Anthropology of the Old Testament*, trans M. Kohl (London, 1974) 241.
8. R. A. Johnson, *The Origins of Demythologizing* (Leiden, 1974).
9. G. Florovsky, 'The Predicament of the Christian Historian' in *Religion and Culture. Festschrift P. Tillich* (New York, 1959) 140-166, esp 141.
10. Cf C. Tresmontant, *La doctrine morale des prophetes d'Israel* (Paris, 1958) 36ff.
11. Henri Corbin, ' "Mundus imaginalis" ou l'imaginaire et l'imaginal', in *Cahiers internationals du symbolisme*, iv (1964) 3-26. The imaginary abandons itself to illusion; the imaginal sees the invisible.
12. T. S. Eliot, *Burnt Norton*, i.
13. J. Barr, *Biblical Words for Time*, 2nd ed (London, 1969) must be the starting point of every discussion of this subject. From the Greek point of view, A. Momigliano, 'Time in Ancient Historiography', *History and Theory*, Beiheft vi (1966) 1-23 should be compulsory reading for all biblical students. For an anthropological point of view, see E. Leach, 'Cronos und Chronos', *Rethinking Anthropology* (London, 1966) 124-132, where the primitive Greek conception of time is argued to have been neither cyclical nor linear, but one of a sequence of oscillations between polar opposites.
14. This having been said, I wholly agree with P. Geach in *Proceedings of the British Academy*, li (1965) 321-336 and *Proceedings of the Aristotelian Society*, Suppl. xlii (1968) 7-16, arguing that time-order and space-order being radically different, 'the more we try to assimilate space and time, the more we shall find ourselves logically impeded from doing so'. Thus, any picture of time is 'limited in usefulness and profoundly dangerous. Nothing is sillier than to think you can settle philosophical problems about time by drawing diagrams.' In *God and the Soul* (London, 1969) 91ff. Professor Geach has shown that for the Bible time *does* exist from 'God's point of view' also, and is neither an illusion, nor an error of mortal mind. The Christian preaching of the Cross as a datable event excludes such metaphysical interpretations — rejections of time of the Spinozean, Bradleyan or McTaggartean kind. Jean Mouroux, *Le mystere du Temps* (Paris, 1962) has rightly spoken of the 'Peregrine temporality of Jesus'.
15. M. Eliade, *Images and Symbols: Studies in Religious Symbolism*, trans P. Mairet (London, 1961) 169-170, 172.
16. E. Muir, 'The Heart could never speak'.
17. T. S. Eliot, *Burnt Norton*, ii, 80-82.
18. G. Florovsky, op cit, 166.
19. Philaret of Moscow (1782-1867) cited by A. Scrima, 'Revelation et Tradition dans la Constitution Dogmatique "Dei Verbum" selon un point de vue orthodoxe', in B. D. Duprey ed, *La Revelation Divine*, ii (Paris, 1968) 523-539. I have found this essay of the eminent Rumanian theologian a great help.
20. Gabriel Marcel's famous words in *Mort de Demain*: 'Aimer un etre, c'est lui dire: toi, tu ne mourras pas'.
21. E. Muir, 'The Incarnate One'.
22. Plato, *Phaedrus*, 274b ff.

23. St Hilary of Poitiers, *ad Constantium Aug. lib. ii*, 9. St Jerome repeated the phrase in *dial.c.Lucifer*, x, 570.
24. St Gregory Palamas, *pro hesychastis*, i, 3, 13.

CHAPTER 1: *AUDI ISRAHEL*
1. W. James, *The Varieties of Religious Experience* (London, 1952) 259.
2. A phrase by A. Farrer.
3. Concerning the 'office' of the prophet in ancient Israel, here it will be sufficient to remark that C. Westermann's otherwise excellent book on the *Basic Forms of Prophetic Speech*, trans H. C. White (London, 1967) suffers, I believe, from a certain partialism, in that it presents the prophet exclusively as a 'messenger of Yahweh' (*mal'ak Yhwh*). Yet the only passage where a prophet is explicitly called *mal'ak* is Mal iii 1.... Before being a 'transmitter' the prophet is an official of the heavenly court who, as a member of Yahweh's 'intimate circle' (*sod*), has a voice in the heavenly lawsuit (*rib*) and, so, can influence Yahweh's decision. See also G. E. Wright, 'The Lawsuit of God: A Form Critical Study of Deuteronomy 32' in *Israel's Prophetic Heritage: Essays in honor of James Muilenburg* (London, 1962) 26-67, esp. the literature cited in nn 33-36.
4. A. J. Heschel, *The Prophets* (New York, 1962) xiv; cf A. Neher, *The Prophetic Existence*, trans W. Wolf (London, 1969) 305ff.
5. I consider J. Muilenburg, 'The "Office" of the Prophet in ancient Israel' in J. P. Hyatt ed, *The Bible in Modern Scholarship* (London, 1966) 74-97, to be by far the finest general essay on the prophetic office. When calling the prophet an 'overseer' I do not take this as an institutionalized office, as H. G. Reventlow, *Wachter uber Israel* (Berlin, 1962). Cf P. Auvray, 'Le prophete comme guetteur, Ez xxxiii 1-20', *RB* lxxi (1964) 191-205 (: a pastoral responsibility). On the prophet as intercessor see N. Johansson, *Parakletoi* (Lund, 1940); F. Hesse, *Die Furbitte im Alten Testament* (Hamburg, 1951); G. von Rad, *Theology*, i, 292. For an opposite view, H. W. Hertzberg in *Tradition und Situation: Festschrift A. Weiser* (Gottingen, 1963) 63ff. See also K. Baltzer, 'Considerations Regarding the Office and Calling of the Prophet', *HTR* lxi (1968) 567-581.
6. M. A. Beek, 'The Meaning of the Expression "The Chariots and the Horsemen of Israel" (2 Kings ii 12)', *OS* xvii (1972) 1-10. Following K. Galling, he considers the title as 'eine Kontrastparallele' to the chariots and horsemen of Pharaoh.
7. Contra J. Lindblom *Prophecy in Ancient Israel* (Oxford, 1962) chap i.
8. R. C. Zaehner, *At Sundry times: An Essay in the Comparison of Religions* (London, 1958) 25-26, 171; *Concordant Discord* (Oxford, 1970) 23.
9. Ernest Hello, quoted by Leon Bloy, *Le Desespere* (Paris, 1969) 124; see also the very useful remarks that E. R. Dodds makes in chap iii of his book *Pagan and Christian in an Age of Anxiety* (Cambridge, 1968) 69ff. esp. what he has to say about the Greek word *ekstasis*, a perpetual source of confusion.
10. The third Theologian of the Orthodox Church, St Symeon the Junior (949-1022), considers ecstasy a feature of 'beginners' — the perfect in the Church being taught continually every hour by the grace of the Spirit that they possess in full 'perception of soul'. The origins of this teaching can be traced in the *Spiritual Homilies* attributed to St Macarius of Egypt, and thence, through St Gregory of Nyssa, to the New Testament itself.
11. G. E. Wright, 'Reflections Concerning O.T. Theology', *Studia Biblica et Semitica Theodoro Christiano Vriezen...dedicata* (Wageningen, 1966) 376-388, esp 378.
12. R. Bultmann, *Primitive Christianity*, trans R. H. Fuller (London, 1956) esp 42ff.
13. Henry de Montherland, *Essais* (Paris, 1968) 422.
14. W. Zimmerli, *The Law and the Prophets*, trans R. E. Clements (Oxford, 1965).
15. W. F. Albright, 'Samuel and the Beginnings of the Prophetic Movement' in H. M. Orlinsky ed, *Interpreting the Prophetic Tradition* (New York, 1969) 149-176.
16. D. F. McCarthy, 'The Inauguration of the Monarchy in Israel: A Form Critical Study of I Samuel 8-12', *Interpretation*, xxvii (1973) 401-412. A detailed bibliography is given on p 401. On the royal traditions in general cf F. M. Cross, *Essays*, chap 9.
17. John Gray, *I & II Kings*, 2nd edn (London, 1970) 476. Cf M. A. Beek, op cit.
18. R. de Vaux, 'Jerusalem and the Prophets' in H. M. Orlinsky ed, *Interpreting the Prophetic Tradition*, 275-300. A revised and augmented version of this important lecture has appeared in *RB* lxxiii (1966) 481-509. The originator of this interpretation is M. Noth in his 1950 study 'Jerusalem and the Israelite Tradition', *Essays*, 132-144.
19. T. S. Eliot, *Notes Towards the Definition of Culture* (London, 1962) 67-68.
20. R. G. Collingwood, *The Idea of History* (Oxford, 1961) 14-20.

21. Mircea Eliade, *Patterns in Comparative Religion*, trans R. Sheed (London, 1958) 2-3.

22. Cf J. Wellhausen, *Geschichte Israels i*, 1st edn (Berlin, 1878) (later edns under the title *Prolegomena zur Geschichte Israels*); *Israelitische und Judische Geschichte*, 1st edn (Berlin, 1894); O. Procksch, *Geschichtsbetrachtung und geschichtliche Uberlieferung bei den vorexilischen Propheten* (Leipzig, 1902); G. von Rad, *Theology*, ii, chap G, mainly 112-119; E. Rohland, *Die Bedeutung der Erwahlungstraditionen Israels fur die Eschatologie der altestamentlichen Propheten* (Heidelberg thesis, 1956); G. Fohrer, 'Tradition und Interpretation im Alten Testament', *ZAW* lxxiii (1961) 1-30; 'Remarks on Modern Interpretations of the Prophets', *JBL* lxxx (1961) 309-319; *History of Israelite Religion*, trans E. Green (London, 1973) esp 282-286; J. Vollmer, *Geschichtliche Ruckblicke und Motive in der Prophetie des Amos, Hosea und Jesaja* (Berlin, 1971).

23. Cf the right reaction of G. Quell, *Wahre und Falsche Propheten* (Gutersloh, 1952) 51f. A case against the existence of cultic prophets was made by M. L. Henry, *Prophet und Tradition* (Berlin, 1969).

24. A. D. Nock, *Conversion* (Oxford, 1961) 161.

25. M. Noth, *A History of Pentateuchal Traditions*, trans B. W. Anderson (Englewood Cliffs, New Jersey, 1972) 156-175.

26. W. F. Albright, *From the Stone Age to Christianity*, 2nd edn (Baltimore, 1964).

27. R. de Vaux, O.P., *Histoire Ancienne d'Israel*, i (Paris, 1971); H. H. Rowley, *Worship in Ancient Israel* (London, 1967) — I would not speak of Moses as a prophet. In his lecture 'New Aspects of Biblical Study', delivered at the Sixth World Congress of Jewish Studies (Jerusalem, 12-19 August, 1973), G. Fohrer was emphatic that the role of Moses should not be minimized, though he contended that there was no conception of a covenant between God and his people in the pre-monarchic period of Israel.

28. For an extensive and authoritative justification of this translation of the divine Name see R. de Vaux, op cit For Israel the only God that really exists is Yahweh: Ex iii 14 is not a dogmatic definition, but the injunction of a practical monotheism. For a complementary view see A. Alt, 'Ein agyptisches Gegenstuck zu Ex 3. 14', *ZAW* lviii (1940-41) 159-160 — re-defended by S. Herrmann, *Israel in Egypt*, trans M. Kohl (London, 1973) 51-54.

29. A. D. Nock, op cit, 7.

30. G. Fohrer, op cit, 282-3.

31. I adopt the text offered by S. Amsler in S. Amsler, E. Jacob, C. A. Keller, *Osee, Joel, Amos, Abdias, Jonas* (Neuchatel, 1965) in loc.

32. The most full-scale treatment of the prophetic attitude towards the cult is that of R. Hentschke, *Die Stellung der vorexilischen Schriftpropheten zum Kultus* (Berlin, 1957). But since the prophetic message was conditioned by the concrete situation of the people to whom it was delivered, the author, by not taking into account the exilic and post-exilic prophets, avoids the real difficulty. J. Lindblom (op cit 351-360, esp 360), while agreeing in essentials with Hentschke, arrives at more balanced conclusions in regard to the pre-exilic prophecy. 'These prophets', he says, 'condemned the contemporary cult because of its syncretistic character, because the people who practised it defiled it by their sinfulness, and because it was regarded as a guarantee of salvation and a substitute for ethical reform. Ideas of a reformed and purified cult are rare and rather vague. In view of the catastrophe which was about to befall the nation, the pre-exilic prophets had little interest in sketching a cultic programme for the future. But it seems that sometimes they envisaged a more spiritualized cult, a cult without animal offerings'. Professor J. P. Hyatt, in his Goldenson lecture 'The Prophetic Criticism of Israelite Worship' (H. M. Orlinsky ed, op cit 201-224), gave five factors in the popular worship of pre-exilic Israel that aroused, according to him, the prophets denunciation of their contemporary worship:
    1. Placing the activity of God exclusively or mainly in the past. To the prophets, Yahweh was the lord of the present and of the future as well as of the past. 'The priests spoke of what Yahweh is, because of what he had done. The prophets spoke of what Yahweh will do because of what he is. They confronted men in the present with the God of Israel's past.'
    2. Many elements in the cult, as it was actually carried out, made it appear magical or quasi-magical. Prophets opposed the *opus operatum* and the *do ut des*.
    3. Prophets opposed a certain worship which was too much centred around man and his wishes and needs, rather than around the demands of God.
    4. Prophets criticized a worship which contained elements of extreme anthropomorphism and had little concern about God's transcendence and sovereign majesty.

5. Prophets objected to a worship which took place only within the formal cult and not in the whole of Israel's life. (On this point all scholars will agree.)

33. Cf the 'Description de la Jerusalem nouvelle (=2Q24)' published by J. Milik in *DJD* iii (Oxford, 1962) 184-193 and the new fragments from 4Q and 11Q.

34. Cf the balanced judgements of M. Noth, 'God, King, and Nation in the Old Testament', *Essays*, 145-178.

35. For the distinction between 'Deuteronomistic' (Dtr) and 'Deuteronomic' (Dt) see F. M. Cross, *Essays*, 274, n 1. It originates from M. Noth.

36. Following G. von Rad, 'The royal Ritual in Judah', *Essays*, 222-231, esp 229-231, I take the first *Ki* in the sense of 'truly' and the 'we' as referring to God who gives the royal protocol. It is to be noted that the promised Anointed is named prince (*sar*), a viceroy in the Kingdom of Yahweh, who is the only king (*maeleck*). See also W. Beyerlin, *Die Kulttraditionen Israels in der Verkundigung des Propheten Micha* (Gottingen, 1959) esp 35-84.

37. For the translation proposed and the interpretation see J. Bright, *Jeremiah*, The Anchor Bible (1965) 140-146. The name may be an old formula which preserves the original verbal force of *Yahweh*. . . . But this was probably not understood in the sixth century B.C., when it could have been taken as 'Yahweh is our righteousness' (i.e. the vindication of our right).

38. T. W. Overholt, *The Threat of Falsehood: A study in the Theology of the Book of Jeremiah* (London, 1970).

39. G. Quell, *Wahre und falsche Propheten* (Gutersloh, 1952); E. Osswald, *Falsche Prophetie im Alten Testament* (Tubingen, 1962); J. L. Crenshaw, *Prophetic Conflict: Its Effect upon Israelite Religion* (Berlin, 1971); F. L. Hossfeld and I. Meyer, *Prophet gegen Prophet: Eine analyse der Alttestamentlichen Texte zum Thema: Wahre und falsche Propheten* (Fribourg, 1973).

40. Cf H. J. Kraus, *Prophetie in der Krisis* (Neukirchen, 1964) esp 91; G. Quell, op cit, 55ff, 59, 61, etc.

41. T. W. Overholt, op cit, 40.

42. J. Bright, *A History of Israel*, 2nd edn (London, 1972) 285-6; J. H. Hayes, 'The Tradition of Zion's Inviolability', *JBL* lxxxii (1963) 419-426.

43. Cf G. von Rad, 'The City on the Hill', *Essays*, 232-242; *Theology*, ii, 155-169 (Isaiah never preached Zion's inviolability); Th. C. Vriezen, 'Essentials of the Theology of Isaiah', *Muilenburg Festschrift*, 128-146 (of the same view). See also K. Seybold's important study *Das Davidische Konigtum im Zeugnis der Propheten* (Gottingen, 1972): fidelity to the engagement is for Isaiah a *sine qua non*. More generally, cf Jorg Jeremias, 'Lade und Zion: Zur Entstehung der Ziontradition', *Probleme biblischer Theologie. G. von Rad zum 70. Geburtstag* (Munich, 1971) 183-198; J. Schreiner, *Sion-Jerusalem: Jahwes Konigssitz* (Munich, 1957).

44. A. S. van der Woude, 'Micah iv 1-5: An Instance of the Pseudo-Prophets Quoting Isaiah', *Symbolae Biblicae et Mesopotamicae F.M.T. de Liagre Bohl dedicatae* (Leiden, 1973) 396-402, puts forward the view that Mic ii-v is a dialogue between the prophet and some pseudo-prophets. This I find extremely improbable.

45. T. S. Eliot, *Burnt Norton*, v, 145-147.

46. O. Eissfeldt, 'The Promises of Grace to David in Isaiah 55: 1-5', Muilenburg Festschrift, 196-207; C. Westermann, *Isaiah 40-66*, trans D. M. G. Stalker (London, 1969) 280-86.

47. Cf F. M. Cross, *Essays*, chap 10: 'The Themes of the Book of Kings and the Structure of the Deuteronomistic History'.

48. G. von Rad, *Essays*, 232.

49. G. Fohrer, *Introduction to the Old Testament*, trans D. Green (London, 1968) 358.

50. The literature on O.T. covenant is enormous. Extensive surveys are provided by D. J. McCarthy, *Old Testament Covenant* (Oxford, 1972) 51, and M. Weinfeld, *berit* in *TWAT i*, col 781-808. A good introduction to the problem is F. M. Cross's 'Brief Excursus on berit "Covenant"' in his *Essays*, 265-273. G. Fohrer's and E. Kutsch's approach (recently summarized in the latter's *Verheissung und Gesetz: Untersuchungen zum sogennanten "Bund" im Alten Testament* (Berlin, 1973) is characterized by Professor Cross as a 'neo Wellhausenist interpretation', which, according to him, distorts the biblical data and stands in plain contradiction to the extra-biblical evidence. Obviously the discussion will continue.

51. M. Noth, 'Old Testament Covenant-making in the light of a text from Mari', *Essays*, 108-117.

52. Mainly in G. Mendenhall, *Law and Covenant in Israel and the Ancient Near East* (Pittsburgh, Pa, 1955).

53. G. M. Tucker, 'Covenant Forms and Contract Forms', *VT* xv (1965) 487-503. The fullest treatment remains D. J. McCarthy, *Treaty and Covenant: A Study in Form*

in the Ancient Oriental Documents and the Old Testament (Rome, 1963).

54. K. Baltzer *The Covenant Formulary in Old Testament, Jewish, and Early Christian Writings*, trans D. E. Green (Oxford, 1971) 91.
55. R. E. Clements *Prophecy and Covenant* (London, 1965) 25, 124. In his later book *Prophecy and Tradition* (Oxford, 1975) Dr Clements seems to have modified his earlier opinions on this point.
56. For possible relations between prophetic threat and treaty curse, see D. H. Hillers, *Treaty Curses and the Old Testament Prophets* (Rome, 1964).
57. In the following two paragraphs I draw on C. Westermann, as in n.46 above.
58. Is liv, 13 could be taken as an imperfect parallel, if we do not read *bonayik* (builders) instead of *banayik* (sons). But *bonayik* is certainly to be preferred.
59. J. Coppens, 'La nouvelle alliance en Jer. 31: 31-34', *CBQ* xxv (1963) 12-21, p 17. I am greatly indebted to this essay, as well as to J. Bright, *Jeremiah*, and R. Martin Achard, 'La nouvelle alliance, selon Jeremie', *RTP* xii (1962) 81-92. Useful information is given also by W. D. Davies, *Torah in the Messianic Age and/or the Age to Come* (Philadelphia, Penn, 1952) 13-28. For more recent literature: P. Buis, 'La nouvelle alliance', *VT* xviii (1968) 1-15; B. Chiesa, 'La "Nuova Alleanza" (Ger. 31-34)', *BO* xv (1973) 173-184. J. Swetnam's paper 'Why was Jeremiah's New covenant New?' in *Studies on Prophecy*, *VTS* xxvi (1974) seems to me eccentric. (He argues that Jeremiah's new covenant is the synagogue as against the Temple.) For the later fates of the notion, see A. Jaubert, *La notion de l'alliance dans le judaisme aux abords de l'ere chretienne* (Paris, 1963).
60. Cf H. H. Rowley, *The Biblical Doctrine of Election* (London, 1950); T. C. Vriezen, *Die Erwahlung Israels nach dem Alten Testament* (Zurich, 1953); H. H. Rowley, *Worship in Ancient Israel* (London, 1967) 254 n.6.
61. A. J. Festugiere, *La revelation d'Hermes Trismegiste*, iv (Paris, 1954) 267.
62. St. Augustine, *de Genesi ad litteram*, xii, 18.
63. Wellhausen's ironical picture of the Chronicler's point of view, quoted by G. Fohrer, *Introduction*, 357 n.15.
64. G. von Rad, *Theology*, ii, 114ff. On the debate cf H. P. Mueller, *Ursprunge und Strukturen alttestamentlicher Eschatologie* (Berlin, 1969).
65. L. Ramlot, *DBS*, viii, col 1002.
66. P. Claudel, *Cent phrases pour eventails* (Paris, 1942).
67. Cf A. Jepsen, 'Gottesmann und Prophet. Ammerkungen zum Kapitel 1. Konige 13', in G. von Rad Festschrift 171-182.
68. T. S. Eliot, *Selected Essays* (London, 1972) 22. Eliot speaks of the true poet.
69. idem, *Ash Wednesday*, v.

CHAPTER 2: *ADVENTUS*

1. See J. D. Purvis, *The Samaritan Pentateuch and the Origin of the Samaritan Sect* (Cambridge, Mass., 1968). A general survey is offered by R. J. Coggins, *Samaritans and Jews: The Origins of Samaritanism Reconsidered* (Oxford, 1975).
2. *DBS* v, col 1267-8.
3. F. M. Cross, *Essays*, 343.
4. See, e.g., F. M. Cross, 'The Contribution of the Qumran Discoveries to the Study of the Biblical Text', *IEJ* xvi (1966) 81-95; W. Lemke, 'The Synoptic Problem in the Chronicler's History', *HTR* lviii (1965) 349-363; T. Willi, *Die Chronik als Auslegung. Untersuchungen zur literarischen Gestaltung der historischen Uberlieferung Israels* (Gottingen, 1972).
5. W. D. Davies in *Christian History and Interpretation: Studies Presented to John Knox* (Cambridge, 1967) 137 n.5.
6. J. M. Schmidt, *Die Judische Apokalyptik: Die Geschichte ihrer Erforschung von den Anfangen bis zu den Textfunden von Qumran* (Neukirchen, 1969).
7. K. Koch, *The Rediscovery of Apocalyptic*, trans M. Kohl (London, 1972).
8. G. von Rad, *Theology*, 4th German ed (Munich, 1965) 315ff; *Wisdom in Israel*, trans J. D. Martin (London, 1972) 263-283.
9. G. Fohrer, *History of Israelite Religion*, trans D. E. Green (London, 1973) 370; 'Die Struktur der altestamentlichen Eschatologie', *TLZ* lxxxv (1960) 401-420.
10. S. Amsler, 'Zacharie et l'origine de l'apocalyptique', *VTS* xxii (1972) 227-231; R. North, 'Prophecy to Apocalyptic via Zechariah', *VTS* xxii (1972) 42-71.
11. Op cit, 91-111; 112-144.
12. J. Wellhausen, *Israelitische und judische Geschichte* (9th ed, 1958, 288ff) was the first, to my knowledge, to express similar views. W. Bousset and E. Stauffer had close insights, and though the apocalypses cannot be accepted today as 'folk-books', they certainly contain a great deal of folklore. Nor must A. Schlatter and J. Jeremias's theories on the apocalypses as the esoteric literature of the

Rabbis be rejected. The character of apocalyptic is esoteric by definition, even if not rabbinical. Cf, on the lines of F. M. Cross, P. D. Hanson, 'Jewish Apocalyptic Against Its Near Eastern Environment', *RB* lxxviii (1971) 31-58; 'Old Testament Apocalyptic Reexamined', *Interpretation*, xxv (1971) 454-479; *The Dawn of Apocalyptic* (Philadelphia, Pa, 1975).

13. G. L. Davenport, *The Eschatology of the book of Jubilees* (Leiden, 1971) 16.

14. G. L. Davenport, (op. cit, 5-8) gives a good introduction to the problems of the prophetic and apocalyptic eschatologies, and I should like to mention also the extremely important philological work of J. Carmignac, 'La notion de l' eschatologie dans la Bible et a Qumran', *RQ* vii (1969) 17-31, and the older article of J. Licht, 'Time and Eschatology in Apocalyptic Literature and in Qumran', *JJS* xvi (1965) 177-182. See also H. P. Muller, *Ursprunge und Strukturen alttestamentlicher Eschatologie* (Berlin, 1969); J. van der Ploeg, 'Eschatology in the Old Testament', *OS* xvii (1972) 89-99. In general it must always be borne in mind that in this period the words 'end', 'time of the end', 'end of the days' etc., mean 'in the sequence of the days' ('in future'), rather than 'the end', and *never* 'the end of the world'. Many misjudgments could be avoided if scholars were alert to this. N. Perrin's, *The New Testament: An Introduction* (New York, 1974) is an example of notorious confusion on this point, with very grave consequences for the general interpretation of the phenomenon of the New Testament.

15. J. T. Milik, 'Milki-sedeq et Milki-resa' dans les anciens ecrits juifs et chretiens', *JJS* xxiii (1972) 95-144.

16. J. Jeremias, *New Testament Theology* i, trans J. Bowden (London, 1971) 80-82. Cf R. Leivestad, 'Das Dogma von der Prophetenlosen Zeit', *NTS* xix (1973) 288-299.

17. Cf W. D. Davies, 'Reflexions on Tradition: the Aboth Revisited' in *J. Knox Festschrift*, 127-159, esp 129-137; 131.

18. Michel Testuz, *Les idees religieuses du Livre des Jubiles* (Geneva, 1960) 118-119.

19. For another possible motive see M. Delcor, 'Le Docteur de Justice, nouveau Moise, dans les Hymnes de Qumran' in R. de Langhe ed, *Le Psautier* (Louvain, 1962).

20. I am not certain whether 1 Macc iv 46 and xiv 41 refer to the eschatological prophet; ix 27 shows that the general belief of the party was that prophecy had long since disappeared. It is natural that its reappearance would be expected in the ideal future, but this does not necessarily envisage *the* Prophet. In any case, if iv 46 and xiv 41 refer to him, my general argument is reinforced.

21. O. Ploger, *Theocracy and Eschatology*, trans S. Rudman (Oxford, 1968) is always useful, though the author's original insight becomes rigid and one-sided and there are too many extrapolations. D. Rossler, *Gesetz und Geschichte* (Neukirchen, 1960) presents his thesis by excluding Qumran and interpreting Pharisaic orthodoxy contemporary to apocalyptic on the basis of rabbinical writings later by several centuries.

22. See E. M. Laperrousaz, 'Les "ordonnances premieres" et les "ordonnances dernieres" dans les manuscrits de la mer Morte', *Hommages a Andre Dupont-Sommer* (Paris, 1971) 405-419.

23. Cf J. Coppens, 'Le Prophete eschatologique. L'annonce de sa venue. Les relectures', *ETL* xlix (1973) 5-35; idem, 'La releve prophetique et l'evolution spirituelle de l'attente messianique et eschatologique d'Israel', ibid, 775-783. On messianism in general see idem, *Le messianisme royal. Ses origines. Son developpement. Son accomplissement* (Paris, 1972) and the same author's studies in the *ETL* of the early 1970s. Note also the very important study of M. de Jonge, 'The Role of Intermediaries in God's Final Intervention in the Future According to the Qumran Scrolls', O. Michel *et al*, *Studies on the Jewish Background of the New Testament* (Assen, 1969) 44-63.

24. The anti-Hasmonaean note is unmistakable. Both *1QS* ix 11 and the CD messianic references belong to the Hasmonaean era. See J. Starcky, 'Les quatres etapes du messianisme a Qumran', *RB* lxx (1963) 481-505, and the precisions and minor corrections of R. Brown, *CBQ* xxviii (1966) 51-57, and J. Fitzmyer, *Essays*, 127-160.

25. See the legend of *bBM* 59b quoted by G. Vermes, *Jesus the Jew* (London, 1973) 81-82, and 243 n.116 for an exceptional case.

26. 'When the last prophets, Haggai, Zechariah and Malachi, died, the holy spirit ceased out of Israel; but nevertheless it was granted them to hear communications from God by means of a *Bath Qol*.'

27. G. Vermes, op cit, 93.

28. P. R. Ackroyd, 'The Vitality of the Word of God in the Old Testament', *Annual of the Swedish Theological Institute* i (1962) 7-23.

29. R. Bloch, *DBS* v, col 1266.

30. A. Robert, *DBS* v, col 411.

31. R. Bloch, *Cahiers Sioniens* ix (1955) 193-223; cf G. Vermes, *Scripture and Tradition in Judaism* (Leiden, 1961) esp. chap vi for the author's opinion of P as already 'midrashic'; R. le Deaut, 'Apropos a Definition of Midrash', *Interpretation* xxv (1971) 454-479: a review of A. G. Wright, *The Literary Genre Midrash* (State Island, 1967). According to le Deaut, genres in ancient Judaism were not rigorously limited. The Midrash is for him a way of thinking and of reasoning, rather than a literary genre.

32. See S. Sowers, 'On the Reinterpretation of Biblical History in Hellenistic Judaism', *Oikonomia ... Oscar Cullmann zum 65* (Hamburg, 1967) 18-25; P. Geoltrain, 'Une vision de l'histoire dans le Judaisme intertestamentaire', ibid, 26-31.

33. W. H. Brownlee, *The Meaning of the Qumran Scrolls for the Bible* (New York, 1964) 72-73.

34. See A. Szorenyi, 'Das Buch Daniel ein kanonisierter Pescher?', *VTS* xv (1966) 278-294.

35. J. Carmignac 'Le document de Qumran sur Melkisedeq', *RQ* vii (1970) 343-378, esp 360-362. For a different view: I. Rabinowitz, '"Pesher/Pittaron". Its Biblical Meaning and its Significance in the Qumran Literature', *RQ* viii (1973) 219-232. According to Rabinowitz the Peshers are not exegetical works, but presage-literature.

36. E. Slomovic, 'Towards an Understanding of the Exegesis in the Dead Sea Scrolls', *RQ* vii (1969) 3-15.

37. I use the most recent edition of the text by J. T. Milik, as in n.15 above, 97-109. In p 126 the author identifies the Anointed-with-the-Spirit with the Teacher of Righteousness. But his argument is based on very heavy textual restoration.

38. Cf the judgement of J. Fitzmyer, *Essays*, 463-4: 'The Qumran sect not only held to the strict observance of the Torah, but also regarded the prophets of the OT with great esteem. This is evident not only from statements of 1QS (1:3; 8:16), 4QpIIosa (2:5), CD (7:17), 1QpHab (2:9), but also from the way they quote the prophets (CD 7:10; 9:5) and from the writings they composed to interpret the biblical prophets (e.g., the *pesharim*, 1QpHab, 1QpMic, 1QpZeph, 3QpIs, 4QpIsa-e, 4QpHosa-b, 4QpNah, 4QpMic, 4QpZeph, 5QpMal'.

39. See, e.g., D. S. Russell, *The Method and Message of Jewish Apocalyptic* (London, 1964) chap vii.

40. D. S. Russell, op cit, 196; P. Grelot, 'Soixante-dix semaines d'annees', *Biblica* l (1969) 169-186.

41. J. Weingreen, 'Rabbinic-Type Glosses in the Old Testament', *JSS* ii (1957) 149-162 (revised in idem, *From Bible to Mishnah* Manchester, 1976, 32-54).

42. G. R. Driver, 'Glosses on the Hebrew Text of the Old Testament', *L'Ancien Testament et l'Orient* (Louvain, 1957) 123-161.

43. *DJD* iv (Oxford, 1965) 87; M. Delcor, 'L'hymne a Sion du rouleau des Psaumes de la grotte 11 de Qumran', *RQ* xxi (1967) 71-88. Dan ix 24 is at the origin of the verses cited.

44. On the possible role of the Levites in matters of mesorah (clear enunciation of the text) see M. Gertner 'The Masorah and the Levites', *VT* x (1960) 241-272.

45. See G. Stemberger, *Der Leib der Auferstehung. Studien zur Anthropologie und Eschatologie des palastinischen Judentums im neutestamentlichen Zeitalter (ca. 170 v.Chr.-100 n. Chr.)*, (Rome, 1972); idem, 'Das Problem der Auferstehung im Alten Testament', *Kairos* xiv (1972) 273-290; idem, 'Zur Auferstehungslehre in der rabbinischen Literatur', ibid xv (1973) 238-266; G. W. Nickelsburg, *Resurrection, Immortality and Eternal Life in Intertestamental Judaism* (Cambridge, Mass, 1972); P. Grelot, 'L'eschatologie de la Sagesse et les apocalypses juives', *Memorial Albert Gelin* (Paris, 1961) 165-178; J. J. Collins, 'Apocalyptic Eschatology as the Transcendence of Death', *CBQ* xxxvi (1974) 21-43.

46. R. Tournay 'Relectures bibliques concernant la vie future et l'angelologie', *RB* lxix (1962) 481-505.

47. E. Lipinski, 'Le *s'r yswb* d'Isaie vii 3', *VT* xxiii (1973) 245-246.

48. E. Lipinski, *Biblica* li (1970) 533-537.

49. This follows the version in J. F. Stenning, *The Targum of Isaiah* (Oxford, 1949) 14.

50. W. H. Brownlee, as in n.33 above.

51. Modern commentators endeavour to trace this procedure of Jewish re-reading of the prophets. See P. E. Bonnard, *Le second Isaie, son disciple et leurs editeurs* (Paris 1972).

52. H. Gunkel and I. Begrich, *Einleitung in die Psalmen* (Gottingen) 1933.

53. P. E. Bonnard, *Le Psautier selon Jeremie* (Paris, 1960). They are Pss: i, vi, vii, xvi, xvii, xxii, xxvi, xxxi, xxxv, xxxvi, xxxviii, xl, xli, xliv, li, lv, lxix, lxxi, lxxiii, lxxiv, lxxv, lxxvi, lxxviii, lxxix, lxxxi, lxxxiii, lxxxvi, xcix, cvi, cix, cxix, cxxxv, cxxxix.

54. J. B. Pritchard ed, *Ancient Near Eastern Texts Relating to the Old Testament*, 3rd ed (Princeton, 1969) 422.

55. See H. Cazelles, 'Une relecture du Psaume xxix?', *Memorial Gelin* (as in n.45 above) 119-128.

56. S. P. Brock, 'The Phenomenon of the Septuagint', *OS* xvii (1972) 11-35; idem, 'The Phenomenon of Biblical Translation in Antiquity', *Alta* (Birmingham) ii 8 (1969) 92-102.

57. See L. M. Pasinya, *La notion de 'Nomos' dans le Pentateuque grec* (Rome, 1972); J. C. M. das Neves, *A theologia da traducao grega dos Sententa no Livro de Isaias (Cap.24 de Isaias)* (Lisbon, 1973).

58. Cf M. Hengel, *Judaism and Hellenism: Studies in Their Encounter in Palestine During the Early Hellenistic Period*, trans J. Bowden (London, 1974) (from the 2nd German ed, Tubingen, 1973). For the Hellenist's point of view see C. Schneider's monumental *Kulturgeschichte des Hellenismus*, 2 vols, (Munich, 1967, 1969).

59. Cf D. Barthelemy, 'L'Ancien Testament a muri a Alexandria', *TZ* xxi (1965) 358-70; idem, 'La place de la Septante dans l'Eglise', Ch. Hauret *et al* eds, *Recherches bibliques vii: Aux grands carrefours de la revelation et de l'exegese de l'Ancien Testament* (Paris, 1967) 13-28. Pere Barthelemy, like Pere Benoit, insists that the Masoretic text ('forme sclerosee et archaisante') is not *the* Bible of the Church.

60. D. Barthelemy, 'Les tiqqune sopherim et la critique textuelle de l'Ancien Testament', *VTS* ix (1963) 285-301.

61. On the Sadducees see J. le Moyne, *Les Sadduceens* (Paris, 1972); on the Pharisees before A.D.70, J. Neusner, *The Rabbinic Tradition about the Pharisees before 70* (Leiden, 1971).

62. See the relevant discussion between R. E. Brown and J. Fitzmyer in the latter's *Essays*, 56f. I find myself unable to agree wholly with either of these outstanding Roman Catholic scholars. The Second Vatican spoke of *significatio plenior*.

63. The first occurences of the word in Greek and Hebrew (*Aristeas* xii 316; 1QS vi 7) denote the law.

64. A phrase from a sermon preached by John Donne to the Queen at Denmark-house, December 14, 1617.

CHAPTER 3: *ECCE*

1. J. Mouroux, *Le mystere du temps. Approche theologique* (Paris, 1962) 159-60.

2. Paul Ricoeur, *Le conflit des interpretations. Essais d'hermeneutique* (Paris, 1969) 374-75.

3. T. S. Eliot, Choruses from '*The Rock'* (1934) vii.

4. I am not convinced by arguments to the contrary.

5. Melito of Sardis, *de Pascha*, 7.

6. J. Jeremias, *Theology of the New Testament* i, trans J. Bowden (London, 1971) 211.

7. Cf J. G. Gibbs, *Creation and Redemption: A Study in Pauline Theology* (Leiden, 1971).

8. When I say 'a present person' I do not mean just 'being there'. This is the way of objects. I use this phrase having in mind Gabriel Marcel and his characteristically New Testament understanding of 'presence' in the interpersonal as *disponibilite*, availability. Christ is never unavailable to anyone, and the early Church never seems to have felt him as unavailable. This *attitude accueillante* (Fr C. Spicq's description of the *agape*) cannot allow fidelity (*fidelite*, the second key-word in Marcel's understanding of the interpersonal) to be doubted. The experience of Christ's continuous love cannot allow the Christian to doubt Christ's loyalty. This experience makes wild *Parusieverzogerung* theories about the early Church to sound as if they come from an 'other world' : a world where the Holy Spirit is not known.

9. H. de Lubac, *Exegese medievale*, ii.i (Paris, 1961) 558.

10. J. Lebreton, *La vie et l'enseignement de Jesus-Christ notre Seigneur*, i (Paris, 1931) 8. Cited by X. Leon Dufour, *Les evangiles et l'histoire de Jesus* (Paris, 1963) 314 n.27.

11. For an account of research in quest of Jesus see W. G. Kummel, 'Das Problem des geschichtlichen Jesus in der gegenwartigen Forschungslage', in *Heilsgeschechen und Geschichte; Ges. Aufsatze 1933-1964* (Marburg, 1965) 392-405.

12. Hippolytus, *Traditio Apostolica*, 41.

13. The unknown solitary of Farne quoted by W. A. Pantin, 'The Monk-Solitary of Farne: a Fourteenth Century English Mystic', *EHR* lix (1944) 162-186, 178.

14. See N. Perrin, *The New Testament: An Introduction* (New York, 1974) 208ff.

15. R. Bultmann, *L'histoire de la tradition synoptique*, trans A. Malet (Paris, 1973) 679, 680 *Postface*.

16. Cf D. Hill 'On the Evidence for the Creative Role of Christian prophets', *NTS* xx (1973/4) 262-274.

17. F. W. Beare, 'Sayings of the Risen Jesus in the Synoptic Tradition: An Inquiry into their Origin and Significance' in *Christian History and Interpretation: Studies Presented to John Knox* (Cambridge, 1967) 161-181, 175.

18. B. Englezakis, 'Thomas, Logion 30', *NTS* xxv (1978/9) 262-72.

19. R. Bultmann, *The History of the Synoptic Tradition*, trans J. Marsh (Oxford, 1968) 162.

20. J. Jeremias, *Theology* §17.

21. C. H. Dodd's suggestion that the Matthean saying is an adaptation of the *Abhoth* saying was taken up by M. D. Goulder, *Midrash and Lection in Matthew* (London, 1974) 154f, who argues that the scribe (?) Matthew read also 'the whole Pauline corpus' and treated Paul as an authority. Shall we suppose that Dodd forgot that the *Abhoth* and their rabbis are subsequent to Mt, and that Goulder forgot that the Pauline corpus is later than the 60s or 70s, or even the 80s? Otherwise, we have seen that Mt xviii 20, though a legal saying, is not a juridical one, but a liturgical one. In 1 Cor v, Paul speaks of the courts of the Church of Corinth. What is interesting and significant is that the Apostle stands above the *pleiones* themselves.

22. E. Cothenet, 'Les prophetes chretiens dans L'Evangile selon Matthieu', in M. Didier ed, *L'Evangile selon Matthieu: redaction et theologie* (Gembloux, 1972) 281-308. A very learned bibliography on our subject is given on p. 281 n. 2.

23. For the exact terminology see Morton Smith, 'Zealots and Sicarii. Their Origins and Relation', *HTR* lxiv (1971) 1-19. The party of the Zealots *sensu stricto* came into existence in the winter of A.D. 67-8.

24. For a different point of view see S. van Tilborg, *The Jewish Leaders in Matthew* (Leiden, 1972).

25. Concerning the state of the question of 'Paul and Jesus' a terse re-statement is given by D. L. Dungan, *The sayings of Jesus in the Churches of Paul* (Oxford, 1971) xvii-xxix, and authoritative accounts by W. G. Kummel, *Ges. Aufsatze 1933-1964* (Marburg, 1965) 81-106, 439-456; cf ibid 169-191; G. N. Stanton, *Jesus of Nazareth in New Testament Preaching* (Cambridge, 1974), chap 4: 'Jesus in Paul's Preaching'; B. Fjarstedt, *Synoptic Tradition in 1 Corinthians: Themes and Clusters of Theme Words in 1 Corinthians I-IV and IX* (Uppsala, 1974).

26. R. Bultmann, *Theology of the New Testament*, trans K. Grobel (London, 1952) 35, 188.

27. A. Schweitzer, *Die Mystik des Apostels Paulus*, trans W. Montgomery (London, 1931) 173.

28. J. M. Robinson in J. P. Hyatt ed, *The Bible in Modern Scholarship*, (London, 1966) 114-150.

29. D. Georgi, *Die Gegner des Paulus im 2. Korintherbrief* (Neukirchen, 1964) 282ff cited by J. M. Robinson, op cit, 142.

30. C. F. D. Moule, 'Jesus in New Testament Kerygma', *Verborum Veritas: Festschrift fur Gustav Stahlin* (Wuppertal, 1970) 15-26. See the pertinent observation of P. Pokorny in p. 26 n. 21. If we had no Fourth Gospel, the Johannine Epistles might have given us the impression that Johannine Christianity ignored the Jesus tradition.

31. Cf the distinguished judgement of H. van Campenhausen in *Die Begrundung Kirchlicher Entscheidungen beim Apostel Paulus*, 2nd ed, (Heidelberg, 1965); *Ecclesiastical Authority and Spiritual Power*, trans J. A. Baker (London, 1969); *The Formation of the Christian Bible*, trans J. A. Baker (London, 1972) chap 4.

32. R. Bultmann, 'Die Bedeutung des geschichtlichen Jesus fur die Theologie des Paulus', *TB* viii (1929) 137-151, translated into English in R. Bultmann, *Faith and Understanding* (London, 1969) 220-246.

33. R. Bultmann, *Theology* i 238f.

34. R. Bultmann, *Exegetische probleme des Zweiten Korintherbriefes* (Uppsala, 1947).

35. W. Schmithals, 'Zwei gnostische Glossen im 2. Korintherbrief', *EvTh* xviii (1958) 552-573, esp 552-54.

36. D. Georgi, as in n. 29 above.

37. W. G. Kummel, *The Theology of the New Testament*, trans J. E. Steely (London, 1974) 165-166.

38. M. Hengel, 'Christologie und neutestamentliche Chronologie. Zu einer Aporie in der Geschichte des Urchristentums' in *Neues Testament und Geschichte ... Oscar Cullman zum 70. Geburtstag* (Zurich/Tubingen, 1972) 43-68, esp 65.

39. The fact that in several places in this chapter I distinguish between Paul's opponents in 1 and 2 Corinthians does not mean that I agree with Georgi's

theories about Paul's 'divine man' opponents in 2 Cor. That one proclaims his powers and boasts of his miracles does not make one de facto a *theios aner*. The crucial characteristic of the Greek 'divine man' is his claim that he is an 'immortal god, no longer a mortal man' (Empedocles, fr.112: *ego d'humin* (dativus ethicus) *theos ambrotos, ouketi thnetos poleumai meta pasi tetimemenos, hosper eoika,* etc.). 'Mensch gewesen, Gott geworden': this is what makes Empedocles, Apollonius of Tyana, Lucian's Alexander *pseudomantis,* etc. 'divine men', and it is not the case, I think, with Paul's opponents in 2 Corinthians.

For a critique of L. Biehler, *Theios Aner,* 2 vols, (Vienna, 1935, 1936) see D. L. Tiede, *The Charismatic figure as Miracle Worker* (Montana, 1972). G. Petzke, *Die Tradition uber Apollonius von Tyana und das Neue Testament* (Leiden, 1970) can offer no true parallel in fact. Miracle-working, healing, and exorcism were in great esteem among the Hasidic circles, and we must not forget Philo's *therapeutai* and the interpretation Essenes Healers proposed by G. Vermes, 'The Etymology of Essenes', *RQ* ii (1960) 427-443; 'Essenes and Therapeutai', ibid, iii (1962) 495-504. Also idem, *Jesus the Jew* (London, 1973) 58-82. (Note that Noah, Abraham, Moses, David and Solomon, and the great prophets, were presented in certain Jewish circles as miracle-workers). In view of this Jewish evidence there is no need, I believe, to have recourse to the hellenistic *theioi anthropoi* in NT exegesis. For a very strong criticism of this tendency of Bultmann and his school see O. Betz, 'The Concept of the So-called "Divine Man" in Mark's Christology', in *Studies in New Testament and Early Christian Literature: Essays in Honor of Allen P. Wikgren* (Leiden, 1972) 229-240.

40. Cf the Hebrew expression *nasa' panim* as used in Gal ii 6: God receives, admires (Deut x 17 LXX) no man's power, rank, or external position.

41. J. Duncan M. Derrett, 'Romans vii 1-4: The Relationship with the Resurrected Christ' in *Law in the New Testament* (London, 1970) 461-471.

42. Here lies the *prote plane* of J. Louis Martyn, 'Epistemology at the Turn of the Ages: 2 Corinthians 5:16' in *J. Knox Festschrift,* 269-287. Paul's question is not one of 'epistemology' or 'gnosiology' but one of relation. M. Thrall's interpretation of the verse (in *Christ and Spirit in the New Testament: Studies in Honour of C. F. D. Moule,* Cambridge, 1973, 153ff) seems to me rather eccentric.

43. See B. M. Metzger, 'The Punctuation of Rom. 9:5', *C. F. D. Moule Festschrift,* 95-112.

44. Cf Jn iv 19-24.

45. K. H. Rengstorf, *TDNT* i 666-668; *S-B* iii 340f; E. Sjoberg, 'Wiedergeburt und Neuschopfung im palastinischen Judentum', *ST* iv (1950) 44-85. For an interesting comparison see what M. Delcor has to say on the absence of the notion of *palingenesia* in Qumran in 'Le vocabulaire juridique, cultuel et mystique de l "initiation" dans le secte de Qumran', H. Bardtke ed, *Qumran-Probleme* (Berlin, 1963) 109-134.

46. See J. Dupont, 'La conversion de Paul et son influence sur sa conception du salut par la foi' in *Foi et salut selon S. Paul ... Colloque oecumenique a l'abbaye de S. Paul hors les murs, 16-21 avril 1968* (Rome, 1970) 67-88, 88-100.

47. Cf E. Cothenet, 'Prophetisme dans le nouveau Testament', *DBS* viii col 1222-1337; J. Reiling, *Hermas and Christian Prophecy* (Leiden, 1973) chap 1. Three pioneering studies have influenced all subsequent research: H. Weinel, *Die Wirkungen des Geistes und der Geister im nachapostolischen Zeitalter bis auf Irenaeus* (Freiburg, 1899); H. Gunkel, *Die Wirkungen des Heiligen Geistes nach den popularen Anschauungen der apostolischen Zeit und der Lehre des Apostels Paulus* (Gottingen, 1888, 3rd ed 1909); and E. Fascher, *PROPHETES: Eine sprach-und religionsgeschichtliche Untersuchung* (Giessen, 1927). Weinel is exhaustive and still indispensable. Fascher approaches the problem from the point of view of the *religionsgeschichtliche* School. To Gunkel modern Protestant NT research owes its discovery of the Spirit, as well as many prejudices about the pneumatic character of early Christianity.

48. See H. Dorries, *Geist und Geschichte bei G. Arnold* (Gottingen, 1963); T. Stahlin, *Gottfried Arnolds geistliche Dichtung: Glaube und Mystik* (Gottingen, 1966); J. Buchsel, *Gottfried Arnold: Sein Verstandnis von Kirche und Wiedergeburt* (Witten, 1970).

49. Leipzig, 1884.

50. Vol I (Leipzig, 1882). This is not to deny that Sohm, like Harnack, can, and did, act as a catalyst. See Y. Congar, 'R. Sohm nous interroge encore', *RSPT* lvii (1973) 263-294. (A seven-page bibliography on Sohm is appended at the end.)

51. J. A. Robinson, 'The Christian Ministry in the Apostolic and Sub-Apostolic Periods', in H. B. Swete ed, *Essays on the Early History of the Church and the Ministry,* 2nd ed, (London, 1921) 57-92, esp 75. For an impressive list of those who

have opposed Harnack's romantic scheme see A. Lemaire, *Les ministeres aux origines de l'Eglise* (Paris, 1971) 191 n 2. More generally, J. Delorme ed, *Le ministere et les ministeres selon le Nouveau Testament: dossier exegetique et reflexion theologique* (Paris, 1974).

52. J. A. Robinson, as above.

53. 'Speaking in tongues' is the only translation that renders the participle *lalon*. Paul refers to glossolaly; he is not semitizing, or using a stylistic effect, the so called *figura etymologiae (elalese legon)*. This is one reason why in the first half of the verse I follow the Byzantine tradition, *'LEGEI ANATHEMA IES'*, which joined by P[46] and the western witnesses is more often right than wrong. The difference in manuscript is minor (the last letter of the *nominum sacrum*), and the reading *'ANATHEMA IES'* can be explained as an assimilation to *'KS IES'*.

54. For its history see G. de Broglie, 'Le texte fondamental de Saint Paul contre la foi naturelle', *RSR* xxxix (1951) 253-266; W. C. van Unnik, 'Jesus: Anathema or Kyrios', C. F. D. Moule Festschrift, 113-126 (a stimulating paper which, however, does not convince me).

55. W. F. Albright and C. S. Mann, 'Two texts in 1 Corinthians', *NTS* xvi (1970) 271-276. They reconstruct: *'dio gnorizo humin hoti oudeis lalon legei Ana athe maran atha Iesous ei me'*, etc.

56. W. Schmithals, *Die Gnosis in Korinth*, 2nd ed, (Gottingen, 1965). Schmithals has been adequately refuted, among others by B. A. Pearson, 'Did the Gnostics Curse Jesus?', *JBL* lxxxvi (1967) 301-305; *The pneumatikos-psychikos Terminology in 1 Corinthians: A Study in the Theology of the Corinthian Opponents of Paul and Its Relation to Gnosticism* (Missoula, Mont, 1973). That the Corinthian opponents of Paul were Gnostics was first suggested by W. Lutgert in 1908. I would rather agree with A. D. Nock, *Essays* ii 940-959, that Paul's opponents were individual Christians who 'came from or came into contact with esoteric Judaism'. According to Pearson they were Hellenistic Jews who held a 'well attested' Jewish Hellenistic belief that man has within himself the 'spiritual' capacity to achieve by 'wisdom', the higher, heavenly plane of existence. Consequently, they denied the resurrection of the dead and valued greatly ecstatic prophecy as a feature of the 'perfect'.

57. I take *pneumatika* as neutral, mainly because of xiv 1 (B. A. Pearson, op cit 138, suggests also ix 11 and xiv 12, but I do not find them relevant). xiv 37 could be said to advocate the masculine, but Paul in these chapters is not talking and judging about people, but rather about spiritual gifts and manifestations — 'charismata', 'ministries', 'operations', etc.... At any rate, I do not think the difference is important. I prefer 'manifestations' rather than 'gifts', because Paul speaks of *pneumatika* that are not from God.

58. The participle *lalon* (cf n.53 above) makes it difficult for me to take the sentence as a pure antithetic parallelism, where the first part is introduced just in order to give greater relief to the second. For Paul's belief that Satan can use 'light' in order to produce 'darkness' cf 2 Cor xi 13ff.

59. This concept of *dunamis* (historical, creative, and salvific) is extremely important for the notion of the spirit in both Testaments. Cf P. Biard, *La puissance de Dieu* (Paris, 1960).

60. I believe that *hoti* here is primarily declarative, but, at the same time, causal too.

61. J. Leenhardt, *Romains* (Paris, 1957) 119. Kummel's discussion: *Theology*, 167.

62. J. D. G. Dunn, '2 Corinthians iii 17: "The Lord is the Spirit"', *JTS* xxi (1970) 309-320; D. Greenwood, 'The Lord is the Spirit: Some Considerations on 2 Cor iii, 17', *CBQ* xxiv (1972) 467-472; C. F. D. Moule, '2 Cor 3: 18b, *Kathaper apo Kuriou pneumatos*' in *Neues Testament und Geschichte* (as in n.38 above) 231-237; M. McNamara, *The New Testament and the Palestinian Targum to the Pentateuch* (Rome, 1966) 168-188; J. Jervell, *Imago Dei. Gen I, 26f. im Spatjudentum, in der Gnosis und in den paulinischen Briefen* (Gottingen, 1960) 173-197; E. Larsson, *Christus als Vorbild:.Eine Untersuchung zu den paulinischen Tauf und Eikontexte* (Uppsala, 1962) 275-293 (against Jervell's gnostic interpretation). Especially valuable are the long discussions of A. Feuillet, *Christologie paulinienne et tradition biblique* (Paris, Bruges, 1973) 32-433; *Le Christ Sagesse de Dieu d'apres les epitres pauliniennes* (Paris, 1966) 113-161. For the opposite view see I. Hermann, *Kyrios und Pneuma: Studien zur Christologie der paulinischen Hauptbriefe* ii (Munich, 1961). More generally on Paul's Christocentrism, see W. Thusing, *Per Christum in Deum: Studien zur Verhaltnis von Christozentrik und Theozentrik in den paulinischen Hauptbriefen* (Munster, 1965) esp. chap iv: 'Pneuma und Theozentrik', 151-163 (154-5).

63. See J. A. Fitzmyer, *Essays*, 26 n.37. Note that Paul like the Qumranic authors sometimes accommodates the OT text which he tries to modernize. The main

change is that of the verb *eisporeuesthai* into *epistrephein*. This will be explained later.

64. Note the verb *atenizein* in iii 13. See A. Feuillet, op cit; idem, *RB* lxxxi (1974) 166-169. J. Jervell, op cit, 183ff; E. Larsson, op cit, 275ff; Ch. Mugler, *Dictionnaire historique de la terminologie optique des Grecs* (Paris, 1964), *s.v.*; especially J. Dupont, 'Le chretien, miroir de la gloire divine d'apres II Cor., III, 18', *RB* lvi (1949) 392-411.

65. I take *Kurion* in iii 18 not as substantive, but as an adjectival title (cf the titles of the wisdom-pneuma in Wi vii). In predicating the Pneuma as *Kurion* Paul wants, I believe, to underline the fact that there is no distance between it and God: the Spirit is not of the order of the servants, as Moses (in the OT and Judaism the Servant *par excellence*) and Paul (iv 5).

For a right interpretation of this passage the context of the opposition must not be forgotten. In Judaism, especially in Hellenistic Judaism, Moses was considered not only as the Servant and Apostle *(saliah)* of God *par excellence*, but also as the image of God, a 'second Adam' on whom the name of God *('elohim)* was bestowed. See W. A. Meeks, 'Moses as God and King' in *Religions in Antiquity: Essays in Memory of E. R. Goodenough* (Leiden, 1968) 354-371 (in relation to our passage note the relief of a man [Moses?] with a *memorah* on his head discussed on pp 362-3). Paul retorts that the glory of Moses was external and, so, condemned to be waning (v.3), fearful, and allowing no *parresia* (cf v.12): the glory of a servant, *pneuma douleias eis phobon* (Rom viii 15). The new glory, on the other hand, is inward (v.3 Ezek xi 17; Jer xxxi 33=Ezek xxxvi 27), and so destined to be always waxing ('from one degree of glory to another'), transfiguring, and liberating: the glory of a free and freeing Lord, *pneuma huiothesias*. Cf Gal iv 24ff — the two covenants: the one (the son according to the flesh) unto slavery, the other (the son according to the spirit) unto filial freedom. Behind the opposition *gramma — eleutheria* (to which I will presently return) lies a Hebrew pun on *harut* (engraved) and *herut* (freedom), used by the rabbis in connection with Ex xxxii 16 (the 'engraved' tables as the tables of 'freedom').

66. J. D. M. Derrett, as in n.41 above, 469.

67. The reading cited by I. de la Potterie in *Foi et salut selon St. Paul* (as in n.46 above), 134-5 (*hou de Kurios to Pneuma. . .*), seems to me an ingenious ancient attempt to correct the annoying Paul.

68. See E. Kasemann, 'The Spirit and the Letter', *Perspectives on Paul*, trans by M. Kohl (London, 1971) 138-166. Kasemann shows well the intrinsic link between this antithesis and that of law-gospel and the Pauline theology of justification.

69. The modern dilemma about who is God's image, the earthly Jesus or the exalted Lord (cf J. Jervell, op cit, 332, 'Nicht der irdische Jesus, sondern der auferstandene und erhohte Herr, der Geist ist, ist die wahre Eikon Gottes') is non-existent for Paul: his Christ is pre-existent (cf Phil ii 6ff, 'who being in the form [*morphe-selem*] of God. . .'; 1 Cor viii 6; Gal iv 4; Rom viii 3; 1 Cor ii 7f, etc.). The oversight of this point by some NT scholars is very curious.

70. The same link between filiation, vision, and likeness is found in 1 Jn iii 2. For the link between *pneuma* and *doxa* cf 1 Pet iv 14 ('Beide sind eschatologische Grossen', E. Larsson, op cit, 292); 'Das Pneuma verlangt danach, sein tiefstes Wesen als *doxa* zu offenbaren', R. Schnackenburg, *Das Heilsgeschehen bei der Taufe nach dem Apostel Paulus: Eine Studie zur paulinischen Theologie* (Munich, 1950) 199.

71. A. Lacomara, 'Deuteronomy and the Farewell Discourse (Jn 13: 31-16:33)', *CBQ* xxxvi (1974) 65-84.

72. For this Deuteronomic phraseology cf M. Weinfeld, *Deuteronomy and the Deuteronomic School* (Oxford, 1972).

73. See A. D. Nock's old but still very valid study, 'The Vocabulary of the New Testament', *Essays* i 341-347; idem, 'Word-Coinage in Greek', *Essays* ii 642-652.

74. Concerning the 'paraclete' and Qumran my attitude is that of G. Quispel, 'Qumran, John and Jewish Christianity' in J. H. Charlesworth ed, *John and Qumran* (London, 1972) 137-155, esp 146-149. For an opposite view see A. R. C. Leaney, 'The Johannine Paraclete and the Qumran Scrolls, ibid, 38-61; O. Betz, *Der Paraklet* (Leiden, 1963).

With regard to Bultmann's old theories in relation to the so called 'helper' of the Mandaic scriptures, I will only say that *yawar* does not mean 'helper', as Noldeke was the first to conjecture from the Persian, but, as Lady E. S. Drower has shown, 'one who blinds, or dazzles with light'. See E. S. Drower, *The Canonical Prayerbook of the Mandaeans* (Leiden, 1959) 252 n.2 and index *s.v*; idem and R. Macuch, *A Mandaic Dictionary* (Oxford, 1963), *s.v. iauar*. G. Quispel, op cit, seems to incline towards translating 'the brilliant one'. K. Rudolph continues to translate 'the helper'.

75. A. J. Festugiere, *Observations stylistiques sur l'Evangile de S. Jean* (Paris, 1974) 68. One of the greatest pillars of Bultmann's literary theory, the prologue as the hymn-like introduction to the *Aramaic* discourses, has been brought down by another great contemporary classical philologist, J. Irigoin, 'La composition rythmique du prologue de Jean (i 1-18)', *RB* lxxviii (1971) 501-514. After a minute and exemplary investigation M. Irigoin arrives at the, I think indisputable, conclusion that, 'far from being simply a translation, paraphrase or recasting of a previous hymn [the prologue that we have] is an original composition, responding to precise rules'. For once, in these two outstanding works, we have seen realized again in recent years R. Reitzenstein's 'altes Ideal, das Zusammenarbeiten von Theologen und Philologen'.

76. This Johannine interpretation of the Spirit is further illustrated in 1 Jn. Cf M. -E. Boismard, 'La connaissance dans l'Alliance nouvelle, d'apres la Premiere lettre de saint Jean', *RB* lvi (1949) 365-391; I. de la Potterie, 'La connaissance de Dieu dans le dualisme eschatologique d'apres 1 Jn 2, 12-14', in *Au service de la parole de Dieu. Melanges offerts a Mgr Andre-Marie Charue* (Gembloux, 1968) 77-99. Here comes, of course, the important Johannine concept of *chrisma*. Loisy, Windisch, Buchsel, Charue, Michel, Schnackenburg, Nauck, Lazure, Bultmann and F.-M. Braun understood this as 'the unction of the Holy Spirit.' I. de la Potterie, 'L'onction du chretien par la foi', *Biblica* xl (1959) 12-69, is more subtle: the unction is Christ's word, the gospel preached in the Church (ii 24, 27), inwardly received through the action of the Spirit. On the parallels between the Paraclete sayings and 1 Jn, cf F.-M. Braun, *Jean le Theologien* iii 2: *Le Christ, notre Seigneur* (Paris, 1972) 43ff and the tables in p 46ff:

77. St Augustine, *tract* 93 1. Cited by M.-F. Berrouard in his very fine essay 'Le Paraclet, defenseur du Christ devant la conscience du croyant (Jn 16 8-11)', *RSPT* xxxiii (1949) 361-389.

78. In a specifically Hebraic metaphor *halak* can mean 'to depart from life' (Gen xv 2; Ps xxxix 14, etc.). The Aramaic verb *selak*, 'to ascend', used in the Ithpael *'istallek'* can mean 'to go away', 'depart', 'die', although literally it would mean 'to be raised up', 'exalted'. M. McNamara, 'The Ascension and the Exaltation of Christ in the Fourth Gospel', *Scripture* xix (1967) 65-73, has shown that this word might lie behind the Johannine expression *hupsothenai*, 'to be lifted up', 'crucified'. If this is so, it can very well also lie behind the verbs *aperchomai* and *poreuomai* here.

79. The word is taken here in its specific legal sense: 'something which is to be tried or proved'. Cf *O.E.D., s.v.*, iii 7b.

80. The negative idea is predominant in *dikaiosune* here. Christ is declared 'guiltless' and, so, 'victorious'. For another point of view see B. Lindars, 'DIKAIOSUNE in Jn 16.8 and 10', *Melanges bibliques en hommage au R. P. Beda Rigaux* (Duculot, 1970) 275-285.

81. *Kai* consecutivum (very rare in Jn).

82. *Krinein* in the condemnatory sense.

83. *Hodegesei en*. See B. M. Metzger, *A Textual Commentary on the Greek New Testament* (London, 1971) 247. Cf the phrase 'walk in (the) truth' in 2 Jn 4 and 3 Jn 3-4; compare 'walk in the commandment' in 2 Jn 6. 'Truth' and 'light' being isomorphous, it must also be noted that Jn always speaks of 'walking in the darkness (night)' or 'in the day'.

84. *Kai* copulative, joining to the general idea something particular. What Strabo describes as '*sunkatalegein to meros to olo*'.

85. *Eme* emphatic.

86. *Hoti* recitativum.

87. Cf 1 Jn iv 6: the Spirit of perversity, of deceiving (the active sense is to be preferred, I believe). The Scrolls seem to support the translation of *plane* as 'perversity', *ta'ut* being a synonym of *awel*.

88. T. Preiss, *Life in Christ*, trans H. Knight (London, 1954).

89. As in n 77 above.

90. R. Brown, *The Gospel According to John* ii (London, 1970) 715.

91. For this translation of *exegesato*, see A. -J. Festugiere, as in n.75 above, 131ff.

92. R. Brown, op cit, 716.

93. P. Jauon, 'Le verbe *ANANGELLO* dans saint Jean', *RSR* xxviii (1938) 234-235. If the Alexandrian reading *apangelo* is adopted in xvi 25, the two verbs are synonymous in Jn xvi. But I am inclined to believe that *apangelo* in v 25 is a later Alexandrian Atticism, and that the original reading is the Byzantine and Western one, viz *anangelo*. John's propensity towards the Atticizing use of the perfect tense and of a noble vocabulary is well known, but I think that the Byzantine Text

could have hardly missed such an Atticism, had it been original.

94. So among modern exegetes Archbishop Bernard, A. Wikenhauser, F.-M. Braun, and B. Lindars.
95. C. Westermann, *Isaiah 40-66: A Commentary*, trans D. M. G. Stalker (London, 1969) 141.
96. *Erchomena epi tina* — adversities, afflictions.
97. A detailed justification of this translation of Rev xix 10 will be offered in a future study. On the 'spirit of prophecy' as a term interchangeable with the 'holy spirit' see J. P. Schafer, 'Die Termini "Heiliger Geist" und "Geist der Prophetie" in den Targumim', *VT* xx (1970) 304-314; idem, *Die Vorstellung vom Heiligen Geist in der rabbinischen Literatur* (Munich, 1972) 21-26; M. McNamara, *Targum and Testament* (Shannon, 1972) 107ff, esp 113.
98. See the excellent study of A. Vanhoye, 'L'oeuvre du Christ, don du Pere (Jn 5, 36 et 17, 4)', *RSR* xlviii (1960) 377-419.
99. On Jn vii 37-38 and Jn xix 34ff see P. Grelot, 'Jean vii 38: eau du rocher ou source du Temple,' *RB* lxx (1963) 43-51. See also H. Rahner, 'Flumina de ventre Jesu. Die patristische Auslegung von Joh vii 37-39', *Biblica* xxii (1941), 269-302; 367-403. J. Wilkinson, 'The Incident of the Blood and Water in John 19.34', *SJT* xxviii (1975) 149-172, is right when he says that for John the meaning of the incident of xix 34 is literal, but he is wrong when he adds, 'not symbolical'.

AFTERWORD: *SPONSA*

1. E. Muir, *The Killing*.
2. Cf Irenaeus, *adv. haer.* i xxiii I; Theodoretus, *haer. fab.* i I. Among the recent literature, W. Foerster, 'Die "ersten Gnostiker" Simon und Menander', in U. Bianchi ed, *Le Origini dello Gnosticismo: Colloquio di Messina 13-18 Aprile 1966* (Leiden, 1967) 190-196; K. Beyschlag, 'Zur Simon-Magus Frage', *ZTK* lxviii (1971) 395-426.
3. See A. F. J. Klijn and G. F. Reinink, *Patristic Evidence for Jewish Christian Sects* (Leiden, 1973), Part I.
4. Clem. Alex., *exc. ex Theod.* xxiii 2-3.
5. See P. Labriolle, *La crise montaniste* (Paris, 1913) 472.
6. The testimony of al-Nadim's *Kitab al-Fihrist* has now been corroborated by P. Colon. *inv. nr. 4780.* See A. Heinrichs and L. Koenen, 'Ein griechischer Mani-Codex', *ZPE* v (1970) 97-216; K. Rudolph, 'Die Bedeutung des Kolner Mani-Codex fur die Manichaismusforschung. Vorlaufige Ammerkungen' in *Melanges d'histoire des religions offerts a Henri-Charles Puech* (Paris, 1974) 471-486.
7. See H. Corbin, 'L'idee du Paraclet en philosophie iranienne', in Academia Nazionale dei Lincei, *Convegno sul tema 'La Persia nel Medioevo'* (Rome, 1970); and 'Le shi'isme et la philosophie prophetique' in *Histoire de la philosophie islamique* (Paris, 1964) 41-151 (esp 101-109).

BIBLIOGRAPHY

A complete bibliography of a subject such as this would be a monumental undertaking.
All that is attempted here is a list of the principal works cited in the book. For further
bibliographical information, recourse may be had to the following:
Elenchus Bibliographicus Biblicus, Biblical Institute Press, (Rome, 1920ff.)
Internationale Zeitschriftenschau fur Bibelwissenschaft und Grenzgebiete,
  Katholischer Bibelwerk, (Stuttgart, 1951/52ff.)
Marrow, S. B., *Basic Tools of Biblical Exegesis*, Biblical Institute Press, (Rome, 1976).
New Testament Abstracts, Weston College School of Theology, (Cambridge, Mass.,
  1956).

Ackroyd, P. R., 'The Vitality of the Word of God in the Old Test ment', *Annual of the
  Swedish Theological Institute*, i (1962) 7-23.
Albright, W. F., 'Samuel and the Beginnings of the Prophetic Movement', in Orlinsky,
  H. M., ed, *Interpreting the Prophetic Tradition*, (New York, 1969) 149-176.
and Mann, C. S., 'Two Texts in I Corinthians', *NTS* xvi (1970) 271-276.
Alt, A., 'Ein agyptisches Gegenstuck zu Ex 3.14', *ZAW* lviii (1940-41) 159-160.
Amsler, S., Jacob, E., Keller, C. A., *Osee, Joel, Amos, Abdias, Jonas*, (Neuchatel, 1965).
'Zacharie et l'origine de l'apocalyptique', *VTS* xxii (1972) 227-231.
Auvray, P., 'Le prophete comme guetteur, Ez xxxiii, 1-20', *RB* lxxi (1964) 191-205.
Baltzer, K., 'Considerations Regarding the Office and Calling of the Prophet', *HTR* lxi
  (1968) 567-581.
  The Covenant Formulary in Old Testament, Jewish, and Early Christian Writings,
  trans D. E. Green, (Oxford, 1971).
Barr, J., *Biblical Words for Time*, 2nd edn, (London, 1969).
Barthelemy, D., 'Les *tiqqune sopherim* et la critique textuelle de l'Ancien Testament',
  VTS ix (1963) 285-304.
'L'Ancien Testament a muri a Alexandrie', *TZ* xxi (1965) 358-370.
La place de la Septante dans l'Eglise', Ch. Hauret *et al.*, *Aux grands carrefours de la
  revelation et de l'exegese de l'Ancien Testament*, (Paris, 1967) 13-28.
Beare, F. W., 'Sayings of the Risen Jesus in the Synoptic Tradition: An Inquiry into
  their Origin and Significance', in Farmer, W. R., Moule, C. F. D., Niebuhr, R. R., eds,
  Christian History and Interpretation: Studies presented to John Knox,
  (Cambridge, 1967) 161-181.
Beek, M. A., 'The Meaning of the Expression "The Chariots and the Horsemen of
  Israel" (II Kings ii 12)', *OS* xvii (1972) 1-10.
Berrouard, M. -F., 'Le Paraclet, defenseur du Christ devant la conscience du croyant
  (Jn. 16, 8-11)', *RSPT* (1949) 361-389.
Betz, O., *Der Paraklet; Fursprecher im haretischen Spatjudentum, im
  Johanneservangelium und in neu gefundenen gnostischen Schriften*, (Leiden,
  1963).
'The Concept of the So-called "Divine Man" in Mark's Christology', in Aune, D. E.,
  ed, *Studies in New Testament and Early Christian Literature: Essays in Honor of
  Allen P. Wikgren*, (Leiden, 1972).
Beyerlin, W., *Die Kulttraditionen Israels in der Verkundigung des Propheten Micha*,
  (Gottingen, 1959).
Beyschlag, K., 'Zur Simon-Magus Frage', *ZTK* lxviii (1971) 395-426.
Biard, P., *La puissance de Dieu*, (Paris, 1960).
Biehler, L., *Theios Aner. Das Bild des 'gottlichen Menschen' in Spatantike und
  Fruhchristentum*, 2 vols, (Wien, 1935, 1936).
Bloch, R., 'Midrash', *DBS* v, col 1267-68.
Boismard, M. E., 'La Connaissance dans l'Alliance nouvelle, d'apres la premiere lettre
  de saint Jean', *RB*, lvi (1949) 365-391.
Bonnard, P. E., *Le Psautier selon Jeremie*, (Paris, 1960).
Le second Isaie, son disciple, et leurs editeurs, (Paris, 1972).
Braun, F. -M., *Jean le Theologien*, t.III, vol.2: *Le Christ, notre Seigneur*, (Paris, 1972).
Brock, S. P., 'The Phenomenon of the Septuagint', *OS* xviii (1972) 11-35.
Broglie, G. de, 'Le texte fondamental de saint Paul contre la foi naturelle', *RSR* xxxix
  (1951) 253-266.
Brownlee, W. H., *The Meaning of the Qumran Scrolls for the Bible, with Special
  Attention to the Book of Isaiah*, (New York, 1964).
Buchsel, J., *Gottfried Arnold; sein Verstandnis von Kirche und Wiedergeburt*, (Witten,
  1970).

Buis, P., 'La nouvelle alliance', *VT* xviii (1968) 1-15.

Bultmann, R., 'Die Bedeutung des geschichtlichen Jesus fur die Theologie des Paulus', *TB* viii (1929) 137-151.

Exegetische Probleme des Zweiten Korintherbriefes, (Uppsala, 1947).

Theology of the New Testament, 2 vols, trans K. Grobel, (London, 1952).

Primitive Christianity, trans R. H. Fuller, (London, 1956).

The History of the Synoptic Tradition, trans J. Marsh, (Oxford, 1968).

Faith and Understanding, trans L. F. Smith, (London, 1969).

L'histoire de la tradition synoptique, trans A. Malet, (Paris, 1973).

Campenhausen, H. von, *Die Begrundung Kirchlicher Entscheidungen beim Apostel Paulus*, 2nd edn, (Heidelberg, 1965).

Ecclesiastical Authority and Scriptural Power, trans J. A. Baker, (London, 1969).

The Formation of the Christian Bible, trans J. A. Baker, (London, 1972).

Carmignac, J., 'La notion d'eschatologie dans la Bible et a Qumran', *RQ* vii (1969) 17-31.

'Le document de Qumran sur Melkisedeq', *RQ* vii (1970) 343-378.

Cazelles, H., 'Une relecture du Psaume xxxix?' in Jourjon, M., ed, *Memorial Albert Gelin*, (Le Puy/Lyon, 1961) 119-128.

Charlesworth, J. H., ed, *John and Qumran*, (London, 1972).

Chieza, B., 'La "Nuova Alleanza" (Ger.31, 31-34)', *BO* xv (1973) 173-184.

Clements, R. E., *Prophecy and Covenant*, (London, 1965).

Prophecy and Tradition, (Oxford, 1975).

Coggins, R. J., *Samaritans and Jews: The Origins of Samaritanism Reconsidered*, (Oxford, 1975).

Collins, J. J., 'Apocalyptic Eschatology as the Transcendence of Death', *CBQ* xxxvi (1974) 21-48.

Congar, Y., 'R. Sohm nous interroge encore', *RSPT* lvii (1973) 263-294.

Coppens, J., 'La nouvelle alliance en Jer. 31:31-34', *CBQ* xxv (1963) 12-21.

Le messianisme royal. Ses origines. Son developpement. Son accomplissement, (Paris, 1972).

'Le Prophete eschatologique. L'annonce de sa venue. Les relectures', *ETL* xlix (1973) 5-53.

'La releve prophetique et l'evolution spirituelle de l'attente messianique et eschatologique d'Israel', *ETL* xlix (1973) 775-783.

Corbin, H., *Histoire de la philosophie islamique*, (Paris, 1964).

'"Mundus Imaginalis" ou l'imaginal', in *Cahiers internationals du symbolisme* iv (1964) 3-26.

'L'idee du Paraclet en philosophie iranienne', Academia Nazionale dei Lincei, *Convegno sul tema 'La Persia nel Medioevo'*, (Rome, 1970).

Cothenet, E., 'Les prophetes chretiens dans l'Evangile selon Matthieu', in Didier, M., ed, *L'Evangile selon Matthieu: redaction et theologie*, (Gembloux, 1972).

'Prophetisme dans le Nouveau Testament', *DBS* viii, col 1222-1337.

Crenshaw, J. L. *Prophetic Conflict: Its Effect upon Israelite Religion*, (Berlin, 1971).

Cross, F. M., 'The Contribution of the Qumran Discoveries to the Study of the Biblical Text', *IEJ* xvi (1966) 81-95 (Reprinted in Cross, F. M., and Talmon, S., eds, *Qumran and the History of the Biblical Text*, [Cambridge, Mass., 1975] 278-292).

Canaanite Myth and Hebrew Epic: Essays in the History of the Religion of Israel, (Cambridge, Mass., 1973).

Cullmann, O., *Christ and Time: The Primitive Christian Conception of Time and History*, trans F. V. Filson, 2nd edn, (London, 1962).

OIKONOMIA. Heilsgeschichte als Thema der Theologie; Oscar Cullman zum 65, Christ, F., ed, (Hamburg — Bergstedt, 1967).

Neues Testament und Geschichte: historisches Geschehen und Deutung im Neuen Testament; Oscar Cullman zum 70 Geburtstag, Baltensweiler, H. and Reiche, B., eds, (Zurich — Tubingen, 1972).

Davenport. G. L., *The Eschatology of the Book of Jubilees*, (Leiden, 1971).

Davies, W. D., *Torah in the Messianic Age and/or the Age to Come*, (Philadelphia, Pen., 1952).

'Reflections on Tradition: the Aboth Revisited', eds, Farmer, W. D., Moule, C. F. D., Niebuhr, R. R., *Christian History and Interpretation: Studies presented to John Knox*, (Cambridge, 1967) 127-159.

Deaut, R. le, 'Apropos a Definition of Midrash', *Interpretation* xxv (1971) 454-479.

Delcor, M., 'Le Docteur de Justice, nouveau Moise, dans les Hymnes de Qumran', in Langhe, R. de, ed, *Le Psautier*, (Louvain, 1962).

'Le Vocabulaire juridique, cultuel et mystique de l'"initiation" dans le secte de Qumran', in Bardtke, H., ed, *Qumran-Probleme*, (Berlin, 1963) 109-134.

'L'hymne a Sion du rouleau des Psaumes de la grotte 11 de Qumran', *RQ* xxi (1967) 71-88.

Delorme, J., ed, *Le ministere et les ministeres selon le Nouveau Testament: Dossier exegetique et reflexion theologique*, (Paris, 1974).

Derrett, J. D. M., *Law in the New Testament*, (London, 1970).

Dodds, E. R., *Pagan and Christian in an Age of Anxiety*, (Cambridge, 1968).

Dorries, H., *Geist und Geschichte bei G. Arnold*, (Gottingen, 1963).

Driver, G. R., 'Glosses on the Hebrew Text of the Old Testament' in *L'Ancien Testament et l'Orient*, (Louvain, 1957) 123-161.

Dungan, D. L., *The Sayings of Jesus in the Churches of Paul*, (Oxford, 1971).

Dunn, J. D. G., '2 Corinthians iii, 17: The Lord is the Spirit', *JTS* xxi (1970) 309-320.

Dupont, J., 'Le chretien, miroir de la gloire divine d'apres II Cor. III, 18', *RB* lvi (1949) 392-411.

'La conversion de Paul et son influence sur sa conception du salut par la foi', in *Foi et salut selon saint Paul ... Colloque oecumenique a l'abbaye de Saint Paul hors-les-murs, 16-21 avril, 1968*, (Rome, 1970) 67-88, 88-100.

Durr, L., *Die Wertung des gottlichen Wortes im Alten Testament und im antiken Orient*, (Leipzig, 1938).

Eissfeldt, O., 'The Promises of Grace to David in Isaiah 55:1-5', in Anderson, B. W., and Harrelson, W., eds, *Israel's Prophetic Heritage: Essays in Honor of James Muilenburg*, (London, 1962) 196-207.

Eliade, M., *Patterns in Comparative Religion*, trans R. Sheed, (London, 1958).

Images and Symbols. Studies in Religious Symbolism, trans P. Mairet, (London, 1961).

Englezakis, B., 'Thomas, Logion 30', *NTS* xxv (1978/1979) 262-272.

Farmer, W. R., Moule, C. F. D. and Niebuhr, R. R., eds, *Christian History and Interpretation: Studies presented to John Knox*, (Cambridge, 1967).

Fascher, E., *PROPHETES. Eine sprach-und religionsgeschichtliche Untersuchung*, (Giessen, 1927).

Festugiere, A. J., *La revelation d'Hermes Trismegiste*, 4 vols, (Paris, 1944-1954).

Observations stylistiques sur l'Evangile de S. Jean, (Paris, 1974).

Feuillet, A., *Christologie paulinienne et tradition biblique*, (Paris/Bruges, 1973).

Le Christ Sagesse de Dieu d'apres les epitres pauliniennes, (Paris, 1966).

Fitzmyer, J. A., *Essays on the Semitic Background of the New Testament*, (London, 1971).

Fjarstedt, B., *Synoptic Tradition in I Corinthians: Themes and Clusters of Theme Words in I Corinthians i-iv and ix*, (Uppsala, 1974).

Florovsky, G., 'The Predicament of the Christian Historian', in Leibrecht, W., ed, *Religion and Culture: Essays in Honor of Paul Tillich*, (New York, 1959) 140-166.

Foerster, W., 'Die "ersten Gnostiker Simon und Menander"', in Bianchi, U., ed, *Le Origini dello Gnosticismo: Colloquio di Messina 13-18 Aprile 1966*, (Leiden, 1967).

Fohrer, G., 'Die Struktur der altestamentlichen Eschatologie', *TLZ* lxxxv (1960) 401-420.

'Tradition und Interpretation im Alten Testament', *ZAW* lxxiii (1961) 1-30.

'Remarks on Modern Interpretations of the Prophets', *JBL* lxxx (1961) 309-319.

Introduction to the Old Testament, trans D. Green, (London, 1968).

History of Israelite Religion, trans D. Green, (London, 1973).

Gazelles, H., 'Une relecture du Psaume XXXIX?', *Memorial Albert Gelin*, Jourjon, M., ed, (Paris, 1961) 119-128.

Geach, P., 'Some Problems About Time', *Proceedings of the British Academy* li (1965) 321-336.

'What Actually Exists', *Proceedings of the Aristotelian Society*, Suppl. xlii (1968) 7-16.

God and the Soul, (London, 1969).

Geoltrain, P., 'Une vision de l'histoire dans le Judaisme intertestamentaire', in Christ, F., ed, *OIKONOMIA: Heilsgeschichte als Thema der Theologie; Oscar Cullmann zum 65*, (Hamburg/Bergstedt, 1967) 26-31.

Georgi, D., *Die Gegner des Paulus im 2. Korintherbrief*, (Neukirchen, 1964).

Gertner, M., 'The Masorah and the Levites', *VT* x (1960) 241-272.

Gibbs, J. G., *Creation and Redemption: A Study in Pauline Theology*, (Leiden, 1971).

Greenwood, D., 'The Lord is the Spirit: Some Considerations on 2 Cor. III, 17', *CBQ* xxiv (1972) 467-472.

Grelot, P., 'L'eschatologie de la Sagesse et les apocalypses juives', in Jourjon, M., ed, *Memorial Albert Gelin*, (Le Puy/Lyon 1961) 165-178.

'Jean VII, 38: eau du rocher ou source du Temple', *RB* lxx (1963) 43-51.

'Soixante-dix semaines d'annees', *Biblica* l (1969) 169-186.

Gunkel, H., *Die Wirkungen des Heiligen Geistes nach dem popularen Anschauungen der apostolischen Zeit und der Lehre des Apostels Paulus*, (Gottingen, 1888, 3rd edn 1909).

Hanson, P. D., 'Jewish Apocalyptic Against Its Near Eastern Environment', *RB* lxxviii (1971) 31-58.

'Old Testament Apocalyptic Reexamined', *Interpretation* xxv (1971) 454-479.

The Dawn of Apocalyptic, (Philadelphia, Pen., 1975).

Hasel, G. F., *The History and Theology of the Remnant Idea from Genesis to Izaiah*, (Berrien Springs, Mich., 1972).

Hayes, J. H., 'The Tradition of Zion's Inviolability', *JBL* lxxxii (1963) 419-426.

Heinrichs, A. and Koenen, L., 'Ein griechischer Mani-Codex', *ZPE* v (1970) 97-216.

Hengel, M., 'Christologie und neutestamentliche Chronologie. Zu einer Aporie in der Geschichte des Urchristentums', in Baltensweiler, H., and Reicke, B., eds, *Neues Testament und Geschichte: historisches Geschehen und Deutung im Neuen Testament; O. Cullmann zum 70. Geburtstag*, (Zurich/Tubingen, 1972) 43-68.

Judaism and Hellenism. Studies in their Encounter in ·Palestine during the Early Hellenistic Period, trans J. Bowden, (London, 1974).

Henry, M. L., *Prophet und Tradition*, (Berlin, 1969).

Hentschke, R., *Die Stellung der vorexilischen Schriftpropheten zum Kultus*, (Berlin, 1957).

Hermann, I., *Kyrios und Pneuma: Studien zur Christologie der paulinischen Hauptbriefe*, 2 vols, (Munchen, 1961).

Hermann, S., *Israel in Egypt*, trans M. Kohl, (London, 1973).

Heschel, A. J., *The Prophets*, (New York, 1962).

Hesse, F., *Die Furbitte im Alten Testament*, (Hamburg, 1951).

Hill, D., 'On the Evidence for the Creative Role of christian Prophets', *NTS* xx (1973/4) 262-274.

Hillers, D. H., *Treaty Curses and the Old Testament Prophets*, (Rome, 1964).

Hossfeld, F. L. and Meyer, I., *Prophet gegen Prophet: Eine analyse der alttestamentlichen Texte zum Thema: Wahre und falsche Propheten*, (Fribourg, 1973).

Hyatt, J. P., ed, *The Bible in Modern Scholarship: Papers Read at the 100th Meeting of the society of Biblical Literature, December 28-30, 1964*; (London, 1966).

'The Prophetic Criticism of Israelite Worship', in Orlinsky, H. M., ed, *Interpreting the Prophetic Tradition*, (New York, 1969) 201-224.

Irigoin, J., 'La composition rythmique du prologue de Jean (I, 1-18)', *RB* lxxviii (1971) 501-514.

Jaubert, A., *La notion de l'alliance dans le judaisme aux abords de l'ere chretienne*, (Paris, 1963).

Jepsen, A., 'Gottesmann und Prophet. Ammerkungen zum Kapitel 1. Konige 13', in Rad, G. von, ed, *Das opfer des Abraham; mit texten von Luther, Kierkegaard, Kolakowski und Bildern von Rembrandt*, (Munchen, 1971) 171-182.

Jeremias, J., *New Testament Theology*, vol. i, trans J. Bowden, (London, 1971).

Jeremias, Jorg, 'Lade und Zion; zur Entstehung der Ziontradition', in Wolff, H. W., ed, *Probleme biblischer Theologie; G. von Rad zum 70. Geburtstag*, (Munchen, 1971) 183-198.

Jervell, J., *Imago Dei. Gen I, 26f. im Spatjudentum, in der Gnosis und in den paulinischen Briefen*, (Gottingen, 1960).

Johansson, N., *Parakletoi: Vorstellungen von Fursprechen fur die Menschen vor Gott in der alttestamentlichen Religion, im Spatjudentum und Urchristentum*, (Lund, 1940).

Johnson, R. A., *The Origins of Demythologizing*, (Leiden, 1974).

Jonge, M. de, 'The Role of Intermediaries in God's Final Intervention in the Future According to the Qumran Scrolls', in Micher, O., *et al.*, *Studies on the Jewish Background of the New Testament*, (Assen, 1969).

Jouon, P., 'Le verbe ANANGELLO dans saint Jean', *RSR* xxviii (1938) 234-235.

Jourjon, M., ed, *A la rencontre de Dieu, Memorial Albert Gelin*, (Le Puy/Lyon, 1961).

Klijn, A. F. J. and Reinink G. F., *Patristic Evidence for Jewish Christian Sects*, (Leiden, 1973).

Koch, K., *The Rediscovery of Apocalyptic*, trans M. Kohl, (London, 1972).

Kraus, H. J., *Prophetie in der Krisis*, (Neukirchen, 1964).

Kummel, W. G., *Heilsgeschechen und Geschichte; Ges. Aufsatze 1933-1964*, (Marburg, 1965).

The Theology of the New Testament, trans J. E. Steely, (London, 1974).

Kutsch, E., *Verheissung und Gesetz; Untersuchungen zum sogennanten 'Bund' im Alten Testament*, (Berlin, 1973).

Labriolle, F., *La crise montaniste*, (Paris, 1913).

Lacomara, A., 'Deuteronomy and the Farewell Discourse (Jn 13:33-16:33)', *CBQ* xxxvi

(1974) 65-84.
Laperrousaz, E. M., 'Les "ordonnances premieres" et les "ordonnances dernieres" dans les manuscrits de la mer Morte', *Hommage a Andre Dupont-Sommer*, (Paris, 1971) 405-419.
Larsson, E., *Christus als Vorbild; Eine Untersuchung zu den paulinischen Tauf-und Eikontexte*, (Uppsala, 1962).
Leach, E., *Rethinking Anthropology*, (London, 1966).
Leaney, A. R. D., 'The Johannine Paraclete and the Qumran Scrolls', in Charlesworth, J. H., ed, *John and Qumran*, (London, 1972) 38-61.
Leivestad, R., 'Das Dogma von der Prophetenlosen Zeit', *NTS* xix (1972/1973) 288-299.
Lemaire, A., *Les ministeres aux origines de l'Eglise*, (Paris, 1971).
Lemke, W., 'The Synoptic Problem in the Chronicler's History', *HTR* lviii (1965) 349-363.
Leon-Dufour, X., *Les evangiles et l'histoire de Jesus*, (Paris, 1963).
Licht, J., 'Time and Eschatology in Apocalyptic Literature and in Qumran', *JJS* xvi (1965) 177-182.
Lindars, B., 'DIKAIOSUNE in Jn 16. 8 and 10', in Descamps. A. and Halleux, R. P. A. de, eds, *Melanges bibliques en hommage au R. P. Beda Rigaux*, (Gembloux, 1970).
   with Smalley, S. S., eds, *Christ and Spirit in the New Testament: Studies in honour of C. F. D. Moule*, (Cambridge, 1973).
Lindblom, J., *Prophecy in Ancient Israel*, (Oxford, 1962).
Lipinski, E., *Essais sur la Revelation et la Bible*, (Paris, 1970).
   'De la reforme d'Edras au regne eschatologique de Dieu (Is 4, 3-5a)', *Biblica* li (1970) 533-537.
   'Le s'r yswb d'Isaie VIII, 3', *VT* xxiii (1973) 245-246.
McCarthy, D. J., *Treaty and Covenant: A Study in Form in the Ancient Oriental Documents and the Bible*, (Rome, 1963).
   Old Testament Covenant, (Oxford, 1972).
   'The Inauguration of Monarchy in Israel. A Form-Critical Study in I Samuel 8-12', *Interpretation*, xxvii (1973) 401-412.
McNamara, M., *The New Testament and the Palestinian Targum to the Penateuch*, (Rome, 1966).
   'The Ascension and Exaltation of Christ in the Fourth Gospel', *Scripture* xix (1967) 65-73.
Martin-Achard, R., 'La nouvelle alliance selon Jeremie', *RTP* xii (1962) 81-92.
Martyn, J. L., 'Epistemology at the Turn of the Ages: 2 Corinthians 5:16', in Farmer, W. R., Moule, C. F. D., Niebuhr, R. R., eds, *Christian History and Interpretation:Studies Presented to John Knox*, (Cambridge, 1967) 269-287.
Mendenhall, G., *Law and Covenant in Israel and the Ancient Near East*, (Pittsburgh, Pa., 1955).
Milik, J., 'Milki-sedeq et Milki-resa dans les anciens ecrits juifs et chretiens', *JJS* xxii (1972) 95-144.
Momigliano, A., 'Time in Ancient Historiography', *History and Theory*, vi (1966) 1-23.
Moule, C. F. D., 'Jesus in New Testament Kerygma', in Bocher, O. and Haacker, H., eds, *Verborum Veritas: Festschrift fur Gustav Stahlin*, (Wuppertal, 1970) 15-26.
   '2 Cor 3:18b, *Kathaper apo Kuriou pneumatos*', in Baltensweiler, H., and Reicke, B., eds, *Neues Testament und Geschichte: Historisches Geschehen und Deutung im Neuen Testament; O. Cullmann zum 70. Geburtstag*, (Zurich/Tubingen, 1972) 231-237.
Mouroux, J., *Le mystere du temps: Approche theologique*, (Paris, 1962).
Moyne, J. le, *Les Sadduceens*, (Paris, 1972).
Muilenburg, J., 'The "Office" of the Prophet in Ancient Israel', in Hyatt, J. P., ed, *The Bible in Modern Scholarship*, (London, 1966) 74-97.
Muler, H. P., *Ursprunge und Strukturen alttestamentlicher Eschatologie*, (Berlin, 1969).
Muller, W.E., *Die Vorstellung vom Rest im Alten Testament*, Preuss, H. D., ed, (Neukirchen, 1973).
Neher, A., *The Prophetic Existence*, trans W. Wolf, (London, 1969).
Neusner, J., *The Rabbinic Traditions About the Pharisees Before 70*, (Leiden, 1971).
Neves, J. C. M. das, *A theologia da traducao grega dos Sententa no Livro de Isaias (Cap. 24 de Isaias)*, (Lisbon, 1973).
Nickelsburg, G. W., *Resurrection, Immortality and Eternal Life in Intertestamental Judaism*, (Cambridge, Mass., 1972).
Nock, A. D., *Conversion*, (Oxford, 1961).
   Essays on Religion and the Ancient World, 2 vols, (Oxford, 1972).
North, R., 'Prophecy to Apocalyptic Via Zechariah', *VTS* xxii (1972) 47-71.
Noth, M., *The Laws in the Pentateuch and Other Studies*, trans D. R. Ap-Thomas,

(Edinburgh, 1966).
A History of Pentateuchal Traditions, trans B. W. Anderson, (Englewood Cliffs, N. J., 1972).
Ohler, A., *Mythologische Elemente im Alten Testament; eine motivgeschtichliche Untersuchung*, (Dusseldorf, 1969).
Orlinsky, H. M., ed, *Interpreting the Prophetic Tradition*, (New York, 1969).
Osswald, E., *Falsche Prophetie im Alten Testament*, (Tubingen, 1962).
Overholt, T. W., *The Threat of Falsehood: A Study in the Theology of the Book of Jeremiah*, (London, 1970).
Pasinya, L. M., *La notion de NOMOS dans le Pentateuque grec*, (Rome, 1972).
Pearson, B. A., 'Did the Gnostics Curse Jesus?', *JBL* lxxxvi (1967) 301-305.
  The pneumatikos-psychikos Terminology in I Cornithians: A Study in the Theology of the Corinthian Opponents of Paul and Its Relation to Gnosticism, (Missoula, Mont., 1973).
Petzke. G., *Die Tradition uber Apollonius von Tyana und das Neue Testament*, (Leiden, 1970).
Ploeg, J. van der, 'Eschatology in the Old Testament', *OS* xvii (1972) 89-99.
Ploger, O., *Theocracy and Eschatology*, trans S. Rudman, (Oxford, 1968).
Potterie, I. de la, 'L'onction du chretien par la foi', *Biblica* xl (1959) 12-69.
  'La connaissance de Dieu dans le dualisme eschatologique d'apres I Jn 2, 12-14', in *Au service de la parole de Dieu. Melanges offerts a Mgr Andre-Marie Charue*, (Gembloux, 1968) 77-99.
Preiss, Th., *Life in Christ*, trans H. Knight, (London, 1954).
Procksch, O., *Geschichtsbetrachtung und geschichtliche Uberlieferung bei den vorexilischen Propheten*, (Leipzig, 1902).
Purvis, J. D., *The Samaritan Pentateuch and the Origin of the Samaritan Sect*, (Cambridge, Mass., 1968).
Quell. G., *Wahre und Falsche Propheten*, (Gutersloh, 1952).
Quispel, G., 'Qumran, John and Jewish Christianity', in Charlesworth, J. H., ed, *John and Qumran*, (London, 1972) 137-155.
  'Mani, the Apostle of Jesus Christ', in Fontaine J. et Kannengiessez C., eds, *EPEKTASIS. Melanges patristiques offerts au cardinal Jean Danielou*, (Paris, 1972) 667-672.
Rabinowitz, I., ' "Pesher/Pittaron": Its Biblical Meaning and its Significance in the Qumran Literature', 2RQ viii (1973) 219-232.
Rad, G. von, *Old Testament Theology* trans D. M. G. Stalker, 2 vols, (Edinburgh, 1962, 1965).
  The Problem of the Hexateuch and Other Essays, trans E. W. Trueman Dicken, (Edinburgh, 1966).
  Wisdom in Israel, trans J. D. Martin, (London, 1972).
Rahner, H., 'Flumina de ventre Jesu. Die patristische Auslegung von John VII, 37-39', *Biblica* xxii (1941) 269-302; 367-403.
Reiling, J., *Hermas and Christian Prophecy* (Leiden, 1973).
Reventlow, H. G., *Wachter uber Israel*, (Berlin, 1962).
Ricoeur, P., *Le conflit des interpretations. Essais d'hermeneutique*, (Paris, 1969).
Robinson, J. A., 'The Christian Ministry in the Apostolic and Sub-Apostolic Periods', in Swete, H. B., ed, *Essays on the Early History of the Church and the Ministry*, 2nd edn, (London, 1921) 57-92.
Robinson, J. M., 'Kerygma and History in the New Testament', in Hyatt, J. P., ed, *The Bible in Modern Scholarship*, (London, 1966) 114-150.
Rohland, E., *Die Bedeutung der Erwahlungstraditionen Israels fur die Eschatologie des altestamentlichen Propheten*, (Heidelberg, 1956).
Rossler, D., *Gesetz und Geschichte*, (Neukirchen, 1960).
Rowley, H. H., *The Biblical Doctrine of Election*, (London, 1950).
  Worship in Ancient Israel (London, 1967).
Rudolph, K., 'Die Bedeutung des Kolner Mani-Codex fur die Manichaismusforschung. Vorlaufige Ammerkungen', in *Melanges d'histoire des religions offerts a Henri-Charles Puech*, (Paris, 1974).
Russel, D. S., *The Method and Message of Jewish Apocalyptic*, (London, 1964).
Schafer, J. P., 'Die Termini "Heiliger Geist" und "Geist der Prophetie" in den Targumim', *VT* xx (1970) 304-314.
  Die Vorstellung vom Heiligen Geist in der rabbinischen Literatur, (Munchen, 1972).
Schmidt, J. M., *Die Judisch Apokalyptik. Die Geschichte ihrer Erforschung von den Anfangen bis zu den Textfunden von Qumran*, (Neukirchen, 1969).
Schmithals, W., 'Zwei gnostische Glossen im 2. Korintherbrief', *EvTh* xxviii (1958) 552-573.
  Die Gnosis in Korinth, 2nd edn, (Gottingen, 1965).

Schnackenburg, R., *Das Heilgeschechen bei der Taufe nach dem Apostel Paulus; eine Studie zur paulinischen Theologie*, (Munchen, 1950).

Schneider, C., *Kulturgeschichte des Hellenismus*, 2 vols, (Munchen, 1967, 1969).

Schreiner, J., *Sion-Jerusalem. Jahwes Konigssitz*, (Munchen, 1957).

Schweitzer, A., *The Mysticism of Apostle Paul*, trans W. Montgomery, (London, 1931).

Scrima, A., 'Revelation et tradition dans la Constitution Dogmatique "Dei Verbum" selon un point de vue orthodoxe', in Duprey, B. D., ed, *La Revelation Divine*, ii (Paris, 1968) 523-539.

Seybold, K., *Das Davidische Konigtum im Zeugnis der Propheten*, (Gottingen, 1972).

Slomovic, E., 'Towards an Understanding of the Exegesis of the Dead Sea Scrolls', *RQ* vii (1969) 3-15.

Smith, Morton, 'Zealots and Sicarii: Their Origins and Relation', *HTR* lxiv (1971) 1-19.

Sowers, S., 'On the Reinterpretation of Biblical History in Hellenistic Judaism' in Christ, F., ed, *OIKONOMIA: Heilgeschichte als Thema der Theologie; Oscar Cullmann zum 65*, (Hamburg/Bergstedt, 1967) 18-25.

Stahlin, T., *Gottfried Arnolds geistliche Dichtung; Glaube und Mystik*, (Gottingen, 1966).

Stanton, G. N., *Jesus of Nazareth in New Testament Preaching*, (Cambridge, 1974).

Starcky, J., 'Les quatres etapes du messianisme a Qumran', *RB* lxx (1963) 481-505.

Stemberger, G., *Der Leib der Auferstehung. Studien zur Anthropologie und Eschatologie des palastinischen Judentums im neutestamentlichen Zeitalter (ca. 170 v. Chr. - 100 n. Chr.)*, (Rome, 1972).

'Das Problem der Auferstehung im Alten Testament', *Kairos* xiv (1972) 273-290.

'Zur Auferstehungslehre in der rabbinischen Literatur', *Kairos*, xv (1973) 238-266.

Swetnam, J., 'Why was Jeremiah's New Covenant New?', *VTS* xxvi (1974).

Szorenyi, A., 'Das Buch Daniel ein kanonisierter Pescher?', *VTS* xv (1966) 278-294.

Testuz, M., *Les idees religieuses du Livre des Jubiles*, (Geneve, 1960).

Thusing, W., *Per Christum in Deum. Studien zur Verhaltnis von Christozentrik und Theozentrik in den paulinischen Hauptbriefen*, (Munster, 1965).

Tiede, D. L., *The Charismatic Figure as Miracle Worker*, (Montana, 1972).

Tournay, R., 'Relectures bibliques concernant la vie future et l'angelologie', *RB* lxix (1962) 481-505.

Tucker, G. M., 'Covenant Forms and Contract Forms', *VT* xv (1965) 487-503.

Unnik, W. C. van, 'Jesus: Anathema or Kyrios' in Lindars, B. and Smalley, S. S., eds, *Christ and Spirit in the New Testament: Essays in Honour of C. F. D. Moule*, (Cambridge, 1973) 113-126.

Vanhoye, A., 'L'oeuvre du Christ, don du Pere (Jn 5, 36 et 17, 4)', *RSR* xlviii (1960) 377-419.

Vaux, R. de, 'Jerusalem and the Prophets', in Orlinsky, H. M., ed, *Interpreting the Prophetic Tradition*, (New York, 1969) 275-300 = *RB* lxxiii (1966) 481-509.

The Bible and the Ancient Near East, trans D. McHugh, (London, 1971).

Histoire ancienne d'Israel, i (Paris, 1971).

Vermes, G., 'The Etymology of Essenes', *RQ* ii (1960) 427-443.

Scripture and Tradition in Judaism, (Leiden, 1961).

'Essenes and Therapeutai', *RQ* iii (1962) 495-504.

Jesus the Jew, (London 1973).

Vollmer, J., *Geschichtliche Ruckblicke und Motive in der Prophetie des Amos, Hosea und Jesaja*, (Berlin, 1971).

Vriezen, Th. C., *Die Erwahlung Israels nach dem Alten Testament*, (Zurich, 1953).

'Essentials of the Theology of Isaiah', in Anderson, B. W. and Harrelson, W., eds, *Israel's Prophetic Heritage: Essays in Honor of James Muilenburg*, (London, 1962) 128-146.

Weinel, H., *Die Wirkungen des Geistes und der Geister im nachapostolischen Zeitalter bis auf Irenaeus*, (Fribourg, 1899).

Weinfeld, M., *Deuteronomy and the Deuteronomic School*, (Oxford, 1972).

Weingreen, J., 'Rabbinic-type Glosses in the Old Testament', *JSS* ii (1957) 149-162 = idem, *From Bible to Mishna: The Continuity of Tradition*, (Manchester, 1976) 32-54.

Westermann, C., *Basic Forms of Prophetic Speech*, trans H. C. White, (London, 1967).

Willi, T., *Die Chronik als Auslegung. Untersuchungen zur litterarischen Gestaltung der historischen Uberlieferung Israels*, (Gottingen, 1972).

Woude, A. S. van der, 'Micah IV 1-5: An instance of the Pseudo-Prophets Quoting Isaiah' in *Symbolae Biblicae et Mesopotamicae F. N. T. de Liagre Bohl Dedicatae*, Beek, M. A., Kampman, A. A., Nijland, C., Ryckmans, J., eds, (Leiden, 1973) 396-402.

Wright, A. G., *The Literary Genre Midrash*, (State Island, 1967).

Wright, G. E., 'The Lawsuit of God; A Form-Critical Study of Deuteronomy 32' in

Anderson, B. W. and Harrelson, W., eds, *Israel's Prophetic Heritage: Essays in Honor of James Muilenburg*, (London, 1962) 26-67.

'Reflections Concerning O.T. Theology', in *Studia biblica et semitica Theodoro Christiano Vriezen dedicata*, (Wageningen, 1966) 376-388.

Zaehner, R. C., *At Sundry Times: An Essay in the Comparison of Religions*, (London, 1958).

Concordant Discord, (Oxford, 1970).

Zimmerli, W., *The Law and the Prophets*, trans R. E. Clements, (Oxford, 1965).

INDEX OF PASSAGES CITED

INDEX OF AUTHORS